SMALL BUSINESS START UP MANUAL

John B. Walton, M.S., M.B.A.

WEYBRIDGE PUBLISHING COMPANY
Dallas, Texas 75248

©**Weybridge Publishing Company 1981**

All rights reserved. No part of this publication may be reproduced, stored in a retrieval system, or transmitted, in any form or by any means, electronic, mechanical, photocopying, recording, or otherwise, without the prior written permission of the publisher.

This publication is designed to provide accurate and authoritative information in regard to the subject matter covered. It is sold with the understanding that the publisher is not engaged in rendering legal, accounting, or other professional service. If legal advice or other expert assistance is required, the service of a competent professional person should be sought.

ISBN 0-939356-00-7

Library of Congress Catalog Card Number 81-50038

658.022
W239

SMALL BUSINESS START UP MANUAL

ACKNOWLEDGEMENT

The bookkeeping accounts used on pages 15, 17, 18 and 20 were reprinted from the "Dome Simplified Monthly Bookkeeping Record No. 612" by permission of the publisher, Dome Publishing Company, Inc., Dome Building, Providence, Rhode Island 02903.

Contents

INTRODUCTION
Approach taken, self preparation, business investigation and summary ... 1

Section One   Self Preparation

CHAPTER ONE - ACCOUNTING/FINANCIAL STATEMENTS ... 6

1.1	Accrual Basis Versus Cash Basis Accounting	7
1.2	The Fiscal Year	8
1.3	Single Entry Versus Double Entry Bookkeeping	8
1.4	The Accounting System	9
1.5	Financial Statements	23
1.6	The Balance Sheet	24
1.7	The Income Statement	29
1.8	Cash Flow	31
1.9	Closing Notes	34

CHAPTER TWO - LEGAL ASPECTS ... 43

2.1	The Business Form	43
2.2	Legal Requirements In Business Formation	47
2.3	Insurance	51
2.4	Protecting Your Ideas	54
2.5	The Legal Aspects Of Selling	56
2.6	Laws Concerning Credit	59
2.7	Employment Laws	60

CHAPTER THREE - TAX ASPECTS ... 64

3.1	Signing Up	64
3.2	Tax Calendar	67
3.3	Tax Forms	68
3.4	Record Keeping For Tax Purposes	69
3.5	Tax Aspects Of Business Formation - Corporations	70
3.6	Tax Aspects Of Business Purchase - Subchapter S Corporations	74
3.7	Tax Aspects Of Business Purchase - Partnerships	74
3.8	Tax Aspects Of Business Purchase - Sole Proprietorships	74
3.9	Methods Of Reducing Corporate Income Tax	75

3.10	Income Splitting To Reduce Personal Income Tax	77
3.11	Methods Of Extracting Corporate Income	77
3.12	Tax-Deductible Benefits	78
3.13	Tax Credits	79
3.14	Tax Deductions	79
3.15	Caution	82
3.16	Sources Of Tax Information	83

CHAPTER FOUR - BUSINESS ADVICE 86

4.1	Small Business Administration	86
4.2	Bank Of America Publications	92
4.3	General Sources	93
4.4	Business Operating Guides And Handbooks	94
4.5	Directories	95

CHAPTER FIVE - FINANCIAL SOURCES 98

5.1	Most Common Situations Where Funds Are Required	98
5.2	Equity Financing	99
5.3	Debt Financing	101
5.4	Self Financing	114
5.5	Equity/Debt Financial Finders	115
5.6	Sources Of Financial Information	115

CHAPTER SIX - MARKETING ASPECTS 117

6.1	Marketing Plan	117
6.2	The Marketing Program	123
6.3	Defining Your Marketing Objectives	131
6.4	Measuring Your Marketing Performance	131
6.5	Sources Of Economic And Marketing Information	132

Section Two   Business Acquisition/Start Up

CHAPTER SEVEN - INFORMATION SOURCES 136

7.1	Business Selection	136
7.2	Sources For Business Purchase	139
7.3	Business Information	141

CHAPTER EIGHT - BUYING AN EXISTING BUSINESS 144

8.1	Financial Sources	144
8.2	Balance Sheet Evaluation	145
8.3	Income Statement Evaluation	148
8.4	Ratio Analysis	149
8.5	Use Of Ratio Analysis	153
8.6	Trend Analysis	154
8.7	Market Analysis	154
8.8	Legal Aspects Of Business Acquisition	156
8.9	Valuation Of An Acquired Business	157
8.10	The Purchase Contract	160
8.11	Finalizing The Transaction	161

CHAPTER NINE - STARTING A NEW BUSINESS 163

9.1	Business Analysis	163
9.2	Market Analysis - Non-Unique Business Retailing, Wholesaling, Manufacturing	164
9.3	Market Analysis - Unique Business	166
9.4	New Business Location	168
9.5	Business Formation Plan	173

CHAPTER TEN - FINANCING A BUSINESS 177

10.1	Purchase Of An Existing Business	177
10.2	Starting A New Business	180

CHAPTER ELEVEN - YOUR LOAN PROPOSAL 188

CHAPTER TWELVE - CONCLUSION 216

Introduction

The American free enterprise system encourages anyone with a modest amount of funds to become the owner-manager of a small business. In 1976, for example, an average of over 17,000 new businesses were incorporated every month. It is very easy to get started with a business of your own. Perhaps it is too easy, since the failure rate of new businesses is alarming; within the first two years about 50% of all new businesses fail and only 25% survive beyond seven years. Two factors are important in the prevention of small business failure:

- Careful prior planning of the acquisition or start up of the small business.
- Skillful ongoing management of the small business.

This book concentrates on the start up aspect of the small business since this aspect is where the first wrong steps can be taken. Additionally, there seem to be few sources that the small businessman can turn to for advice in acquiring or starting his business. On the other hand, there are several excellent books dealing in the successful operation of small businesses.

APPROACH

This book will take you through each step in the acquisition or start up of a small business. No one can succeed by pure luck despite what may be believed to the contrary. College education is also not necessarily required. What is required is that you must have the desire and the persistence to properly prepare yourself and to undertake a detailed investigation of the business of your choice. The detailed knowledge acquired during this process will not only be helpful in running the business but will also help convince others in the business world, such as suppliers, bankers, lawyers and accountants, that you are worthy of their respect. This respect is valuable credit and may make the vital difference between success and failure. In summary, the two key aspects in starting a business are:

1. Self preparation.
2. Thorough business investigation.

I. SELF PREPARATION

Self preparation must be tackled first and each aspect will be treated in a separate chapter.

ACCOUNTING/FINANCIAL STATEMENTS

It is extremely important for you to understand and be able to prepare the major financial statements that present the overview of your chosen business. If your business is new you must be able to make projections concerning the future size and shape of its financial statements.

In gaining an understanding of financial statements, you need only get a sure grasp of the fundamentals. You do not really need the detailed knowledge of the accountant. As a successful owner-manager, you can always hire a bookkeeper to keep your accounts and a CPA to prepare your tax return. For long-term success it is recommended that you do just that, but this is not part of the concerns of business start up.

LEGAL ASPECTS

The various forms of business enterprise are described - proprietorship, partnership and the corporate form. The advantages and disadvantages of each form are discussed.

Various legal aspects of business formation are also covered - law of contracts, federal, state and local regulations, insurance and liability.

TAX ASPECTS

All businesses, like it or not, have a silent partner - Uncle Sam. Major tax codes are discussed that can minimize the amount of tax to be paid and maximize any tax to be recovered. Again, the various choices made during business formation can be crucial to how much future tax will be owed.

BUSINESS ADVICE

This chapter is largely given over to describing the assistance and advice that is available from the SBA - the Small Business Administration.

FINANCIAL SOURCES

Under this heading the various sources of capital are described. In particular, the role of the bank and especially the banker himself is described. The banker is a crucial ally to be won over. He can provide great assistance in business start up and in ongoing business management.

MARKETING ASPECTS

In this chapter you will be shown how to define your market, how to set up your marketing program, how to define your marketing objectives and how to measure your marketing results.

The six topics, outlined above, will be covered in sufficient detail to give you a good background in basic business knowledge. You cannot always trust professional advisers to assist you in every matter. Sometimes these advisers themselves are not familiar with a particular business aspect, and, sometimes, they just cannot be bothered to perform as they should. In any case, you should, whilst seeking out the best advice obtainable, know enough to safeguard your own interest, since in the end you must be the master of your own fate.

It is recommended that you establish long term professional relationships with individuals you have interviewed and who have answered your questions satisfactorily. These questions can be compiled in advance for such investigations. Any professional man will, for a reasonable fee, spend some time to give advice to a prospective client. One way to short circuit the trial and error of obtaining advisers is to ask successful businessmen for the names of advisers who have given them good service over the years.

Finally, it must be noted that professional advice is an indispensible ingredient to success and worth every penny spent. Do-it-yourself deals involving verbal contracts, for example, can lead the unwary into all sorts of trouble. No, the best way to ensure that you gain good advice is to understand the basics and let the advisor help you with the finer points.

It is worth the effort to understand the basics before getting into a small business. After all, you plan to be in business a long time and a short course of preparation may avoid the loss of years of hard-earned savings.

II. BUSINESS INVESTIGATION

In parallel with the task of becoming acquainted with business fundamentals, you should thoroughly investigate the business you are entering. The second section of this book will contain information on how to find out the particulars of any business venture. Of course, it is possible that you are thoroughly familiar with every aspect of your future business and are able to discuss it from A to Z. That is good. However, the next steps will also be crucial to any business investigation.

Investigation of business costs, the financial ratios and the market data are vital to the build up of a financial projection of the business performance during its start up period. How much, for example, should be spent on advertising, on repair and maintenance, on insurance, and so forth. The tabulation of this data will enable you to establish how much a business is worth, how much inventory is needed, how much cash in hand you will need and how much debt service you can afford to carry.

Finally, you will be shown how to package the data collected above in the form of a concise loan proposal, should you require a bank loan to start your enterprise. Even if you have sufficient start up funds of your own, the loan proposal format will provide the basic document required to ask for business expansion funding in the future.

SUMMARY

The entrepreneur, with little cash and no other resources, cannot afford to learn by making mistakes. Mistakes made during business formation are often fundamental and cannot easily be rectified. Such mistakes can prove fatal to the health of the fledgling business. This book was written as an honest attempt to help the new businessman avoid making such fundamental mistakes. It stresses self preparation and then thorough business investigation. At least then the new businessman will understand just what he is getting into and be able to assess his chances of success in a rational, systematic manner. Too often, the unprepared are carried along by overly optimistic judgements based purely on wishful thinking. While optimism is a strong ally in providing motivation, only careful planning and hard work will provide a secure foundation for business success.

SECTION ONE

SELF PREPARATION

1

Accounting/Financial Statements

1.0 This first chapter discusses a subject that is unpopular with many would be businessmen. It contains material that is, perhaps, the most challenging of all the chapters on self preparation. However, it is presented first when you are fresh, with the promise that the later material is far easier.

The accounting system provides an accurate record of the finanical activity of a business on a daily basis. It records purchases, sales, merchandise inventories, credit owing, accounts to be paid, equipment and buildings owned and so on. The financial statements of a business provide an accumulated status of the financial activity of a business over a specific time period, which is usually one year.

There are three major reasons why it is important for the businessman to go to the extra effort of keeping up-to-date, neat and accurate financial records.

- Business Management

    Accurate records are essential to good business management, especially in the difficult start up period. Good records provide information on sales trends, expenses, cash flow and so on - all in one centralized location. The businessman can constantly know where he is and can plan ahead with confidence all his financial commitments. After all, any business can only stay solvent and provide a good living for its owner if it makes a satisfactory profit. Good records provide one of the best tools in ensuring that the business performs profitably. Thus, the businessman should thoroughly familiarize himself with his financial records and use them extensively in making business decisions.

- Tax Records

    The I.R.S. requires every business to maintain a set of books. However, there is more to it than that. If the businessman is subjected to a tax audit and the business records are neatly kept, it has carefully filed sales slips and invoices, etc., the I.R.S. cannot fail to be favorably impressed. Missing or partially updated records give the impression of sloppy management and, at worst, legitimate tax deductions may be dissallowed through lack of appropriate records.

1/Accounting/Financial Statements

- Employee Fraud

    Poor record keeping provides an open invitation for employee fraud. An accurate financial records system, with adequate built-in safeguards, will do much to reduce the potential for this type of problem.

.1 ACCRUAL BASIS VERSUS CASH BASIS ACCOUNTING

In setting up his books, the small businessman must decide between three methods of accounting:

- Cash Basis
- Accrual Basis
- Hybrid Basis

Cash Basis

In this method of accounting, income is only recognised and recorded when cash is actually transfered in payment or receipt. If, for example an item is sold on credit, that sale is only recognized when a check arrives in payment, perhaps 30 or 60 days after the actual sale. Similarly, expenses are only recognised and recorded on the day the cash payment is made. For example, taxes might be owing for 90 days, but will only be recorded when paid.

Accrual Basis

In this accounting method income and expenses are recognized and recorded as they are incurred, rather than when cash is received or paid. For example, all credit sales would be recognised on the day of sale. Similarly, insurance expense is recorded as occuring, and its value being used up, month by month over the entire year, rather then, say, when the payment was made.

Hybrid Basis

In this method sales and purchases of merchandise are recorded on an accrual basis, whereas expenses are recorded on a cash basis.

Which method should the small businessman choose? Most large businesses elect the accrual basis, since this method most accurately reflects the true financial picture of business operations over a specific period. However, before deciding on the accrual basis, there are distinct advantages in electing the cash basis. The most important advantage is that the businessman can time income and expenditures in order to delay some of his tax liability from one tax year to the next. The cash method is also somewhat more straightforward and cheaper as an accounting technique.

The hybrid method is one that certain businesses, which would otherwise use the cash basis, are required to use by the I.R.S. The I.R.S. restrictions involve those businesses where capital improvements or sale of merchandise (largely retail operations) is a major factor in their income.

The tax aspect of accounting will be explored more thoroughly in a later chapter. Note, however, that once an accounting basis is chosen, it requires prior consent from the I.R.S. Commissioner to change it - but it can be changed later if desired. It is the author's recommendation that the cash basis be chosen, where possible, and that the benefits of the full accrual system be left until the business is large enough to warrant them.

1.2 THE FISCAL YEAR

The fiscal year is the annual period over which a business measures its income for tax purposes. The fiscal year does not necessarily have to coincide with the calendar year; that is it can, for example, run from September 1 of one year to September 1 of the following year. It is often advantageous for tax payers to arrange that the fiscal year of their business is different from their personal tax year. Thus, if the fiscal year of the business ends on January 31, the owner can receive his salary as owner-operator in January with tax consequences deferred for an entire year, and so forth. Unfortunately, this arrangement applies only to incorporated businesses, so proprietorships and partnerships must use the same fiscal and tax years.

It is recommended that the fiscal year of a new business be set up with the tax effects in mind. The fiscal year can be altered once it has been established, but it does require prior approval from the I.R.S. Commissioner.

1.3 SINGLE-ENTRY VERSUS DOUBLE-ENTRY BOOKKEEPING

Most books on accounting present the double-entry method of bookkeeping as the only method to consider. It is indeed the perfect method since it provides cross checking and automatically balances all the accounts. This balancing is achieved since every financial transaction is recorded in two separate places, one in a "debit" entry and one in a "credit" entry. Thus, the sum of all "debits" must equal all the "credits". However, this bookkeeping method cannot be explained easily in a single chapter and really requires a course at an evening college to understand fully. But for those who are already knowledgeable, or whose wife/husband/bookkeeper is knowledgeable, and want to spend the extra time and expense, then there are packaged systems that can be used. One such system is:

Wilmer "Start A Set"

This is a complete double-entry bookkeeping system comprising:

- 120 forms including General Ledgers, Record of Journal Entries, Records for Invoices, Cash Received, Cash Disbursed, etc.
- Set of numbered accounts.
- A heavy cam-lock binder.

This can be obtained from your local bookstore/stationer or directly from:

Accountant Stationers and Printers
712 East Washington Blvd.
Los angeles, CA 90021

The price for this system is roughly $20 and additional sheets are available.

The single entry system is far simpler than double-entry and is cheaper to keep up. It does not provide quite the sophistication of the double-entry method but does provide enough information for tax records and for business management.

1/Accounting/Financial Statements

Two systems are in common use:

Dome Publishing Company

This single-entry system was designed by a group of CPA's and is a quality approach, if adequate for your needs. You can check with your legal advisor to see whether or not it contains sufficient detail for your type of business. It comes as a single spiral-bound book the "Dome Simplified Monthly (or Weekly) Bookkeeping System" and costs about $5. It comprises numbered accounts for receipts and expenditures, summary sheets and year-end financial statement sheets. It also provides a payroll section for 15 employees. It can be obtained locally or from:

> Dome Publishing Co, Inc.
> Dome Building
> Providence, R.I. 02903

The Ideal System

This is not quite so simplified as the Dome method, but follows the more usual columnar accounting convention. There are special ledgers for several specific businesses, although the "General Business" ledger (number 3611) is quite suitable for most small business situations.

The Ideal System includes sections for each specific account - sales, purchases, etc., and costs about $13. It can be obtained locally, or from:

> The Ideal System
> P.O. Box 1568
> Augusta, Georgia 30903

Any of these three systems can be used with success. You might try starting with the cheapest and simplest (the Dome System - as the author did) and graduating to a more complex system as the need arises.

1.4 THE ACCOUNTING SYSTEM

The accounting systems described in the previous section are not quite complete in themselves, and there will be need for some additional paperwork to provide your new business with a full information system.

The type of system I will describe is, of course, the simplest possible. However, in order to make it as general as possible a hybrid basis - part cash, part accrual will be described. Such a system would apply to a retail store, say a bookshop. The single entry system will be the one described, since again it is the simplest and cheapest to use.

1.4.1 Business Checkbook

One of the first steps the new businessman should take is to open a checking account in the name of the new business. After this point, all the cash flow of the new business can pass through that account. This prevents the possibility of combining the owners personal checks with those of his business. Thus, the owner can track the critical balance of his cash flow in a precise manner.

The business bank account should have at least two people authorized to sign checks for the business. The checkbook often comes with three checks per page, each check numbered, as is its corresponding stub. The stub is large enough to record:

- The number of the check
- The date of the check
- The name of the payee/purpose
- The amount of the check

It is important to pay as many bills as possible by check and enter the number of the check used in the appropriate payment account in your books.

A machine called a "check writer" can be used to speed up the writing of checks and also to make the alteration of the check amount almost impossible.

1.4.2 Invoices—Sales And Expenses

Above and beyond your Bookkeeping ledgers, you will need some system for handling the recording of sales and certain expenses. This is because there can be hundreds of small sales made during the day, and yet at the end of the day only the day's total sales needs to be recorded in the income ledger. Similarly with expenses; you will receive invoices from your merchandise suppliers and, perhaps, pay them 30 days later. Thus, you still need a filing system to hold sales and payment invoices until you have recorded or paid them.

Sales

The type of invoice/filing system you need for recording sales depends on the number (not the dollar amount) of sales made per week, and also to some extent the type of business.

Infrequent Sales

A small manufacturing business may, for example, ship an order every few days. The sale, in this case, is invariably a credit sale and a billing invoice is required to obtain payment from the customer. Packages of preprinted invoices can be purchased cheaply, and will perform the billing function with the minimum of effort. These forms come in triplicate or even quadruplicate, with interleaved carbon papers. The first and second copy of the invoice can be sent to the customer, the third and fourth being kept in a file in numerical sequence. The fourth copy can always be sent to be buyer who has failed to pay the invoice within the stipulated time period.

Convenient, packaged invoice forms are sold by the Wilson Jones Company and are in the Grayline (R) "Snap-a-way" series. The four part invoice form is #44-401-4part.

1/Accounting/Financial Statements

bmh
BRACE MUELLER HUNTLEY INC.

P. O. BOX 1340, SYRACUSE, NEW YORK 13201 • (315) 463-3341

STEEL ALUMINUM BRASS PLASTICS

INVOICE	
DATE	NUMBER
03/28/73	BW 05335

D-U-N-S 00-495-2099

DUPLICATE INVOICE

SOLD TO:
RICHMOND MFG CO
367 ORCHARD ST
ROCH NY 14606

SHIP TO: SAME

TERMS
ALUMINUM AND PLASTICS - NO DISCOUNT
30 DAYS NET
STEEL and BRASS - ½ - 10 - NET 30

SHIP VIA: BMH   FROM: BUFF   1/2% DISC

REQUISITION NO.	CUSTOMER ORDER NUMBER	F.O.B.	B.M.H. NO.	DATE	SALES #	ACCOUNT NO.
		DLVD	54306	03/23/33	27	24000

Quan. Ordered	DESCRIPTION	PRODUCT CODE	QUAN. SHIPPED	WEIGHT	PRICE	AMOUNT
1 PC	CF STL BAR C1018 BLACK	2025730				
	1 X 8 X 20	2025730	1	44	30590	1346
	CUTTING	2025730				300

DISCOUNT	TOTAL AMOUNT
9	1546

MATERIAL PROVING DEFECTIVE WHEN USED FOR THE PURPOSE SPECIFIED WILL BE REPLACED. NO CLAIMS FOR LABOR OR DAMAGES WILL BE ALLOWED AND NO RESPONSIBILITY ASSUMED FOR DELAYS OF CARRIERS OR DELAYS ARISING FROM FIRES, STRIKES OR OTHER CAUSES BEYOND THE CONTROL OF THE COMPANY. PRICES ARE SUBJECT TO CHANGE WITHOUT NOTICE. WE HEREBY CERTIFY THAT THESE GOODS WERE PRODUCED IN COMPLIANCE WITH ALL APPLICABLE REQUIREMENTS OF SECTIONS 6, 7 AND 12 OF THE FAIR LABOR STANDARDS ACT, AS AMENDED, AND OF REGULATIONS AND ORDERS OF THE UNITED STATES DEPARTMENT OF LABOR ISSUED UNDER SECTION 14 THEREOF.

TYPICAL CREDIT INVOICE

These invoices can be marked paid when payment is received. Where several repeat customers are usual, a card can be made up for each customer that indicates the customer's current balance against each order. The file of unpaid invoices represents your Accounts Receivable; that is, amounts owed to you for goods you have sold on credit. The invoice is reasonably self explanitory but should contain:

- Your company name, address, phone number
- Customer's name, address, order number
- Date of invoice, date shipped, shipment method
- Merchandise description, amount, with sales tax shown separately
- Payment terms

The payment terms are of special note. The "net 30 days" means that you require full payment within 30 days. "1% 10 days, net 30 days" means that if your customer pays within 10 days from the date of shipment he can deduct 1% from the total invoice amount; if he pays after 10 days, the net amount applies.

Infrequent cash sales, that is say five to ten an hour, can be handled satisfactorily by the use of the familiar cash receipt. A book of pre-numbered cash receipts can be purchased in duplicate format. Your company name can be printed on the top of each form. Such sales slips can also be used for credit sales, where say Master Charge is used, and can be so marked. The top copy is given to the customer and a duplicate kept for your records. At the end of the day, the cash sales can be separated from the credit sales and filed in numerical sequence. All sales slips should be filed, even those voided, so that complete records can be kept.

The sales for each employee can be tracked by giving each salesperson a separate receipt book, identified by number.

Frequent Sales

Frequent credit sales would require a modified version of the sales invoice previously described. Some form of automation would probably be required for optimum efficiency - perhaps a word processing machine with a prestored list of customer names and addresses programmed with their current orders. The word processor can print both the invoices and their attached envelopes using an automatic paper feeder.

Even larger businesses, of course, use punched cards, which when returned with payment can be automatically processed. The Public Utility Companies typically use such automated system.

Frequent cash sales call for the use of a cash register. Cash registers come in a variety of forms of complication. However, it is probably worth the extra expense of a register that provides partial automation of the accounting system. Such a register would probably contain microelectronics and sell for about a thousand dollars. A partial list of the features of such a cash register is:

- Contains a double tape, which provides a receipt for the customer

1/Accounting/Financial Statements

SCANDINAVIA HOUSE
651-4676
501 Weybridge Ave
Dallas, Texas 75240

A1375

Date: July 7, 79

Sold To: John B. Walton
Address: 15917 Broadridge Dr.
Dallas, TX 75216
Phone: H. 233 6141 / W. 654 1160

KIND OF SALE: COD
DELIVERY INFORMATION: WPU
X 2230

QUAN	DESCRIPTION	PRICE	AMOUNT
1	3700 EX swivel tilt chrome base desk chair Gr. #4 Gunstock Russet	(186.00)	186 00
		less 10%	18 60
			167 40
		tax	8 37
			175 77
	Final Sale		

Signature: John B. Walton

TYPICAL CASH RECEIPT

- and a record for the shopkeeper.
- Maintains separate totals for those items requiring sales tax, those that do not, and the amount of sales tax accumulated.
- Will print out sales totals, tax totals and can be cleared and set to zero after each day's use.

Obviously, such a cash register greatly simplifies the task of tracking daily sales. The various totals for each day can be entered directly into the total receipts column of your accounts ledger (as will be discussed later).

Expenditures

Expenditures are easier to deal with than sales and should be segregated into two major categories:

1. Merchandise and materials
2. Other expenditures (for example rent, office supplies, heating, etc.)

The first category reflects the cost of goods sold, whereas the second reflects the cost of business operations (overhead). Both categories can be paid either by cash or by check.

You will be sent invoices by your suppliers, by your utility company, by the city tax office, and so on. You should segregate the incoming invoices into the two expenditure categories and file them separately using two box files or two-ring binders. The file containing your unpaid invoices for merchandise and materials is your Accounts Payable file. The file containing your unpaid operating expenses is your Accrued Expenses file.

It is important to keep and file the invoice or receipt for any type of expenditure both for tracking accounts payable and also for verifying expenditures to the I.R.S. Where items are paid by check, the invoice should be marked "PAID", it should be dated, and the number of the payment check should also be added. This latter step will help to avoid later confusion if payment controversies arise.

1.4.3 Recording Income

As indicated earlier, the accounting system of a retail store will be used as an example. Remember that I.R.S. requirements call for the use of an accrual system for recording the sales of a retail operation.

For our purposes, the accounting system devised by Dome Publishing will be used and several of the ledgers will be referred to by way of illustration.

At the end of each business day all sales, both cash and credit, are totalled up and entered into the section "Total Receipts From Business Or Profession". The total sales tax on merchandise sold (both for cash and credit) is entered in one column; and total sales (including tax) is entered in the next column.

Note: All ledger entries should be made in pencil – to easily correct the inevitable mistakes.

1/Accounting/Financial Statements

MONTH OF JANUARY, 1975

DAY	TOTAL RECEIPTS FROM BUSINESS OR PROFESSION				ACCT. NO.	ACCOUNT	EX... THIS
	SALES TAX		AMOUNT				
1	22	50	450	00		**DEDUCTIBLE**	
2	31	25	625	00	1	MDSE.-MATERIALS	
3	35	00	700	00	2	ACCOUNTING	
4	25	00	500	00	3	ADVERTISING	
5	48	00	960	00	4	AUTO EXPENSE	
6	SUNDAY		—		5	CARTONS, ETC.	
7	12	50	250	00	6	CONTRIBUTIONS	
8	18	50	370	00	7	DELIVERY EXP.	
9	25	00	500	00	8	ELECTRICITY	
10	34	50	690	00	9	ENTERTAINMENT	
11	21	75	435	00	10	FREIGHT & EXP.	
12	44	50	890	00	11	HEAT	
13	SUNDAY		—		12	INSURANCE	
14	23	00	460	00	13	INTEREST	
15	26	25	525	00	14	LAUNDRY	
16	35	00	700	00	15	LEGAL EXPENSE	
17	48	00	960	00	16	LICENSES	
18	42	50	850	00	17	MISC. EXP.	
19	62	00	1240	00	18	OFFICE EXP.	
20	SUNDAY		—		19	POSTAGE	
21	27	50	550	00	20	RENT	
22	32	00	640	00	21	REPAIRS	
23	36	00	720	00	22	SHOP EX	
24	35	50	710	00	23	TAX —	
25	32	50	650	00	24	TAX —	
26	46	00	920	00	25	TAX -	
27	SUNDAY		—		26	SELL	
28	12	50	250	00	27	SUP	
29	15	00	300	00	28	TEL	
30	23	50	470	00	29	TR	
31	19	25	385	00	30	T	
TOTAL THIS MONTH	835	00	16,700	00	31		
TOTAL UP TO LAST MONTH	—		—		32		
TOTAL TO DATE	835	00	16,700	00	3?		

TYPICAL INCOME LEDGER

(Used by permission-DOME PUBLISHING CO., INC)

You will, of course, have goods returned and either have to repay the cash paid or remove the credit charge to the customer.

A sales slip for the returned goods is then prepared, which is exactly the same as the original sales slip except that it is stamped RETURNED GOODS or REFUND. The sales amount and tax for the refund is then subtracted from that day's totals. In this way, a record is kept as an invoice and an adjustment made to the income ledger that a refund/returned goods situation has occurred.

At the end of each month the totals for sales tax and receipts are calculated for that month and entered. In our case a total of $16,700 of goods were sold, of which $835 was state sales tax. These amounts are added to the totals up to the end of the previous month to provide the two totals to date. The totals to date calculated in the last month of the business' fiscal year provide the total income for the year and ease the tasks of preparing financial statements (to be covered later) and your income tax return.

1.4.4 Recording Expenditures

The I.R.S. allows the retail store owner to choose which accounting method he prefers for recording expenditures. We will choose the cash method, since it provides a tax advantage. Thus, overall, our accounting system is the hybrid basis - part cash and part accrual.

The Dome "Detail of Monthly Expenditures" ledger, shown below, is divided into two sections. Section one, on the left side of the page is for merchandise and materials, whereas section two, on the right side of the page covers everything else. Expenditures should be entered on a daily basis and include the following information:

- Date
- To Whom Paid
- Check Number
- Amount
- Account Number

The account number corresponds to a particular category of expense. Dome has created two major cateories of expenditure:

- Expenditures deductible for tax purposes - #1-35
- Expenditures non-deductible for tax purposes - #51-57

Each category is explained in detail in the Dome Bookkeeping Record Book. For example:

Account No. 1 - Merchandise and Materials

This includes all mechandise and materials purchased for resale.

Account No 15 - Legal Expense

Again a distinction must be made between legal expense incurred as the result of business transactions and legal

1/Accounting/Financial Statements

expense incurred for non-business purpose. The former should be shown under No. 15, and the latter under No. 55 - Personal.

Account No. 52 - Federal Income Tax

By law, Federal Income Tax payments are not deductable and therefore must be entered here.

DETAIL OF MONTHLY EXPENDITURES — JANUARY

\multicolumn{4}{c}{MDSE. AND MATERIALS PAID BY CASH AND CHECKS}	\multicolumn{5}{c}{OTHER EXPENDITURES BY CHECKS AND CASH}
DAY	TO WHOM PAID	CHECK NO.	AMOUNT	DAY	TO WHOM PAID	CHECK NO.	ACCT. NO.	AMOUNT
1	Apex Supply Co.	305	360 90	1	Nicky Oil Co.	306	11	13 81
2	General Mdse Co.	307	250 78	2	Natl. Bank of Amer.	313	53	50 —
3	Lacy Co.	309	59 82		ditto	313	13	2 56
3	Natl. Supply Corp.	310	32 44	3	L.B. Repair Co.	314	21	16 50
3	Wholesalers, Inc.	311	57 13	3	Joe's Serv. Station	316	4	25 55
4	U.S. Sales Co.	315	41 77	3	Gen'l Adver., Inc.	317	3	27 50
4	Cash Purchases	—	46 20	3	Standard Ins. Co	318	12	40 —
				4	Watt Transport	319	10	22 78
				4	Speedy Service	320	7	24 08
				4	Main Office Supply	321	18	11 59
				6	Payroll (net Paid)	322	31	185 31
				6	Owner's Salary	323	55	100 —

DETAIL OF MONTHLY EXPENDITURES

(Used by permission-DOME PUBLISHING CO.,INC)

At the end of each month the total for each account is entered into the "Expenditures" summary sheet (shown below). In this manner, the total deductible expenses and total overall expenses, including non-deductible items, are entered into the ledger.

Note that the current month's expenditures are added to the column of "Total Up To Last Month" expenditures to provide the total to date.

MONTH OF JUNE, 19 77

EXPENDITURES

ACCT. NO.	ACCOUNT	TOTAL THIS MONTH	TOTAL UP TO LAST MONTH	TOTAL TO DATE
	DEDUCTIBLE			
1	MDSE.-MATERIALS	8,400	38,000	46,400
2	ACCOUNTING	-0-	55	55
3	ADVERTISING	350	1,750	2,100
4	AUTO EXPENSE	70	350	420
5	CARTONS, ETC.	-0-	0	-0-
6	CONTRIBUTIONS	-0-	0	-0-
7	DELIVERY EXP.	-0-	-0-	-0-
8	ELECTRICITY	-0-	-0-	-0-
9	ENTERTAINMENT	-0-	-0-	-0-
10	FREIGHT & EXP.	-0-	-0-	-0-
11	HEAT	-0-	-0-	-0-
12	INSURANCE	-0-	600	600
13	INTEREST	190	950	1140
14	LAUNDRY	-0-	-0-	-0-
15	LEGAL EXPENSE	10	400	410
16	LICENSES	-0-	-0-	-0-
17	MISC. EXP.	-0-	26	26
18	OFFICE EXP.	0	-0-	0
19	POSTAGE	-0-	62	62
20	RENT	1000	5,000	6,000
21	REPAIRS	60	260	320
22	SHOP EXP.	80	360	440
23	TAX — SOC. SEC.	-0-	560	560
24	TAX — STATE U. I.	-0-	176	176
25	TAX — OTHER	2,310	4,100	6,410
26	SELLING EXP.	0	-0-	-0-
27	SUPPLIES	240	1100	1340
28	TELEPHONE	150	600	750
29	TRADE DUES, ETC.	-0-	-0-	-0-
30	TRAVELING EXP.	-0-	170	170
31	WAGES & COMM.	810	4,800	5610
32	WATER	-0-	-0-	-0-
33				
34				
35				
	SUB-TOTAL	13,670	59,319	72,989
	NON-DEDUCTIBLE			
51	NOTES PAYABLE	-0-	-0-	
52	FEDERAL INC. TAX	-0-	3,600	3,600
53	LOANS PAYABLE	200	1,000	1,200
54	LOANS RECEIV.	-0-	-0-	-0-
55	PERSONAL	-0-	21,000	21,000
56	FIXED ASSETS	-0-	1,700	1,700
57				
	TOTAL THIS MONTH	13,870		
	TOT. UP TO LAST MO.		86,619	
	TOTAL TO DATE			100,489

MONTHLY EXPENDITURE SUMMARY

(Used by permission—DOME PUBLISHING CO., INC)

1/Accounting/Financial Statements

Not every account is used, and you can name up to three additional deductible accounts and one non-deductible account if the accounts provided do not fit your needs. Also, some months certain accounts, such as Tax - Soc. Sec., have no entries. This is because our system is on a cash basis and we pay the Social Security Tax due only every quarter (taxation will be dealt with in detail in a later chapter).

At the end of the fiscal year, the cumulative total to date provides the total expenditures, deductibles and non-deductibles, that have been made during the year. The totals for every expense catagory are useful, since they show you how much has been spent on various items and where effective cost cuts can be made.

1.4.5 Credit-Credit Cards

Most small stores, although not all, decide that they have to extend credit to gain extra sales volumn. Most businesses are too small to make the extra bookkeeping and extra hassle of managing their own credit system worth while. It is best to accept one or more of the major credit cards - usually Master Charge and Visa. The advantages of credit cards are:

- The bank handles all collections and credits your account each month.
- The bank is responsible for unpaid accounts, lost or stolen cards.

The disadvantages to the businessman are:

- Usually, an initial fee (approxiamtely $30) and an annual charge for renting each imprinting machine are required.
- A fee is charged for each credit sale - usually three percent.

The businessman is required to obey certain conditions:

- The customers signature on the sales slip must be compared with that on the card.
- Telephone approval must be obtained for card sales over a specific amount.
- The card must not have expired.

If you provide your own credit system and if, at the end of the year, there are credit accounts which are obviously uncollectible, the same procedure is followed as with returned goods, except that the invoice and ledger are stamped "Uncollectible Accounts".

1.4.6 Payroll Accounting

The Dome Monthly Bookkeeping Record contains a payroll section for 15 employees. Another Dome publication (#650) will cover up to 50 employees.

The information for each employee is carried an two pages. The first page, shown partially below, provides information on hours worked, etc.

Week No.	WEEK ENDED	HOURS						Regular Time	Over. Time	RATE		Regular Wages	Overtime Wages	Paid by Check No.
		SUN.	MON.	TUE.	WED.	THU.	FRI.	SAT.			Amount	Per.			
1	Jan. 7		7	7	7	7	7	3	38		200	wk	200		2341
2	14		7	7	7	7	7	3	38		200	wk	200		2401
3	21		7	7	7	7	7	3	38		200	wk	200		2460
4															
13															
	Totals—1st Qtr.												2,600		

NAME Norma C. Glenn ADDRESS 44 Humboldt Ave., Boston, Mass.

The second page, again partially shown below, provides a record of various payroll deductions. Note that total wages equals net pay plus all the deductions.

SOCIAL SECURITY NO. 035-41-4673   NO. OF EXEMPTIONS 1   / SINGLE ☑ MARRIED ☐

Week No.	TOTAL WAGES (a)	DEDUCTIONS						NET PAY (h)	Week No.
		Social Security (b)	U.S. With. Tax (c)	State With. Tax (d)					
1	200 —	12 26	29 10	5 90				152 74	1
2	200 —	12 26	29 10	5 90				152 74	2
3	200 —	12 26	29 10	5 90				152 74	3
4									4
TOTALS 14	2,600 —	159 38	378 30	76 70				1,985 62	TOTALS 14

The task of entering the various deductions for each wage can be simplified by the purchase of a Combination Tax Chart. This chart provides the various deductions corresponding to salary level and number of exemptions. A convenient four page plastic covered chart is provided by:

>Redi-Record Payroll Systems
>Oceanside
>New York

After the amounts for each employee have been entered, the totals for each category of deduction and pay are entered into a master control sheet for that week. For example, the total amount of social security deducted from all employees is entered into the appropriate column of the control sheet. This control sheet is illustrated below.

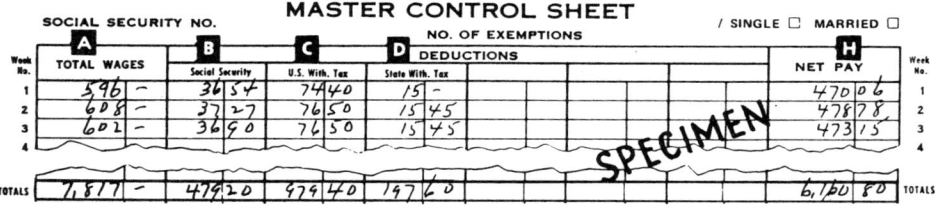

MASTER CONTROL SHEET

SOCIAL SECURITY NO.   NO. OF EXEMPTIONS   / SINGLE ☐ MARRIED ☐

Week No.	TOTAL WAGES A	DEDUCTIONS						NET PAY H	Week No.
		Social Security B	U.S. With. Tax C	State With. Tax D					
1	596 —	36 54	74 40	15 —				470 06	1
2	608 —	37 27	76 50	15 45				478 78	2
3	601 —	36 90	76 50	15 45				473 15	3
4									4
TOTALS	7,817 —	479 20	979 40	197 60				6,160 80	TOTALS

Dome also provides a separate sheet on which details of the various tax deposits can be recorded. The timing of the various tax deposit payments will be covered later in the chapter on taxation.

1.4.7 Petty Cash

Petty Cash is a fund specially set up, in bills and coins, for the purpose of quickly providing cash to employees so that they can make small emergency purchases for the business. Typical of such situations is the purchase of stamps, payment of shipping charges and payment of donations.

If the small business can survive without a petty cash fund another headache will have been avoided. If, however, it becomes necessary then a simple system should be set up. Since, the petty cash system is open to employee abuse certain rules must be followed:

1. A small ledger book should be purchased that has at least six ruled columns, together with a box (with key) for keeping the fund. These should be kept in a safe place and entrusted to only one senior employee besides the owner.
2. A check is written "Payable to Petty Cash" for not more than $20, and the cash drawn placed in the box.
3. Whenever the fund is used the following should be entered in the petty cash book:
   o   Date
   o   Payee
   o   Employee
   o   Amount and purpose
4. The employee <u>must</u> obtain a receipt and it should be placed in the box.
5. When the fund gets low another $20 check can be drawn.
6. At the end of each month, the individual expenditures are entered into the regular expenditures ledger and the remaining balance calculated. Obviously, the total petty cash expenses for the month plus the balance should equal the prior balance plus any petty cash paid into the fund.

At the end of any accounting period the cash in the business is the sum of the petty cash balance plus the amount in the business checking account.

1.4.8 Fiscal Year-End Accounting

At the end of each fiscal year it is necessary to prepare your financial statements, which indicate the year's profits, the business' assets and liabilities. The financial statements will be covered in detail later on in this chapter, but before they can be prepared a certain amount of "tidying up" has to take place with your accounts. Remember that our accounting system for the retail shop and for illustration is on a <u>hybrid</u> basis - part cash, part accrual. We must, therefore, make sure that the year-end cash balance and accrual balance are correct.

Accrual Items

1. Sales

   Since both cash and credit sales were recorded in the "Receipts From Business" ledger the total year-end balance shown for sales is on the accrual system.

2. Accounts Receivable

   Pull out your accounts receivable file and make a list of all those still unpaid at year end (Dome provides a special sheet for this entitled "Schedule of Accounts Receivable). Total these up and the amount will be your year-end balance of accounts receivable.

3. Purchases

   You will remember that we chose to keep <u>all</u> our expenditures on a cash basis. Thus, purchases of merchandise for resale are also on a cash basis (Dome Account #1). We need to convert the cash basis for purchases to the accrual basis to comply with I.R.S. requirements. But first, we must total up our year-end accounts payables. This is done in exactly the same manner as accounts receivables (Dome provides a "Schedule of Accounts Payable). Then, a few mathematical steps are required:

   Purchases For The Year (Accrual Basis)

   1. Merchandise - Materials (Acct. No 1) $ _____
   2. Deduct - Beginning of Year of Accounts Payable - _____
   3. Balance   _____
   4. Add-End of Year Accounts Payable   + _____
   5. Purchases for Year   = _____

   As we shall see later, the subtraction of purchases from sales provides the amount of gross profit for the year.

4. Inventories

   The amount of goods in inventory is an important matter to any retail operation and year-end values are an important accounting item. The goods in inventory are valued at cost or lower. The latter situation occurs when the merchandise has lost value because it has been damaged, is out-of-date, or cannot be sold for some reason. The amount of decrease in value below cost must be added to business expenses for that year and is added to the cost of merchandise and materials.

   The accounting situation for a manufacturer is a little more complicated and will be dealt with later.

5. Fixed Assets

   Dome Account Number 56 (Fixed Assets) is the sum of the following items that may have been purchased during the year.
   - Machinery and Equipment
   - Autos and Trucks
   - Other Equipment
   - Buildings
   - Land

1/Accounting/Financial Statements

You will notice from the "Monthly Expenditure Summary" ledger, see Section 1.4.4, that #56, Fixed Assets is listed under non-deductable expenditures. This is because the full cost of these items cannot be deducted as a business expense in the year of purchase. However, what can be deducted is an item known as depreciation. Depreciation is the amount that the fixed asset has lost in value during the year through wear and tear. Land does not loose value and <u>cannot</u>, therefore, be depreciated. The complicated rules for calculating depreciation will be covered in the chapter on taxation.

6. Cash Items

  - Cash

    The year-end cash balance is the amount in the business checking account plus the amount in petty cash.

  - Expenditures

    All expenses in accounts numbered 2 through 35 are on the cash basis. It is wise to check that the totals of deposited employee deductions for taxes given in the year-end expenditure ledger sheet equals the amounts shown as the tax deposits.

1.5 FINANCIAL STATEMENTS

Financial Statements, which show profits over the year and provide an accurate picture of total assets and total liabilities, are often perceived as merely stale records of the years activity. On the contrary, financial statements are used on many occassions in the life of a small business. If, for instance, a small business is offered for sale it is vital, of course, to be able to understand the sellers books and financial statements. Again, if a small business is being started it will probably be necessary to create projected financial statements in order to establish the basis for credit with a banker or supplier. It is worth noting that estimated financial statements are known as PRO FORMA statements. Tax returns, even for the smallest business, require the completion of an elementary form of financial statements. Finally, it will be necessary for the businessman to create his own estimated financial statements in order to be able to forecaste his cash needs in, for example, buying the business, buying inventory, paying expenses and generally running the business until it is self supporting.

The financial statements of large corporations can be immensely complicated, with many footnotes indicating special accounting conventions that they have used in preparing their statements. Small businesses, on the other hand, do not, in the main, require complicated accounting systems and you should be suspicious of the statements of a small business that appear overly complicated. There are three basic financial statements:

1. The Balance Sheet
2. The Income Statement (sometimes called the Profit and Loss Statement)
3. The Cash Flow Statement

The first two of these statements are the ones normally requested by banks and normally given in corporate annual reports. These two are interrelated and must be consistent from year to year.

The third statement, the Cash Flow, is often far more informative since it shows the actual cash flow into and out of the business on a month by month basis. As you will see later, it is quite possible to show very satisfactory profits on the income statement, but actually be going broke. The Cash Flow statement would pick up this discrepancy and, therefore, it is an extremely important document to have in the analysis of any business.

1.6 THE BALANCE SHEET

A simple example will serve to demonstrate how the balance sheet is used. Suppose that Mr. Smith buys an existing retail store for $30,000. Smith has $20,000 of his own money and has to borrow $10,000 from his bank to pay the rest. You can quickly see that a balance can be made between the $30,000 value of the business (the assets) and the funds used to buy the business. The funds needed divide into two parts; firstly, the $20,000 - the owner's capital contribution (owner's equity) and, secondly, the $10,000 - funds owed to outsiders (the liabilities).

In every business, therefore, a simple balance sheet equation always applies:

$$\text{Assets} = \text{Liabilities} + \text{Owner's Equity}$$

In this case,

$$\$30{,}000 \text{ (assets)} = \$10{,}000 \text{ (liabilities)} + \$20{,}000 \text{ (owners equity)}$$

The first important thing to realise about a balance sheet is that it is true only at the end of a particular day, and, therefore, balance sheets are always dated. Take Mr. Smith's business as an example. His balance sheet at the end of the day he bought it would appear as follows:

TABLE ONE
SMITH RETAIL STORE
Balance Sheet
June 15, 1980

ASSETS		EQUITIES	
	$30,000	Liabilities	$10,000
		Owner's Equity	$20,000
Total Assets	$30,000	Total Equities	$30,000

Note that the total of liabilities and owner's equity is called the equity.

Suppose that on the next day Smith acquires $4,000 worth of merchandise from a supplier on credit. Smith's balance sheet that evening would be as follows:

1/Accounting/Financial Statements

SMITH RETAIL STORE
Balance Sheet
June 16, 1980

ASSETS		EQUITIES	
	$34,000	Liabilities	$14,000
		Owner's Equity	$20,000
Total Assets	$34,000	Total Equities	$34,000

Thus each side of the balance sheet has increased by the extra $4,000 worth of merchandise.

Naturally, this balance sheet does not provide the reader with much information and would not be an acceptable description of the business. What is needed is a more detailed breakdown of the assets and equities.

Let us go back and look at a more detailed version of Smith's balance sheet on the day he bought his store. It is assumed that the previous owner paid off all prior debts including any for merchandise on hand. Smith, however, will have to collect payment on the outstanding balance of any merchandise sold on credit. He will, as you will see, allow a small amount for uncollectible accounts. The prior owner also pays Smith $3,210, which will cover the past quarter's Sales Tax and Federal Income Taxes, which are due to be paid within the next month.

The full balance sheet now appears as follows:

TABLE TWO
SMITH RETAIL STORE
Balance Sheet (Accrual Basis)
June 15, 1980

ASSETS		EQUITIES	
Current Assets		Current Liabilities	
Cash	$ 3,210	Accounts Payable	$ 0
Marketable Securities	$ 0	Notes Payable	$ 0
Accounts Receivable	$11,300	Current Portion Of	
Allowance For		Long-Term Loan	$ 2,000
Doubtful Accounts	$ (180)	Accrued Expenses Payable	$ 0
Inventories	$ 7,400	Accrued Income Taxes Pay.	$ 3,210
Total Current Assets	$21,730	Total Current Liabilities	$ 5,210
Long Term Assets		Long Term Liabilities	
Equipment	$ 1,580		
Furniture & Fixtures	$ 9,900	Bank loan, 12% interest,	
	$11,480	5 Years	$ 8,000
Less Accumulated			
Depreciation	$ 0	Owner's Equity	
Net Long Term Assets	$11,480	W. Smith, Capital	$20,000
Prepaid Expenses	$ 0		
Intangible Assets	$ 0		
Total Assets	$33,210	Total Equities	$33,210

Naturally, since Smith has just acquired the business there are many zeroes in the balance sheet. Normally, each account would have some value.

We will explain each account in detail later, but first notice that several of the accounts are called accrual accounts. For example, accrued income taxes payable is an accrual account. This means that the business owes taxes but has not yet paid them. Similary, accounts receivable is another accrual account. Accounts receivables are monies owed to the business for goods purchased on credit for which payment has not yet been received. When the various accounts are listed in this manner, the accounting method used is called <u>accrual basis accounting</u>. Accrual basis accounting is the accounting method used by all large corporations and many small business, since it more accurately reflects the state of the business than the other accounting method called <u>cash basis accounting</u>.

Cash basis accounting lists only those cash transactions that have taken place in each account. Thus, if Smith sells $2,000 worth of goods of which $1,500 are credit sales and $500 are cash sales, He would list;

        Cash $500

He would not list the $1,500 anywhere until he received the $1500 cash payment.

For the moment, only the accrual basis accounting method is discussed, since it is the more difficult to understand.

The next few sections explore each account of the balance sheet, using the accrual basis, in more detail.

ASSETS

Assets are divided into two major categories; current assets and long-term assets. Current assets include cash and other items such as inventory that can be converted into cash reasonably quickly. Long-term assets are those items such as land, buildings and equipment which are not intended for sale, but are permanent items used in the business. For this reason, long-term assets are sometimes called fixed assets. Let us go back to the example of Mr. Smith and his retail store and examine each element of his balance sheet on June 15th. First of all, let us look at his current assets.

Cash

This is the amount of money Smith has on hand in his store plus any money he has in the store's checking account at the bank. The only cash, he has is the sales and income tax due, which was handed to him by the prior owner and is now in his checking account.

        Cash $3,210

Marketable Securities

Any prudent businessman would not keep large sums of money in his checking account. He would for example, invest in Government Securities, such as T Bills, or Commerial Paper (both these financial instruments easily earned 10% interest in 1979). Note, the current minimum value T Bill is $10,000 and the

1/Accounting/Financial Statements

current minumim value good quality commercial paper, such as a General Motors Acceptance Corporation note, is $25,000. For Smith's case he has no marketable securities, thus:

    Marketable Securities (at cost) $0

Accounts Receivable

This represents the amount of goods sold to customers of the store on credit, for which payment has not yet been received. In today's world this would usually be charge card business. In Mr. Smith's case:

    Accounts Receivables $11,300

Allowance For Doubtful Accounts

Whenever credit is extended there will be a certain percentage that will not be repaid. The average unpaid credit over several years is fairly constant and each type of business has its own value. In Mr. Smith's case, let us assume the percentage is 1.5%:

    Allowance For Doubtful Accounts ($180)

Note, that the $180 is only an allowance or expectation of how much of the $11,300 will not be collected. On the balance sheet it is subtracted, denoted by the (180), from the amount of accounts receivables to give the true value of the receivables.

Inventories

This is the value of the merchandise, at cost, that Smith has in his shop. For this case:

    Inventory $7,400

Total Current Assets

The current assets are always totalled up and presented as a separate item on the balance sheet:

    Total Current Assets $22,730

This value is important since it represents the total value of items used in the operating cycle of the business. Inventory is bought on credit, then sold for cash and on credit. The credit later collected as cash, which can be used to pay for the inventory, and so on. For this reason current assets are also known as working assets.

So much for current assets. Long-term assets are normally listed in the balance sheet under that heading. If Mr. Smith had owned his store's building and the land it occupied, these would have been listed under long-term assets. In this case, Smith rented his business premises from a property company. However, he does have equipment, such as a cash register and typewriter:

    Equipment $1,580

Also,

        Furniture and Fixtures $9,900
        Total Long-Lived Assets $11,480

Depreciation

As is obvious, long-lived assets do not last forever and, for example, a typewriter will, over many years, wear out and have to be replaced. Thus, each year it can be said that a little value of that typewriter is lost. This diminishing value is called depreciation and applies to all fixed assets that deteriorate over time. Land, of course, cannot wear out and, therefore, suffers no depreciation.

On Mr. Smith's very first day in business no time has elapsed for any depreciation to accumulate; thus:

    Depreciation $0

Listed at the bottom of the table of assets are any miscellaneous items that do not properly fit under short-term or long term assets.

Prepaid Expenses

If Mr. Smith had prepaid any of his future expenses, such as insurance, heating or telephone, these would be listed under the heading "Prepaid Expenses".

Accounts Payable

These assets have no physical existence, but do provide value to a business. The most common example of such an asset is "Goodwill". Goodwill represents the amount of money a business is bought for over and above the value of its physical assets. Other such intangible assets are valuable trademarks or patents.

LIABILITIES

As with assets, liabilities are divided into two groups; short term and long-term. Short-term liabilities are those which must be repaid during the current year, whilst long-term liabilities are those that must be repaid beyond the current year.

The various sub-catorories of current liabilities will now be explored.

Intangible Assets

The amount listed under Accounts Payable is the sum of all the various amounts owing to the vendors who have supplied merchandise to the business. Normal business conduct requires that these accounts are paid within 30 days. However, many large strong companies will stretch out their accounts payable to 60 or even 90 days. However, a small, perhaps new business would want to retain a good credit rating by paying promptly. Indeed, it can be advantageous to pay earlier especially if suppliers give a cash discount for prompt payment. In this case, the invoice will state something like this:

                2, 10, net 30

This means that if you pay within 10 days from the date of the invoice you can deduct 2%, otherwise you pay the full amount within 30 days.

In Mr. Smith's case, we will assume that the seller has taken the responsibility of paying all the prior suppliers. Thus,

    Accounts Payable $0

Notes Payable
The amount listed under notes payable represents either promissary notes given to suppliers or short term borrowing from banks. Mr. Smith has none of either category:

    Notes Payable $0

Current Portion Of Long-Term Debt
This amount is that portion of the long-term debt that must be repaid during the current year. Smith has borrowed $10,000 over five years and is scheduled to repay $2,000 in principal repayments (excluding interest) over the first year.

Accrued Expenses Payable
This item represents such things as interest or loans, wages earned but not yet paid, insurance premiums due, pensions to be paid out, and so on. These are all amounts that have to be paid out in the current year ahead and, therefore, are a current liability on the business:

    Accrued Expenses Payable $0

Accrued Income Taxes Payable
This item needs almost no explanation. It is, of course, the amount owing for State Sales Tax, Federal Income Tax, and FICA Tax:

    Accrued Income Taxes Payable $3,210

In Smith's case the number of items in <u>long-term liabilities</u> is very small. Normally, these items are either long-term mortgages or loans from commercial banks. We previously noted that the current portion of the long-term debt was $2,000. Clearly, the long-term position is $8,000. Thus,

    Long-Term Liabilities $8,000

Owner's Equity
Owner's Equity is the amount of capital the owner has tied up in his business. The amount of owner's equity varies with time depending on whether the owner puts more capital into the business, or reduces his investment. We will see later just how this comes about.

Smith invested $20,000 of his own money in his retail store. Thus, his balance sheet capital contribution reflects just that:

    W. Smith, Capital $20,000

This concludes the first look at the full balance sheet. We will return to it at the end of the first year of operations, but first the Income Statement will be discussed.

THE INCOME STATEMENT
You will recall that the Balance Sheet always reflects the state of the business at the end of a particular day, as if frozen at an instant in time. The Income Statement, on the other hand, reflects how much profit or loss the business has made over a specific period of time. This period is normally one year, but large companies report their earnings quarterly and half yearly.

Very simply, the income statement indicates how much the sales were and how much was spent in expenses.

Smith's full income statement for his first year of operation (on an accrual basis) is:

TABLE THREE
SMITH RETAIL STORE
Income Statement (Accrual basis)
Fiscal Year Ended June 15, 1981

Total Net Sales	$150,000
Cost Of Sales	84,000
Gross Profit On Sales	$ 65,700
Operating Expenses	
Employee Salaries	$11,460
Telephone	840
Insurance	600
Supplies	2,160
Outside Labor (cleaners, etc.)	600
Repair and Maintenance	840
Advertising and Promotion	2,500
Car and Delivery	1,000
Bad Debts	300
Administration/Legal	1,000
Rent/Utilities	12,000
Taxes (except owner's)	9,940
Interest	1,200
Depreciation	2,650
Total Operating Expenses	$ 47,090
Net Income Before Taxes	$ 18,610
Owner's Taxes	$ 4,260
Net Income After Taxes	$ 14,350

This type of income statement is typical of a retail store type of operation. First the total net sales are given. Net sales are the total sales minus the value of any goods returned. Next, the cost of these goods, that is the price paid by the store owner to the distributor or manufacturer, is subtracted, giving the gross profit on sales. This value is only the gross profit, since all the costs of operating the business must be subtracted in order to obtain the business profit before taxes. These operating costs are grouped under a separate heading.

The purpose of grouping the items in the income statement as shown is to easily assess the effects of a change in the level of sales or expense. Notice, for instance, that the ratio of the cost of goods sold to the value of net sales is $84,300 divided by $150,000 or 56%. This percentage will remain reasonably unchanged over a wide range in net sales. Suppose, for example, that Smith had sold $170,000 worth of goods during the year. His cost of goods would have been approximately $95,000 and his gross profit $75,000. If he had kept the same operating expenses his net income before taxes would have been $75,000 – $45,550 or $29,450.

On the other hand, if his total operating expenses had been 10% higher, then his net income before taxes would have been $65,700 – $50,105 or $15,595, assuming his net sales were still $150,000.

These two simple examples illustrate that relatively small changes in sales or expenses can have a dramatic effect on profit. It is important, therefore, to estimate future sales carefully and budget expenses accordingly.

Two items concerning this income statement are of special interest:

1. Federal Taxation

    The net income before taxes is the amount that the I.R.S. recognizes as income to the business and, since Smith is the sole proprietor, income to him. It does not matter how much of that income he has had to reinvest in the business during the year, the amount shown on the income statement is the taxable income.

2. Cash

    The $18,610 income shown does not mean that Smith will have that amount in cash generated from the business during the year. We will see in the next section just what he will have and how that differs from the income statement amount.

CASH FLOW

The cash flow statement described below shows the flow of funds into and out of the business on a month by month basis. To the small businessman, this is the only meaningful way to present the cash flow. It is normally not shown this way, but is merely a rearrangement of the income statement, separating out the cash from the non-cash items. It is the author's contention that the starting businessman should first fix his attention on month by month cash flow rather than concern himself with year to year flow.

A cash flow example is shown on the next page. The first item shown is the net sales. This represents the amount of goods, less returns and discounts, etc., actually sold. However, collections lag behind sales. It is assumed that one third of the goods are cash sales and, therefore, one third of sales are collected in the month of their sale. It is further assumed that two thirds are credit sales, with one third collected during the month after their sale and the last third collected two months after their sale.

Example

	Month 1	Month 2	Month 3
Sales ($K)	12.0		
Collections (cash)	4.0		
(credit)		4.0	4.0

TABLE FOUR
SMITH RETAIL STORE
12 Month's Cash Flow For The Period Ending June 15, 1981
(In 000's Dollars)

MONTH ITEM	JUN JUL	JUL AUG	AUG SEP	SEP OCT	OCT NOV	NOV DEC	DEC JAN	JAN FEB	FEB MAR	MAR APR	APR MAY	MAY JUN	TOTALS
Net Sales	12.0	11.7	12.4	13.3	15.6	17.4	12.1	10.7	9.7	12.5	11.8	10.8	150.0
Collections	11.6	11.6	12.0	12.4	13.7	15.4	15.0	13.2	10.8	11.0	11.2	11.8	149.7
DISBURSEMENTS													
Employees Salaries	0.80	0.80	0.80	0.95	1.22	1.59	1.3	0.8	0.8	0.8	0.8	0.8	11.46
Purchases	0	6.50	7.20	7.50	8.60	9.80	6.80	5.90	5.30	7.00	6.60	5.70	76.90
Telephone	0.07	0.07	0.07	0.07	0.07	0.07	0.07	0.07	0.07	0.07	0.07	0.07	0.84
Insurance	0.6	0	0	0	0	0	0	0	0	0	0	0	0.60
Supplies	0	0.18	0.18	0.18	0.18	0.18	0.18	0.18	0.18	0.18	0.18	0.18	1.98
Outside Labor	0.05	0.05	0.05	0.05	0.05	0.05	0.05	0.05	0.05	0.05	0.05	0.05	0.60
Repairs & Maintenance	0	0.07	0.07	0.07	0.07	0.07	0.07	0.07	0.07	0.07	0.07	0.07	0.77
Advertising	0	0	0.25	0.25	0.30	0.40	0.40	0	0	0.25	0.25	0.25	0.72
Car & Delivery	0.06	0.06	0.06	0.06	0.06	0.06	0.06	0.06	0.06	0.06	0.06	0.06	1.00
Administrative & Legal	0.70	0.10	0	0.10	0	0	0	0	0	0.10	0	0	1.00
Rent & Utilities	1.00	1.00	1.00	1.00	1.00	1.00	1.00	1.00	1.00	1.00	1.00	1.00	12.00
Principal & Interest	0.27	0.27	0.27	0.27	0.27	0.27	0.27	0.27	0.27	0.27	0.27	0.27	3.24
Taxes	1.67	1.54	0	1.72	1.79	0	2.21	2.09	0	1.69	1.64	0	14.35
Total Disbursements	5.22	10.64	9.95	12.22	13.61	13.49	12.41	10.49	7.8	11.54	10.99	8.45	126.81
Net Cash Flow	6.38	0.96	2.05	0.18	0.09	1.91	2.59	2.71	3.0	(0.54)	0.21	3.35	22.89
Cumulative Cash Flow	6.38	7.34	9.39	9.57	9.66	11.57	14.16	16.87	19.87	19.33	19.54	22.89	22.89

Thus, by the end of his first month Smith has only collected $4,000 of the goods he has sold. Fortunately, he also collects receivables from the prior two months sales made by the former owner (as was agreed in the store purchase agreement). Thus, total collections for the first month are, therefore, $11,600.

His disbursements for expenses begin immediately in the first month, although fortunately again he bought the store stocked with a full inventory and does not, therefore, have to pay for any merchandise in the first month. However, since he will be depleting his stock by sales, he will be ordering more merchandise during his first month. Since he chooses to pay for this merchandise after a 30 day period, he will, in fact, begin paying during his second month in business. As you will note, the cost of goods ordered is $6,500.

Smith pays for his normal monthly expenses, such as labor, telephone and rent etc., as usual. Some of his expenses, advertising for example, are discretionary and he decides to hold off during his first two months. However, some extra expenses, such as insurance and legal expenses, are start up expenses and cannot be avoided. The total of first month expenses is $5,220, which leaves him with a positive cash flow of $6,380 for his first month. In addition, he started the month with $3,210 cash, transfered to him by the prior owner in order to pay the quarterly taxes due. In this case, he pays $1,670 in State Sales Tax on June 20 and $1,540 FICA and Income Taxes on July 31. Thus, his actual cash balance at the end of the first month is $9,590.

As the year progresses, his retail sales rise each month to a Christmas peak, drop off sharply after the New Year, rise a little in early spring to fall moderately through the summer months. If you look, you will notice that his purchases anticipate this trend, thus preserving the best possible cash position. His advertising expenses too are geared to the selling seasons, but are dependent somewhat on Smith's evaluation of his advertising needs. The important thing to note is that his net cash flow each month varies eratically, with a negative cash flow occuring during the tenth month of operation.

The cumulative cash flow is the actual amount of cash he accumulates as the months progress. He pays his own estimated taxes and FICA each quarter, and after one year has earned himself $22,890 in cash (remembering his original $3,200, his actual cash balance is $26,090).

It is worth noting that on an accrual basis Smith has earned $18,610 (pre-tax) versus $22,890 on a cash basis. Thus, if Smith opts for a cash basis, his income taxes will be higher. <u>Note</u>, this will not necessarily always be the case. Usually, the cash basis will lead to lower income and, therefore, lower taxes in most start up business situations.

In fact, the scenario just presented represents <u>the most favorable cash flow situation</u> of taking over an existing business. This was because Smith took over a full inventory of an ongoing business and also had the benefit of existing accounts receivables. New businesses are not so fortunate.

Cash Flow In A New Business

Let us assume that Smith has again invested a total of $30,000 in a retail store, but that it is brand new. He has stocked it with a full inventory, but does not have the benefit of prior accounts receivables, goodwill or prior advertising. Thus, his sales will be low at first and grow gradually as customers become aware of his business. He will usually spend a disproportionate amount in advertising during the first months to increase public awareness and thereby, boost sales.

The cash flow statement shown on the next page indicates the situation in these changed circumstances.

Close study of this new cash flow statement show the dramatic effect of starting a new business. The first few months show large negative cash flows and a positive cash flow is only achieved at the end of the seventh month, after the heavy Christmas sales period. Notice, in particular, that the maximum cumulative negative cash flow is $11,080; that is Smith has to have at least that amount of extra cash to pay into this new business in order to stay in business.

This example demonstrates the severe cash drain on new businesses. In this case, it would have been better if Smith could have employed members of his family without pay during the start up year and so save about $10,000. Even so, he would have been able to draw very little from his new business to support himself and his family. Thus, the new businessman should ensure that he has adequate capital to survive the initial start up period when the business is generating very little cash. It is very important, therefore, that the new businessman carefully forecaste just what the cash flow will be and accurately estimate the value of sales and expenses.

This illustrates a cogent cause of new business failures - inadequate initial sales not generating enough cash for the business to survive through the start up period. The techniques of estimating the income and expenses of a particular type of business will be provided in the later section on business investigation.

1.9 CLOSING NOTES

We will close this section on Financial Statements by considering some further aspects of the Balance Sheet.

1.9.1 Balance Sheet At First Year-End

Smith's balance sheet at the start of his business was discussed in Section 1.6. Let us now take a look at his balance sheet after being in business for one full year. In order to do this various assumptions have to be made. Let us first assume that Smith decided to withdraw $14,000 in cash from the business over the year. Smith's year-end income statement (Section 1.7) shows that his after tax income for the year was $14,350. Thus his additional capital contribution to the business is $350. In terms of his cash balance; he began the year with $3,210, accumulated a further $22,850 and withdrew $14,000. Thus, his ending cash balance stands at a healthy $12,100.

In constructing the rest of the accrual basis balance sheet, Smith normally would have been maintaining the current balance of each account on an accrual basis and would, therefore, be able to list the final balance of each account directly. However, it is possible to construct the year-end

1/Accounting/Financial Statements

TABLE FIVE
SMITH RETAIL STORE
12 Month Cash Flow For Period Ending June 15, 1981
(In 000's Dollars)

MONTH ITEM	JUN JUL	JUL AUG	AUG SEP	SEP OCT	OCT NOV	NOV DEC	DEC JAN	JAN FEB	FEB MAR	MAR APR	APR MAY	MAY JUN
Net Sales	6.0	7.0	8.0	9.0	11.0	13.0	8.0	9.0	9.0	10.0	11.0	11.0
Collections	2.0	4.33	7.0	8.0	9.33	11.0	10.66	10.00	8.66	9.33	10.0	10.66
DISBURSEMENTS												
Employees Salaries	0.85	0.85	0.85	0.95	1.22	1.5	1.0	0.85	0.85	0.85	0.85	0.85
Purchases	0	3.92	4.48	5.04	6.16	7.28	4.48	5.04	5.04	5.60	6.16	6.16
Telephone	0.07	0.07	0.07	0.07	0.07	0.07	0.07	0.07	0.07	0.07	0.07	0.07
Insurance	0.6	0	0	0	0	0	0	0	0	0	0	0
Supplies	0.18	0.18	0.18	0.18	0.18	0.18	0.18	0.18	0.18	0.18	0.18	0.18
Outside Labor	0.5	0.5	0.5	0.6	0.7	0.9	0.4	0.4	0.5	0.5	0.5	0.5
Repairs & Maintenance	0.07	0.07	0.07	0.07	0.07	0.07	0.07	0.07	0.07	0.07	0.07	0.07
Advertising	0.4	0.4	0.3	0.25	0.4	0.4	0	0	0	0.25	0.25	0.25
Car & Delivery	0.06	0.06	0.06	0.06	0.06	0.06	0.06	0.06	0.06	0.06	0.06	0.06
Administration & Legal	1.0	0.05	0.05	0	0	0.05	0.04	0.04	0.04	0	0	0
Rent & Utilities	1.0	1.0	1.0	1.0	1.0	1.0	1.0	1.0	1.0	1.0	1.0	1.0
Principal & Interest	0.28	0.28	0.28	0.28	0.28	0.28	0.28	0.28	0.28	0.28	0.28	0.28
Taxes	0	0.28	0	1.05	0.85	0	1.65	0.95	0	1.30	0.85	0
Total Disbursements	5.01	7.66	7.84	9.55	10.99	11.79	9.23	8.94	8.09	10.16	10.27	9.42
Net Cash Flow	(3.01)	(3.33)	(0.84)	(1.55)	(1.66)	(0.79)	1.43	1.06	0.57	(0.83)	(0.27)	1.24
Cumulative Cash Flow	(3.01)	(6.34)	(7.18)	(8.73)	(10.39)	(11.08)	(9.65)	(8.59)	(8.02)	(8.85)	(9.12)	(7.88)

balance sheet from the cash flow statement shown in Table Four, together with knowing the year beginning balance sheet (Table Two) and the year's income statement (Table Three). It is instructive to see how this can be done, and so each ending balance sheet account will be constructed using these three statements.

Cash

Beginning Balance	3,210	(Table Two)
Cash Accumulated	22,890	(Table Four)
Cash Withdrawn	(14,000)	Assumption
Ending Balance	$12,100	

Marketable Securities

We will assume that Smith did not buy any. However, he probably should have at least bought a $10,000 T Bill in January to use his cumulative cash flow most profitably.

Accounts Receivable

The tables indicate:

Net Sales	$150,000	(Table Three)
Less Bad Debts	300	(Table Three)
Goods Sold	$149,700	
Collections	$149,700	(Table Four)

You will note that he collected the same amount as he sold, which is purely a coincidence. Thus, his beginning accounts receivables of $11,300 (Table Three) is the same as his ending. To further illustrate this; if he had collected only $148,700, his accounts receivables would have been $1000 higher at $12,300. Alternatively, if he had collected $150,700, his accounts receivables would have been $1000 lower at $10,300.

Allowance For Doubtful Accounts

This remains underchanged at $180.

Inventories

Beginning Inventory	$7,400	(Table Two)
Purchases (for sale)	$76,900	(Table Four)
Total	$84,300	
Cost of Goods Sold	$84,300	(Table Three)

Thus by the end of the year Smith has sold all his original inventory and has sold all the goods he has paid for. Let us assume that he has ordered, but not paid for, the goods he plans to sell in June-July. Let us assume that the value of these goods is $6,960, which would have a sales value of about $12,000 (the amount sold in the previous period one year ago).

Long-Term Assets

As Table Four indicates, Smith's disbursements during the year were for ongoing expenses and he did not add any equipment, furniture or fixtures (capital items). Thus the original value of the long term assets is still

1/Accounting/Financial Statements

$11,480. However, Table Three reveals that Smith charged $2,650 to depreciate these assets during the year. Thus, the net value of the long term assets is $11,480 - $2,650 or $8,830.

Prepaid Expenses/Intangible Assets

Both these accounts remain at zero. Smith has, for example, used up the total value of his insurance and will have to buy a further year's policy in late June. If, for example, the balance sheet had been made in mid December, prepaid insurance would have been $300, which was the value of insurance paid for but not yet expired.

Accounts Payable

Going back to the previous paragraph on inventories you will note that Smith had an inventory, but had not paid for, $6,960 worth of merchandise. Thus his accounts payable is $6,960.

Notes Payable

Fortunately for Smith he has not had to borrow any further funds and, therefore, this account is zero.

Current Portion Of Long-Term Debt

Each year, Smith must pay back $2,000 of his $10,000 bank loan. Thus, this account is $2,000.

Accrued Expenses Payable

On some of his ongoing expense accounts, Smith allows himself the full 30 days payment. A study of the disbursements in Table Four and the expenses in Table Three reveals the amount of accrued expenses payable.

Item	Expensed	Cash Paid	Accrued Value
Supplies	$2160	1,980	180
Repairs	840	770	70
Advertising	2,500	2,350	150
Car & Delivery	1,000	720	280
Total Accrued Expenses Payable			$680

Remember, the accrued expenses payable represents the value of goods and services used up during the year that have not yet been paid for.

Accrued Income Taxes Payable

This account is complicated by the fact that the only taxes that Smith can deduct as part of his operating expenses are sales taxes, any state or local property taxes, and employee taxes. He cannot deduct FICA or Income Taxes paid for himself. This is why he expenses $9,940 (Table Three) for operating taxes, but has actually paid out $14,350 (Table Four) in cash. The latter amount includes, of course, $3,210 in taxes owed by the prior owner and an amount for Smith himself.

We will now unravel this complex amalgamation of taxes, which will certainly present the small businessman with a great deal of extra paperwork and headaches.

Sales Tax

Total net sales amounted to $150,000. Thus sales tax at 5.25% (an arbitrarily chosen percentage on before-tax sales of $142,500) is $7,500. He paid sales taxes at the end of the first, fourth, seventh and tenth month of operation (see Table Four). This first month's payment of $1,670 was for the prior owner's sales and, thus, he paid a total of $1,720 plus $2,210 plus $1,690, which equals $5,620 for his own sales. He therefore owes $7,500 minus $5,620 or $1,880 for his own sales. Therefore, his accrued sales tax liability is $1,880.

Employee Taxes

Based on salaries of $11,460, it was somewhat arbitrarily assumed (we will see later that there are published tables for calculating accurate employee tax deductions) that FICA amounts to 10% or $1,140 and income tax withholdings at $1,200 for a total employee tax expense of $2,440 for the year.

Thus the total deductible tax expense for the year, as shown in Table Three, is $7,500 (Sales tax) plus $2,440 (Employee Tax expense) for a total of $9,940.

Smith's Taxes

Smith has also witheld amounts for FICA and estimated income tax on his own pre-tax income of $18,610. Using the same arbitrary deduction percentages, Smith owes $1,860 for FICA and $2,400 for income taxes, which amounts to a total taxation expense of $4,260 (See Table Three - Owner's Taxes).

Examination of the cash flow statement (Table Four) indicates that Smith made tax deposits of $1,790 in October, $2,090 in January, and $1,640 in April towards all his non-sales taxes. This is a total of $5,520. The annual tax expense for both Smith and his employees is $4,260 plus $2,440 respectively, for a total of $6,700. Thus Smith's total accrued employement tax liability is $6,700 minus his cash payment of $5,520, or $1,180, which is split $400 for employees and $780 for Smith himself. This somewhat complicated tax situation is tabulated below.

Tax Types	Tax Expense	Cash Deposited	Accrued Tax Liability
Sales	$7,500	$5,620	$1,880
Employee FICA	1,140		400
Employee Income	1,300	2,040	
Sub Totals	$9,940	$7,660	$2,280
Smith's FICA	$1,860	$3,480	$ 780
Smith's Income	2,400		
Sub Totals	$4,260	$3,480	$ 780
TOTALS	$14,200	$11,140	$3,060

Remember now that Smith cannot deduct his own tax as part of his business expenses, and thus only the Sales and Employee portion of the Accrued Tax Liability appears under current liabilities. Unhappily, Smith's tax still is a current liability as far as cash flow is concerned.

Long-Term Debt

Table Four indicates that Smith paid a total of $3,240 in principal and interest towards the long term debt. $1,200 was paid for interest and, therefore, $2,040 was paid off the long-term debt, leaving $5,960 to be paid off beyond the next year ahead.

Owners's Equity

Table Three indicates that Smith's Income Tax expense was $4,260 and his after-tax earnings was $14,350. As noted in the section on taxes, Smith deposited $3,480 towards his taxes and withdrew $14,000 in cash from the business. Thus, the additional capital left in the business amounts to $1,130, of which $780 is accrued tax liability and $350 represents true capital contribution.

All these accounts can be summarized in the new year-end balance sheet.

TABLE SIX
SMITH RETAIL STORE
Balance Sheet (Accrual Basis)
June 15, 1981

ASSETS		EQUITIES	
Current Assets		**Current Liabilities**	
Cash	$12,100	Accounts Payable	$ 6,960
Marketable Securities	$0	Notes Payable	$ 0
Accounts Receivable	$11,300	Current Portion of	
Allowance for		Long-term Loan	$ 2,000
doubtful accounts	$ (180)	Accrued Expenses Payable	$ 680
Inventory	$ 6,960	Accured Taxes Payable	$ 2,280
Total Current Assets	$30,180	Total Current Liabilities	$11,920
Long-Term Assets		**Long-Term Liabilities**	
Equipment	$ 1,580	Bank Loan, 12% Interest,	
Furniture & Fixtures	$ 9,900	5 years	$ 5,960
	$11,480		
Less accumulated		**Owner's Equity**	
depreciation	$ 2,650		
Net Long-term assets	$ 8,830	W. Smith, Capital	$21,130
Prepaid Expenses	$0		
Intangible Assets	$0		
Total Assets	$39,010	Total Equities	$39,010

1.9.2 Financial Statements For Partnerships

The financial statements for Partnerships are reasonably straightforward. If, for example, three individuals, Brown, Black and White, formed a partnership business contributing 40%, 40% and 20% to the total assets respectively, only the capital contribution section of the balance sheet would change. Assuming that the total owner's equity is $100,000, the owner's equity portion of the balance sheet would appear as follows.

Owner's Equity

A.	Brown, capital contribution	$40,000
B.	Black, capital contribution	$40,000
C.	White, capital contribution	$20,000

Since the exact division of the ownership is indicated by the balance sheet, the net income before taxes of the partnership business is stated in exactly the same manner as a sole proprietorship.

1.9.3 Financial Statements For Corporations

It is sometimes advantageous from the tax and legal aspects for even a quite small business to be incorporated. The particular reasons will be covered in later sections, but suffice it to say that the incorporated small business is quite common and you will certainly come across it.

Again, it is the owner's equity section of the balance sheet that is changed by the new form of ownership. Firstly, this section is renamed "Stockholders Equity", since the owners of the corporation are its stockholders and own capital stock in the corporation. Capital stock, which is represented by the stock certificates issued by the corporation to its share holders, may be of several different classes. Each stock class has distinctly different ownership rights.

Preferred Stock

These shares have preference over other shares in respect to dividend distribution, or in distribution of assets in case of liquidation, or both. A description of the type of preferred stock is normally included; price and dividend percentage. Some preferred stock is cumulative, which means that if the dividend is not paid one year, it accumulates to be paid in later years. Normally, preferred stockholders have no voting power in the management of the corporation, unless the company fails to pay its dividend at the promised rate.

Common Stock

These shares provide their owner with voting power in corporate management and an owner receives dividend payment, but only after the preferred stockholders have been paid. However, there is no limit to the amount of dividend payment each year, so that in prosperous times the dividend can be high.

Capital Surplus

This is the amount paid in by shareholders over the par or legal value of

1/Accounting/Financial Statements

each share. This situation can occur, for example, where an additional shareholder is brought in to provide extra capital to a prospering new business. The par or original value for each share might have been $5, but the increase in the value of the business makes each share worth $8 for the new entrant. The $3 difference would go into the capital surplus account.

Accumulated Retained Earnings

This is the accumulated year after year amount that is not paid out in the form of salaries to employees or dividends to stockholders, but is retained in the corporation after corporate taxes have been paid.

The stockholder's equity portion of the balance sheet might look as follows:

Stockholder's Equity

Capital Stock

- Preferred stock, 5% cumulative, $100 par value each, authorized issued and outstanding 1,000 shares $100,000
- Common stock, $10 par value each, authorized, issued and outstanding 20,000 shares $200,000
- Capital surplus $ 60,000

    Accumulated retained earnings $150,000

    Total Stockholder's Equity $510,000

4 Financial Statements For Manufacturing Companies

The financial statements considered up to now have been for retail operations, in which merchandise manufactured by someone else is bought, stored and sold to customers. The way the inventory of a retail store is handled was described earlier in Section 1.4.8. A manufacturing company, on the other hand, buys its raw materials, processes the raw materials into products, and then stores those products ready for sale. Thus, the inventory can be, and usually is, divided into three separate accounts:

- Raw materials
- Work in process (WIP)
- Finished goods

The raw materials account is the cost of the materials used plus cost of storage. The work in process account is the amount of raw materials being used in current products plus the costs of labor used up to date. The finished goods account represents the total cost of the goods being stored ready for sale. It must be noted that the indirect costs as well as the direct material and labor costs must be included in the cost of finished goods. This I.R.S. law is called "Full Absorbtion Accounting" and applies to manufacturers. Thus, the full indirect costs (or overhead) of manufacture must be added to the value of the finished goods in inventory. The overhead costs are those costs that are "incident to and necessary for the production process". Examples of such overhead costs are rent for the manufacturing space, heat, light, repairs, superivsory labor, short-lived tools, etc.

This I.R.S. ruling really amounts to applying an accrual accounting system to a manufacturer's inventory. He cannot deduct his manufacturing overhead costs as expenses until he has sold those goods. In fact, only his front office non-production costs can be deducted as ongoing expenses - his indirect manufacturing overhead is part of his cost of goods account.

You are no doubt wondering how on earth the average business man is expected to know of this I.R.S. ruling (in fact it is Reg. Section 1.471-11(9)). Well, in the section on taxes you will be shown exactly how to go about looking up such information.

2

Legal Aspects

This chapter is intended to provide an overview of some of the most important legal aspects of starting a new business. Obviously, it is not intended to replace the advice of a competent lawyer, but at least it should make you aware of various legal decisions to be made and pitfalls to be avoided.

THE BUSINESS FORM

There are three major business forms to choose from:
- Sole Proprietorship
- Partnership
- Corporation

Sole Proprietorship

This is the simplest business form and is the easiest and cheapest way to get started. The "sole proprietor" is the person who independently runs a business for profit and who does not incorporate that business. All he need do is to register his business name, if fictious, and comply with city, county and state registration and licensing requirements (covered in detail later).

However, there are some major disadvantages of this type of business form:

- A sole proprietor exposes himself to unlimited liability. He may, of course, be covered by various insurance policies but they cannot cover every eventuality. Business adversaries can, and often do, use the liability threat to force a sole proprietor to comply with their wishes.

- The sole proprietorship dies with the owner and has to be reformed in some manner amongst the heirs. The corporate form lives on irrespective of the death of its stockholders.

- Corporate shareholder — employees can enjoy many tax-deductible fringe benefits (covered in Chapter Three).

- Many legal tax avoidance opportunities available in the corporate form are unavailable, since the business income is reported entirely as being that of the sole proprietor. In fact, the sole proprietor does not file a separate tax return for his business but merely reports the business profit/loss on his own tax return. The fiscal year of the business has to be the same as the sole proprietor (calendar year).

Partnership

The normal form of partnership between two or more individuals is known as <u>general partnership</u>. The responsibilities of the various partners should be spelled out in a partnership agreement - a legal document costing several hundred dollars to prepare. A partnership must file a tax return but does not itself pay taxes - the income attributed to each partner is taxed and paid by that partner. Even if the partnership's income is not distributed, but kept as retained earnings, the tax must still be paid. A partner can, however, deduct business loses, but not beyond the value of his equity in the business.

The general partnership has many of the drawbacks of the sole proprietorship:

- The general partner is exposed to unlimited liability.
- He is liable, too, for the legal consequences of any business act performed by his partners.
- The partnership is automatically dissolved by the death of one partner - it lacks the attributes of continuity and transferability that a corporation has.

Certain other forms of partnerships have been developed to avoid some of the problems of the general partnership.

- <u>Limited Partnership</u>

  This form is composed of one or more general partners and many limited partners. The general partners manage the business and accept liability for its debts. The limited partners take no part in managing the business and are liable only up to the extend of their investment in the business. Any losses are mostly passed on to the limited partners as tax write-offs.

- <u>Family Partnership</u>

  This is used to pass part of an income producing asset to other members of the same family thus spreading the income and reducing the overall tax paid.

- <u>Joint Venture</u>

  This is really a general partnership formed for a specific purpose and time, after which is dissolves.

Note - A partnership agreement is essential to spell out the rights and duties of the various partners. This should be drawn up <u>before</u> the business has started, when good will is at its highest. At the very least the partnership agreement should cover:

- Partners names
- Business name and specific nature
- Amounts contributed
- Amounts to be withdrawn
- Partner's rights and duties

- Procedure for dissolution/valuation methodology
- Procedure for admission of new partners

Corporation

The corporate form of small business is the most expensive to set up and will require the most official paperwork in operation. However, there are some good reasons for even the very small business to incorporate.

- Personal Liability - The owner/stockholder of a small corporation is liable only up to the amount that he has invested in the corporation. As already indicated, the general partnership and sole proprietorship situations provide no limits to personal liability. It is true, however, that if the small corporation borrows funds, the lending institution will almost invariably require that the owner/shareholder pledge his personal collateral against the loan.

- Taxation Advantages - The corporate form offers several advantages not open to other business forms:

    1. Maximum Reinvestment Of Income

        The first $25,000 of corporate income is taxed at 17 percent, the second $25,000 at 20 percent, the third $25,000 at 30 percent, and the fourth $25,000 at 40 percent and the balance at 46 percent. Thus, if you are a high-rate income taxpayer and want to reinvest in your business for expansion, etc., the corporate form will enable you to pay the least amount of tax. In fact, up to $150,000 may be retained by the company for investment.

    2. Minimum Tax On Dividends

        A corporation is granted a tax deduction of 85% of all the dividends it received from other domestic corporations. The tax advantage to the owner/stockholder should be obvious.

    3. Tax-Free Fringe Benefits

        The employee/shareholder can obtain the tax-free benefits of life insurance, health and accident plan, group legal services, death benefits (up to $5,000), certain meals and lodging, certain travel and entertainment, automobiles and even airplanes, employee discounts, interest free loans, qualified pension and profit sharing plans (covered by ERISA Act 1974) and use of corporate facilities.

    4. Transferability Of Interests

        If a corporation grows large enough, it can offer its shares publically, possibly on the local "over-the-counter" market. As well as a vehicle for raising cash, the public stock offering does make possible the eventual sale of stock on the owner/manager's death, since a public market for the stock has been created.

        The corporate form also offers most in the way of estate planning opportunities.

    5. Fiscal Year - Subchapter S Corporation

        A disadvantage of the corporate form just described is that a double-taxation situation exists. The double-taxation occurs when a corporation retains some of its earnings and, of course, pays corporation tax on them. Then, later on, personal tax is paid when those retained earnings are paid out to the owner/stockholders.

The double-taxation can be avoided, of course, by paying out the entire corporation's profits as owner's salaries. The current maximum tax rate on "personal service income" is 50%. However, if this salary is sufficiently large it may be judged by the I.R.S. to be unreasonable (this situation happened to Mary Kay of Mary Kay Cosmetics) and the amount above that reasonable level is then taxed at regular income rates.

Another alternative to paying double-taxation is to elect the form of a "Subchapter S Corporation". This election enables certain small corporations to be taxed as though they were partnerships. They do, however, still have the limited liability protection of a corporation. Subchapter S election for tax purposes is on a year by year basis and can be especially useful in the early years in allowing any losses to flow through fully to the owners as a tax write-off.

Certain requirements must be met for a corporation to take the Subchapter S election:

1. The corporation must be a domestic corporation chartered by any state.

2. The corporation must have no more than 15 shareholders. Husband and wife are treated as one shareholder.

3. No shareholder may be a non-resident alien.

4. Only one class of stock is permitted (this can be a grave tax disadvantage, as will be explained later).

5. It must not be affiliated with a group of corporations.

6. The corporation's gross receipts must not exceed 80% derived from non United State's sources or more than 20% from passive investments (such as rents, royalties, interest, etc.).

Subchapter S corporations, because of their favorable tax status, have other advantages:

- A Subchapter S can adopt <u>any fiscal year</u> it chooses, even though its stockholders are taxed on a calendar year basis. Obviously, opportunities exist for income acceleration or deferal.

- Loss flow through rules are not quite as favorable as those of a partnership, the amount of loss that may be deducted as a Subchapter S stockholder is limited to ownership equity (stock) in the business plus any personal loans made to the corporation.

2/Legal Aspects

- The tax-deduction fringe benefits permitted to an employee of a Subchapter S corporation are exactly the same as those for other corporations, but are not permitted for a partner.

- A personal service income tax of no more than 50% is charged on partnership income. If, however, a large proportion of the partnership's income comes from capital investments (property, etc.), then a partner's personal service income cannot exceed 30% of the partnership's net profits. On the other hand, the entire income of a Subchapter S employee is eligible as personal service income.

    There is no penalty tax for unreasonable accumulation of retained earnings, nor is there a limit placed on "reasonable salary".

    Note - The personal service tax situation just described, which was introduced by the Tax Reform Act of 1969, probably provides the most important reason for selecting the corporate form of business.

- Income Splitting opportunities are easily acheived by allocating stock ownership among the various family members.

Choice Of Business Form

The various pros and cons of the alternative business forms have been discussed. Your own personal situation needs to be fully explored with a competent business lawyer. However, the recommendation of this book is that the corporate form be given preference, unless the business is required to provide losses to the owner that directly flow through to him. In the latter case, such as property investment where items like component depreciation deductions can offset income, the preferred business form is the sole proprietorship or partnership.

LEGAL REQUIREMENTS IN BUSINESS FORMATION

How do you officially proclaim that your new business is established? This depends on the type of business form you decide is best for you. If, for example, you choose to be a sole proprietor and part of the business name contains your own surname, for example "J. Smith's Tastee Donuts", the name is not fictious and you can just open your stores without registering your business name.

2.2.1 Ficticious Name Registration

If you decide to call your business by a fictious name, for example "Super Tastee Donuts" you are required to register that name with the county and pay a filing fee ($10-$30). Details of the filing procedure may be obtained from your local county clerk.

If you form a corporation, it requires to be registered as a corporation and the fictious name statement is not necessary.

2.2.2 Agreements

Documented statements about agreements are unnecessary for sole proprietorships and are not legally required for partnerships. However, in the latter case, it is strongly advisable to have a lawyer create a legally binding partnership agreement.

2.2.3 Incorporation

A corporation is, strangely enough, legally recognized as an artificial person. It is a separate entity in its own right, as distinct from its employees and stockholders, and is responsible for its own debts.

As stated earlier, the corporate form requires more paperwork than the other business forms and this is especially true in the start up formalities:

- Subscription Agreement

    If several of you are joining together to form a corporation, then a subscription agreement is required. This agreement states the value to be contributed by each stockholder and the distribution of the stock and any notes. In addition, the agreement describes the purpose and structure of the corporation.

- Employment Agreements

    In these documents the rights, duties and compensations of the employee/shareholders are described. This agreement may also cover the buy/sell rules of the corporation in selling to outsiders, placing a value on the stock, and so forth.

- Formal Incorporation

    The corporation has to file for formal incorporation in a particular state. Just prior to this, any tax aspect of incorporation can be ruled on by seeking an opinion from the Treasury Department. This latter step is normally required only when incorporating complex existing businesses.

    The corporation's charter - the articles of incorporation - are submitted to the state's Superintendent of Corporations (or similar authority) and he grants a certificate of incorporation. The corporation's life begins upon receipt of this document. If you proceed before gaining certification you will be subject to personal liability for your actions.

- Meetings

    A directors meeting should be held to elect the corporate officers and adopt the bylaws. Approvals are needed for the corporate seal, the issuance of stock certificates, any transfer of property and the opening of the corporation's bank account. A shareholders meeting should also be held immediately and at least annually thereafter.

    Special attention should be paid to keeping detail minutes of these meetings, for they can prove to be valuable in, for example, disputes

2/Legal Aspects

with the I.R.S. For instance, in a dispute concerning excessive retained earnings, a good defence can be established if the directors meeting minutes indicates constructive uses for all the retained earnings.

4 Special Notes On Incorporation

Note One - Incorporating In Delaware

You may have heard that many of the large corporations are incoporated in Delaware instead of their home state - for example United Aircraft (home - Connecticut), Tenneco Inc. (home - Texas), Shell Oil (home - New York). Clearly, there must be certain advantages to incorporating in Delaware that are not obtainable in other states. It is also true, however, that many other states are now closing the gap between their regulations and those of Delaware. The specific advantages offered by Delaware are:

- No minimum capital is required. Share valuation is at the discretion of the directors, who can decide what part of the initial capital contribution goes into capital and what part into surplus.
- There is no corporate income tax levied by Delaware for companies inside or outside the state. There is no tax on shares held by non-residents and also no inheritance tax.
- Any combination of business activities is legal.
- Dividends can be paid out of profits and, of course, out of surplus.
- Your corporation can hold shares of other companies and can hold any type of property in any state. It can purchase its own stock for its own purposes.
- A single individual may incorporate. This individual may also be a corporation.
- Corporate meetings (stockholders and directors) may be held outside the state. The corporation's records do not have to be kept in Delaware.

The key advantages of incorporating in Delaware are for the small corporation that wants an unusual debt to equity balance or that wants to do business in many states with the least hassle.

Note Two - Choice Of Stock Types

In forming a corporation, a taxpayer needs to pay particular attention to the debt to equity mix. If, for example, part of the initial investment in the new business is made in the form of a loan, the necessary groundwork will have been made to extract some of the accumulated income on a tax free basis. This is because the taxpayer/stockholder is merely receiving the repayment of a debt and not additional income.

This strategy has been attacked by the I.R.S. as a "thin corporation". However, ratios of up to 75% debt, 25% equity for owner investment should withstand I.R.S. scrutiny. Here again, expert tax advice is crucial.

This being said, you do need to issue some stock. What choices are there? The two major categories of stock are common stock and preferred stock.

Common stockholders are the legal owners of the corporation and are allowed to vote at stockholder's meetings concerning the election of directors and general corporate policy. Preferred stockholders claim the right of income distribution ahead of common shockholders by way of fixed dividend payments. Usually, the dividend rights of preferred stockholders are cumulative, that is, if the dividend is not paid one year, payment accrues to the next year, and so on. Preferred stockholders have no voting rights, and, therefore, are sometimes regarded as debtors.

The type and amount of stock distributed depends upon the purpose to be served. For example, if five individuals contribute equal amounts to a corporation and desire equal voting rights, then they obviously would each require one fifth of the total distributed common stock. In the case of a family head wanting only to distribute income, but not to surrender control, he might distribute various amounts of common and preferred in such a way that he holds the majority of the common stock. Another variant is to issue two classes of common stock, where class A has voting privileges and class B does not.

It is quite useful to include some preferred stock in your initial stock issue. This is because preferred stock can be used to withdraw capital from your corporation taxed at only the capital gains rate (not as straight income). However, the preferred stock used for this purpose must be issued by a new corporation. Otherwise, is is covered by Section 306 of the Internal Revenue Code and the funds derived from its sale are classified as ordinary income.

It is also vital to issue Section 1244 stock, which can be used to take a loss as a deduction to ordinary income. Up to $500,000 of Section 1244 stock may be issued, with no limits placed on the size of the equity of the corporation. Losses due to the worthlessness of the stock will be treated as ordinary tax-deductable losses; up to $50,000 on a single return and $100,000 on a joint return.

Just these few glimpses of the intricacies of the various types of stock you can use should convince you to use a competent lawyer in incorporating your business. Thousands of dollars of your hard earned money could depend upon it!

2.2.5 Business License And Permits-Local And State

You will, almost certainly, have to obtain a local business license for the city or county in which you do business. The license usually has to be renewed annually and costs vary from $10 up to about $100. The county clerk's office should be able to provide information on just what the local requirements are.

You will also require the local permits which show that you are in compliance with local ordinances - health requirements, zoning restrictions and so forth. Again, the county clerk's office should be visited for information. These local permits are important, especially in businesses such as restaurants, since the police will shut you down if you are in violation.

Certain professional occupations, such as doctors, lawyers, CPA's and so on, have always required licensing. However, recently many other service occupations, such as TV repairmen and auto servicemen, also need state licenses. Further information on such licenses can be obtained from the state government.

Most states require that business owners collect sales tax on all items directly sold to customers. If, however, items are sold to another business sales tax is not required - merely the recording of the sale against the tax-exempt number of the client business. By the same token, where items are purchased from another business, sales tax is not paid.

2.2.6 Business Permits And Regulations-Federal

Sooner or later you will have to hire employees. At that point, you will need a Federal Employer Identification Number. This identification number is obtained at no charge by filling in I.R.S. form, #SS-4.

Certain businesses require a federal government license. For example, meat packaging and investment counseling require such permits. You should check if your business is a candidate for such a license by making an application to:

> Federal Trade Commission
> Sixth Street and Pennsylvania Avenue, N.W.
> Washington, D.C. 20580

Special regulations apply to exporters, and a validated Export License is required from the Department of Commerce for each export shipment. On the other hand, no license is required to import merchandise into the United States. However, you do have to pay import duty on most items, which can vary widely in percentage of value. An informative booklet entitled "Exporting to the U.S." all about importing is available from the:

> Superintendent of Documents
> U.S. Government Printing Office
> Washington, D.C. 20402

INSURANCE

All businesses are exposed to risk of one kind or another. Naturally, the prudent business man protects himself by buying adequate insurance coverage. Here again, the advice from honest, competent professionals is essential since there are several dozen different types of insurance.

2.3.1 Insurance Coverage

A partial listing is presented below of the more common types of insurances small businesses buy.

Accounts Receivable	Medical
Automobile	Payroll
Blanket Contractual	Product Liability
Business Interruption	Property Damage
Disability	Rent
Employers Liability	Security & Life

Fire And Flood	Sole Propertor's Life
General Liability	Security Bonds
Key-Man Life	Vandalism
Machinery And Equipment	Workmen's Compensation

Obviously, with so many types to choose from you need to follow certain rules to avoid being over or under insured:

Rule One

Establish the dollar value of your total legal exposure - all contracts such as leases, delivery commitments, etc. (legal advise may help here), and all valuable property (forget paperclips).

Rule Two

Estimate the probability that various business disasters might occur - fire, theft, breakdown, etc.

Rule Three

Establish, with the help of your insurance adviser, just what risks can be covered, ignoring the petty items.

Rule Four

Get the polices that best seem to cover your needs, but do all you can to guard against having to use them, for any loss can only be partially compensated by insurance.

Rule Five

Make sure that you read the "fine print" of your policies so that you understand what the conditions of insurance are and understand enough so that you do not violate your policies.

2.3.2 Special Business Coverage

Apart from protecting your obvious items of value, such as property, you should consider policies that cover the risks of business interruption. Indirect effects of property loss require coverage of such items as rent payment, accounts receivable, customer bankruptcy and interruptions of commissions.

Apart from a general liability policy, product liability coverage is required for the increasing cases of manufacturers or marketers who provide products that are "unreasonably dangerous".

2.3.3 Business Continuation After Owner's Death

Although not strictly part of the most pressing start up concerns, the businessman should, not too long after his business gets off the ground, consider the consequences of his death. The problem will have to be faced by his heirs (wife and children) and, unless proper thought is given to this somewhat unpleasant subject, they will face some disasterous consequences. If, for example, a wife carries on her husband's business without authority she may be held liable for any debt incurred by that business. Often, the other hiers can sue for loss of their share of the estate.

There are two general types of agreement that enable the business to continue after the death of a sole proprietor. These are a living trust agreement and an agreement to buy and sell. A revocable living trust is useful where there are sons or relatives willing to continue the business immediately after the owner's death. The one problem of the trust is finding a suitable trustee will to take on the arduous duties of administering the trust. A buy-sell agreement is entered into with a person who is willing to buy the business upon the death of the properitor, thus making the full value of the business available to the proprietor's family. Usually, the buyer is one of the employees of the business who would view the purchase and management of the business as a good opportunity. The only completely satisfactory way of financing such a buy-sell agreement is by means of a life insurance carried by the employee(s) on the life of the proprietor. The life insurance premiums paid by the employee are not tax deductible, but the life insurance proceeds are not taxable. Thus, the employee can purchase the business with the full proceeds of the insurance (Interval Revenue Code Section 101).

A similar problem exists with a partnership and without a specific business continuation agreement difficult situations can easily arise. The surviving partner must act as the liquidating trustee. He must account for all property values, and, if anything goes wrong, have the burden of proving that he acted in good faith and with strict adherence to the laws governing partnership dissolution. A continuation plan must be set up in order to avoid such problems. A buy-sell agreement is a satisfactory solution, but must be properly drawn up and financed with life insurance.

As indicated earlier, a corporation does not cease because of the death of a stockholder. However, there can be far-reaching consequences, which depend largely on the porportion of the stock held by the stockholder. If the deceased is a major contributor to the management of the business, the problem of business continuation arises. If the deceased is a minor contributor, the question of a fair price for the stock arises especially with a small closed corporation. Again, a specific plan is required in order to avoid unpleasant consequences.   Several satisfactory plans are available:

- Purchase and sale agreement by which the heirs of the deceased stockholder receive a prearranged price for each share of stock.

- A buy-sell agreement financed by life insurance.

Conclusion

An ounce of prevention on the part of the businessman can save immeasurable financial and emotional hardship on the part of his heirs. It is strongly recommended that he avail himself of good legal advice in this area.

2.4 PROTECTING YOUR IDEAS

There are several different legal devices for protecting your ideas; each device was set up for a particular business asset.

- A <u>copyright</u> protects artistic property from reproduction or use without authorization.
- Business know-how and confidential information can be protected if it qualifies as a <u>"trade secret"</u>. Such confidential assets are protected by common law.
- A unique idea or design can be protected by the use of a <u>patent</u>, which gives the holder the exclusive right to manufacture and sell a product embodying the unique idea.
- The distinguishing mark you use to identify you product brand (it may be a name or a symbol) is protected under the state and federal law of "trademark".

Copyrights

The Federal Copyright Act covers any physical embodiment of artistic expression. In order to qualify for copyright protection, several requirements must be satisfied:

- The work must be in a physical form to qualify and must be of unique content.
- It must fall into one of 15 separate classes ranging from books, through photographs to choreographic and pantomime works.
- The work must have a copyright notice affixed in a given position. The general form used is:

    © , James Smith, 1979

- The work should be registered in the Copyright Office. The specifics can be found by writing to the:

    Register of Copyrights
    Library of Congress
    Washington, D.C. 20559

Trade Secret

Some ideas are not patentable, but are extremely valuable. For example, secret recipes, such as the preparation of the Coca Cola essence, can be protected by laws prohibiting disclosure by employees. The right to privacy also provides protection. There are several obvious steps that can be taken to maintain a trade secret:

- Permit only those employees with a definite need-to-know access to confidential information.
- Ask all employees and any outside consultants or suppliers to sign non-disclosure agreements, which serve as a legal requirement for them to keep any sensitive company information confidential.

2/Legal Aspects

Patent

A patent will provide some protection, but not as complete as commonly supposed. A patent does, for example, disclose the idea and opens the door for someone to improve your invention and claim a new patent for himself. In addition, your own exclusive rights to the idea will expire in a certain period (3.5 to 17 years depending on category). Several important facts should be noted:

- Three categories of patent are permitted - "utility inventions" (a mechanism, process or composition), "ornamental designs", and "asexually reproducible plants".

- Your invention must be filed with the Patent Office and will need the expert guidance of a patent attorney. The entire process is expensive and lengthy.

- Once your patent has been granted via "notice of allowance" you should:
    A) Mark your product with the patent number.
    B) Avoid any marketing action that restrains trade - your patent rights may be terminated.
    C) Report a sale of your patent to the Patent Office within three months of the transaction. If this is not done the buyer will lose the rights to the patent.

Trademark

A recognizable trademark, which will probably be expensive to establish, is legally protected under the laws concerning "unfair competition" in business. Trademarks are protected under both state and federal laws. However, federal protection, under the Lanham Act provides much broader protection. Trademarks may only be federally registered if they are on items used in interstate commerce.

If you market your product in two or more states you can register your trademark with the Patent Office. You can only register after your product has been used in interstate commerce and, once registered, it is protected for 20 years. The registration process is relatively simple and specific information can be obtained from the Commissioner Of Patents, Washington, D.C. 20231.

Once your trademark is registered you must:

- Use your trademark name consistently as a brand name to avoid the problem of it becoming a generic name - like cellophane.

- You must check for any infringement of your mark. The official "Gazette", which is published weekly, provides information on all new registrations.

- After six years of registration you must register your trademark with a "Declaration Of Use".

- You may renew trademarks filed in the "Principal Register" during the twentieth year of their existence. Any change in ownership must also be recorded.

2.5 THE LEGAL ASPECTS OF SELLING

Not all state and federal laws create an unfair burden on small businesses. Some laws are meant to specifically help small business by fostering competition and preventing monopolies from gaining a stranglehold on any market segment. You should, therefore, be familiar with the laws as they generally apply. It could be that you may need them one day!.

- **Sherman Antitrust Act (1890)**

    This act dealt with the growing problem of large industrial combinations and is enforced by the Department of Justice. The act has two major sections:

    I. Every contract, combination or conspiracy in restraint of trade is illegal.

    II. Monopolies or attempts to monopolize are illegal.

    This act is very powerful and was used in 1911 to break up Standard Oil. The courts, in interpreting the Sherman Act, have created what is known as the "Rule of Reason", which states: "every conspiracy should be evaluated on its own merits to determine the extent of the restraint of trade". Note that two activities are always illegal:

    a) Price fixing
    b) Horizontal division of markets, i.e., dividing up, say, the retail sales of an item between a few major retailers.

    Vertical market division (the division between manufacturer, wholesaler or distributor, and retailer) may not always be illegal.

- **Clayton Act (1914)**

    The Sherman Act, just described, deals with monopoly situations in being. The Clayton Act seeks to prevent anti-competitive situations from developing into monopolies. It covers several situations which are only illegal "where the effect may be to substaintially lessen competition or trend to create a monopoly":

    a) Price fixing - arrangements where several suppliers of a given product agree to sell for the same price.
    b) Tying and exclusive agreements - where buyers are required to purchase more than one type of product from a supplier or may only sell the product from a supplier or may only sell the supplier's product in a particular product line.
    c) Reciprocity arrangement - where one party refuses to buy from a second party unless the second party agrees to purchase goods from the first party.
    d) Aquisition of stock in another corporation.
    e) Interlocking directorships - no person can be a director of two competitors having capital, surplus and individual profits of more than $1 million.

The Federal Trade Commission (FTC) and the Department of Justice both have jurisdiction over the Clayton Act.

- **Federal Trade Commission Act (1914)**

    The FTC was created to prevent unfair and deceptive trade practices, which damage competition and small business interests. Specific protection on behalf of the public interest had to wait until 1938 when the Wheeler-Lee Act ammended the original FTC Act. Since then the powers of the FTC have been further strengthened. The Fair Packaging and Labelling Act (1966) requires full disclosures of product ingredients, requires standardization in packaging size, and has been used to introduce the concept of labelling price per unit. The FTC Improvement Act gave the FTC wide powers for consumer protection - it can fund consumer groups, gain restitution for consumers, impose fines on companies violating FTC rules, publish cease and decist orders, and so forth. The Magnuson-Moss Warranty Act simplified and regularized warranty claims.

    Thus, the FTC has wide ranging powers and information about its latest rulings can be obtained from:

    > Bureau of Information
    > Federal Trade Commission
    > Washington, D.C. 205580

    An overview of some of the more important FTC rulings is presented below:

    1) Product attributes
        - You must not use misleading endorsements
        - You must not exaggerate the qualities or benefits of your product.
        - You must not claim affiliation to or endorsement from a company or organization unless it is true.
        - You must state the products correct origin.
    2) Advertising
        - Comparision advertising is permitted, but only if the findings are truthful.
        - You must not mistate the quantity of goods available; your "limited stock" must really be limited.
        - You must not call your product new unless it is less than six months old.
        - "Going out of Business" or "Fire Sale" statements must be true.
        - Loss leaders must not be advertised unless you can supply sufficient demand.

- **The Robinson-Patman Act (1931)** and the **Cellar-Kefauver Act (1950)** ammended the Clayton Act to, respectively, outlaw price discrimination and asset acquisition. In the case of price discrimination; the receiver is equally as guilty as the giver of discounts, brokerage discounts can only be given to independent brokers, advertising allowances must be given to competing firms on a proportionate but equal basis. However, you may give discounts if:

a) There are true manufacturing cost savings
b) There is no interstate commerce involved, (state laws apply in this case)
c) The products are not of like grade or quality
d) There is a lower priced competitor
e) There is normal fluctuation in markets
f) The businesses to which you sell are not in competition

- **Uniform Commercial Code (UCC)**

  The Uniform Commercial Code was drafted by the National Commission on Uniform State Laws to do just that - unify the various laws relating to business matters throughout the United States. The code regulates the sale of goods, commercial paper, particular aspects of banking, letters of credit, warehouse receipts, bills of lading, and investment securities.

  An important aspect of the UCC covers two kinds of implied warranty:

  1. The implied warranty of merchantability requires that any goods sold should function correctly, and that edible items should be fit to eat.

  2. The implied warranty of fitness of purpose requires that a buyer has the right to rely on the seller's expertise in selling a specific item.

  Such an implied warranty holds the seller or manufacturer liable for injuries caused even though no design defector negligence is involved. The terms of any warranty must now be fully disclosed:

  1. Full Warranty - will remedy any defect without charge to the consumer.

  2. Limited Warranty - the seller may modify or exclude any implied warranty, but the disclaimers must be positive, explicit, unequivocal and conspicuous.

  Note - Warranties are limited to the sale of goods. No warranty applies to the performance of a service. Defective service is actionable under the laws concerning negligence.

- **State Laws**

  The laws regulating sales practices in each state vary widely. Perhaps the widest discrepancies are in the so called "Blue Laws", by which certain states forbid the sale of specific items on Sundays. You will certainly need to obtain information from your local Chamber of Commerce on such matters.

  A recent piece of legislation "The Hart-Scott-Rodino Anti-Trust Improvement Act" (1976) gave the Attorney General in any state the right to sue on behalf of the state's citizens in anti-trust and price fixing matters. The implication of the act is that the laws we have briefly covered in this section can now be tackled at the state rather than federal level and are, therefore, more likely to be enforced with increasing frequency.

2/Legal Aspects

LAWS CONCERNING CREDIT

As was indicated previously, any type of extention of credit involves extra problems for the small business. If credit does become necessary, which is not the case in all businesses (dry cleaning for example), then providing charge card facilities is, almost certainly, the best way to go. If, however, you want to venture into providing your own credit service, you should be aware that the credit laws are complex and far reaching.

- **Equal Credit Opportunity Act**

    This act seeks to place limits on the businessman's credit screening process. He may not:
    1) Automatically reject anyone on the grounds of race, religion or age.
    2) Deny credit because of marital status or sex.
    3) Discount any income from part-time employment.
    4) Request any information from a spouse unless the spouse shares the account.
    5) Maintain separate histories of husband and wife who share the same account.

- **Fair Credit Reporting Act**

    The act seeks to regulate the practicies of the various agencies who collect and disseminate information on the credit worthiness of individuals. If you use a report from an agency you must inform the credit applicant and also:
    1) Explain what the report is.
    2) Indicate that he has the right to see a "complete and accurate" account of that credit report.

- **Federal Trade Commission**

    If you deny credit to an applicant based on reports either from a credit agency or another source you must supply him with information concerning that source.

- **Federal Reserve System—Regulation Z**

    Regulation Z protects consumers who receive credit. There are only a few exceptions - agricultural credit, non real-estate credit over $25,000 and transactions with SEC registered stock brokers.

    Two credit categories are specifically dealt with:
    1) Open-ended credit - or revolving charges, such as used with credit cards.
    2) Installment sales or loans.

    Both are covered separately, but both require, in essence, complete breakdown of all sales, complete information on finance charges, beginning and ending balance information, and so forth.

    Often a state's UCC provides even broader consumer protection and should be studied in detail.

Conclusion

Consumer credit has now become a complicated headache for those retailers wishing to provide it. If used, it must be set up by a competent lawyer and the law requires that files are accurately maintained.

2.7 EMPLOYMENT LAWS

Since 1964, with the passage of the Civil Rights Act, the federal laws have grown increasingly harsh on acts of employment discrimination.

- **Civil Rights Act**

    This act prohibits discrimination in employment on the basis of race, creed, color, sex or national origin. It is important to note that this act only applies to employers of 15 or more persons.

- **Equal Employment Opportunity Act**

    This empowers the Equal Employment Opportunity Commission with the power to sue for discriminatory activities covered by the Civil Rights Act. The EEOC monitors companies with 100 employees or more. A few pitfalls to watch out for are listed below:

    1) Many employment tests have been held to be discriminatory. If you do use any, make sure that they are legally valid.

    2) Avoid asking questions pertaining to national origin, marital status, and educational background unless clearly job related, arrest record (not conviction) and credit rating.

    3) Pregnancy and childbirth must be treated as temporary disability and extending special benefits to "heads of households" is also illegal.

    4) Employees should only be fired for specific reasons and reference made to performance as recorded in their personnel files.

- **The Equal Pay Act**

    The act applies to companies employing 25 individuals or more and requires equal payment for men and women based on skill to do a particular job.

- **The Age Discrimination Act**

    This act permits discrimination on grounds only where there is a valid reason for doing so - such as requiring a child actor, and so forth.

    This act and the Equal Pay Act are enforced by the U. S. Department of Labor.

- **The Occupational Safety and Health Act (OSHA)**

    OSHA covers all employees and seeks to establish a safe working environment. Specific industry standards have been created and information about each standard can be obtained from the Government Printing Office. Several booklets are available.

2/Legal Aspects

- The OSHA General Industry Standard
- The General Industry Guide for Applying Safety and Health Standards
- Fact Sheet for Small Businesses in Obtaining Compliance Loans
- What Every Employer Needs to Know About OSHA Recordkeeping

It is wise to set up your own programs in employee safety, and help in this regard can be obtained from your insurance agent and legal advisor.

National Labor Relations Act

The Supreme Court upheld that the NLRA superseded state's rights in labor relations. In fact, Congress has never provided sufficient funds for the National Labor Relations Board (NLRB) to excersie more than a very narrow jurisdiction, and in 1959 Congress allowed state law to operate in those areas where the NLRB had declined to do so.

The two most important parts of the NLRA are Sections 7 and 8. Section 7 gives the right of employees to form a union for the purpose of collective bargaining. Section 8 provides against employer interference in this right. The five prohibited practices are:

1) Interference with efforts of employees to form, join or assist labor organization, or to engage in concerted activities for mutual aid and protection.

2) Domination of a labor organization (no company unions controlled by the company).

3) Discrimination in hire or tenure of employees to influence union affiliation.

4) Discrimination against employees for filing charges or giving testimony under the act.

5) Refusing to bargain collectively with a duly designated representative of the employees.

On the other hand, employers have the right to present their case to their employees concerning unions and collective bargaining. Normally a union representative will have gathered at least 30% of the proposed "bargaining unit" before he visits management to propose the formation of a union. If management refuses to recognize the union, the proposed membership can give authority that the union petition the NLRB for a secret ballot. Note that it is illegal to recognize a union that is comprised of less than 50 percent of the majority. If you are in doubt let the NLRB conduct a ballet to determine the true feeling amongst your employees.

If elections for a union do ensue, the management may follow a campaign on its own behalf:

1) It should stress current employee benefits, and compare them with competitors especially if their own are better than others.

2) It should stress the advantages of dealing with management directly, rather than on the basis of a union member. The costs associated with unionism should also be outlined.

3) Point out that employees are not obliged to speak with union organizers and that a union of their disliking would be difficult to dislodge once elected.

4) Any distortions should be immediately corrected by a statement of the truth.

Management may tell its story in any way that is fair, but every action should be first reviewed by the company's legal adviser(s).

- **The Wagner Act**

This act requires an employer to "bargain collectively with the representatives of his employees" and that such bargaining is to be "in respect to rates of pay, wages, hours of employment, or other conditions of employment". Any hint of bad faith on the part of the employer can result in the NLRB assessing penalties.

- **Labor-Management Relations Act (Taft Hartley)**

The act was passed in 1947 to curtail some of the excessive union power that was thought to have arisen. Unions may not engage in:

1) Restraint or coercion of workers in the exercise of rights guaranteed in Section 7.

2) Attempt to cause an employer to discriminate against an employee except where the employee fails to pay his dues.

3) Refusal to bargain in good faith.

4) Requirement of excessive or discriminatory initiation fees.

5) Strikes and boycotts with unlawful objectives.

6) "Featherbedding" practices of pay without work performed.

In addition, unions can be sued for breaking collective bargaining contracts; can be sued for unlawful secondary boycotts or strikes; and, in a national emergency, be required to halt a strike for an 80 day cooling off period.

Conclusion

A good businessman provides a safe, harmonious working place for his employees, and creates, thereby, a satisfactory return on his investment. Both parties can benefit if the needs of each are recognized and honored.

- **Legal References**

Naturally, you may want to look further into some of the legal aspects covered briefly in this chapter. Firstly, therefore, two general business text books can be recommended:

1) "Business Law" - Ronald A. Anderson and Walter A. Kumpf; published by South-Western Publishing Co.

2) "The Legal Environment of Business" by Michael P. Slitka and James E. Inman; published by Grid.

Secondly, there are two legal reference sources used by lawyers and legal professionals to look up specific legal items in whatever depth they require:

1) "Total Client-Service Library" (TCSL) published by the Lawyers Cooperative Publishing Company. The TCSL comprises 10 different sets of reference books covering all aspects of American Law. Perhaps the most useful general reference is "American Jurisprudence 2d", which is a legal encyclopedia containing statements of law arranged in alphabetical order. Each volume is kept up to date by cumulative pocket supplements, which are found in the back of each volume. In addition, the New Topic Service Section enables the editors to add those new titles of the law that periodically emerge, and to rewrite existing titles or parts of articles that are subject to important changes.

   A guide to the TCSL is published by Lawyers Cooperative under the title "The Living Law".

2) A competing collection of legal research reference books is published by the West Publishing Company and the guide to its system is entitled "West's Law Finder". West also publishes a comprehensive legal encyclopedia under the title "Corpus Juris Secundum". It is arranged by subject in alphabetical order from Vol. 1, Adjective Law, through Vol. 10, Workmen's Comp 782 to end - Zoning. Annual supplements are published and kept in the pockets.

   West also publishes many State Annotated Statutes and Codes, for example:

   > California - West's Annotated California Code
   > New York - McKinney's Consolidated Laws of N.Y. Annotated
   > Texas - Vernon's Annotated Texas Statutes and Codes.

3

Tax Aspects

3.0 Most people are familiar, perhaps too familiar they might say, with Federal and State taxes. However, even in a small business this familiarity will have to grow considerably. The purpose of this chapter is not to make you a tax expert, but rather to give you enough background to talk to accountants, CPA's and so on with enough knowledge to make sure that your best interests are being served.

3.1 SIGNING UP

It is best to find out all the various taxes for which your new business is liable and to apply for the proper identification numbers in order to report those taxes. If you fail to do this you may be liable for penalties and interest charges. You will, of course, have to pay different taxes to the various taxing authorities - Federal, State, County, City, etc. A tax calendar will be provided later on to remind you just when all the various taxes are due.

Federal Taxes

Employer Identification Number - This number is used in reporting all Federal taxes. It is obtained by completing Federal Form SS-4, which can be obtained from your local I.R.S. office. Federal payroll taxes must be collected when the business has one or more employees. If the business is a corporation, the owner is an employee and payroll tax must be paid. An employer is responsible for withholding various taxes from each employee and depositing them in an authorized commercial bank.

Corporation Tax

If your business is incorporated, its profits will be taxed at the following rates:

Income		Tax Rate	
	$0 to $25,000		17%
	$25,00 to $50,000		20%
	$50,000 to $75,000		30%
	$75,000 to $100,000		40%
	Over $100,000		46%

Up to $150,000 of undistributed earnings, which you can use as a corporate investment fund, may be accumulated without tax.

Every corporation, whose estimated tax (i.e., expected income tax liability, less

3/Tax Aspects

credits and exemptions) is expected to be $40 or more, is required to make estimated tax payments. These estimated tax payments are deposited using Form 503, "Federal Tax Deposits, Corporation Income Taxes". The due dates are given in the Tax Calendar (Section 3.2)

Federal Unemployment Tax

If you meet the following tests, you must pay Federal Unemployment Tax.

- $1,500 or more in wages was paid in any calendar quarter, or;
- One or more employees were hired for some portion of at least one day during each of twenty different calendar weeks, not necessarily on a consecutive basis.

The Federal unemployment tax rate in 1974, for example, was 3.2% of wages paid up to $4,200, but any state unemployment tax may be deducted. Deposits are paid quarterly, using the Quarterly Deposit Form 508, and an annual report must be filed using Form 940.

Self Employment Tax

If you are a sole proprietor or a partner you may be liable for Self Employment Tax. Self Employment Tax is to provide Social Security benefits for self employed individuals.

If your income from your self employment activities is $400 per year or more you must file a special tax return, Form 1040 Schedule SE, and pay Social Security taxes.

Note

- An owner-employee of a corporation is not required to pay Self Employment Tax.
- Similarly, a Subchapter S corporation is not required to pay Self Employment Tax.
- A wise move in partnership situations is to make your wife a partner, if she is unemployed, so that she may receive increased Social Security benefits.

Federal Withholding And Social Security Taxes

You, as an employer, are required to withhold various amounts from each employee for Federal Income Tax and Social Security. The amounts withheld depend upon the employee's pay for a specific pay period and his number of exemptions. The exact tax rates are published by the I.R.S. each year under the title "Employer's Tax Guide - Circular E". You will also receive I.R.S. Publication 213, "Are You Up To Date On Your Withholding Information", which should be posted for employees to see.

On hiring a new employee you must:

- Ask him to fill out a Form W-4, withholding exemption certificate, or Form W-4E, exemption from withholding, as the case may be.
- Obtain a Social Security number, if he does not have one, using Form SS-5.

65

The deposit rules for Income Tax withheld and Social Security Taxes are:

	Deposit Rule	Deposit Due
1.	If at the end of a quarter the total amount of undeposited taxes is less than $200.	No deposit required. Either pay balance directly to I.R.S. with quarterly return or make a deposit.
2.	If at the end of a quarter the total amount of undeposited taxes is $200 or more.	On or before last day of next month.
3.	If amounts due are between $200 and $2,000.	Within 15 days after end of month following the quarter.
4.	If amount due is $2,000 or more.	Within 3 banking days after end of quarter-monthly period.

If you are required to make quarterly deposits with an authorized Commercial Bank or Federal Reserve Bank, you use a Federal Tax Deposit Form 501 (Form 511 for Agricultural Labor). Each quarter you must file Form 941, Employers Quarterly Federal Tax Return.

When filing your Form 941 for the last quarter of the year, you must also file copy A of all Forms W-2 issued for the year and Form W-3, Reconciliation of Income Tax Statements. Form W-2, which provides details of wages paid and all deductions (Federal, State, Local, etc.), must be given to each employee no later than January 31 of the following year of his employment. Should he leave during the year, he should be provided with a W-2 no later than 30 days after his last wages were paid.

Excise Taxes

Excise taxes are Federal taxes on certain occupations and on the sale of certain items. A partial list of the kind of items involved is:

- Manufacturers and dealers of beer, wine and liquor
- Local telephone service
- Air transportation
- Gaming devices
- Highway motor vehicles
- Gasoline
- Fishing equipment
- Truck manufacturers
- Pistols, firearms, cartridges

The full list is available from the I.R.S. in publication 510, Information of Excise Taxes for 19XX. If you are required to pay excise taxes you must use Form 720, the Quarterly Federal Excise Tax Return, and make deposits using Form 504, Federal Tax Deposit, Excise Taxes.

Year-End Filing

- Sole Proprietor - as a sole proprietor you show the profits from your business on Schedule C of your Form 1040, the U.S. Individual Income Tax Return. If you have more than one business then you must file a separate Schedule C for each. You will probably also have to file a declaration of estimated tax, Form 1040 - ES, and make estimated tax payments during the year.

- Partnership - an informational return, Form 1065, "U.S. Partnership Return of Income", must be filed on April 17 for calendar year partnerships, or on the 15th day of the 4th month following the close of the fiscal year. Each partner's distributive share is reported on Schedule K, Form 1065. Each partner must also file information on his distributive share on Schedule E & R, Part III, Form 1040.

- Corporation - A corporation must file its income tax return, Form 1120, "U.S. Corporation Income Tax Return", using the same filing schedule defined for Form 1065 above. Subchapter S corporations file Form 1120S.

State Taxes

All states have unemployment taxes, with the rates based on "experience", which will vary from one employer to another. You will have to apply for a State Employer Identification Number. You will also require a State Sales Tax Identification Number for use in reporting withheld sales taxes. The state taxes normally are:

- State Income Tax - this must be withheld from each employee, depending on his salary and exemptions.
- State Unemployment Insurance - this must be paid as indicated above.
- Sales Tax - must be collected and paid to the state tax authorities. Note, even if you are required to collect no state sales tax by the nature of your business, you should always file a null return to avoid a surprise assessment.

Other Taxes

The most common tax not previously mentioned, is property tax if the business owns its premises. If the business leases its premises, the lease may stipulate that the tenant pay property taxes or the amount of increase in property taxes. In addition, most leases will stipulate that the tenant is responsible for paying any special taxes that might be applied on property by any government agency.

.2 TAX CALENDAR

Listed below are the important tax dates for the various business forms. As you can see, reporting and paying taxes is a year-round activity.

Jan. 1 Form W4 - employee status determination date.
     15 Amended declaration return of estimated tax may be filed.
     15 Farmers may file declaration return and pay estimated tax in full.
     15 Final payment of estimated tax by individuals who have previously made declarations.
     31 Employer furnishes each employee Form W-2, showing amount of taxes withheld during past year.

	31	Form 941 - quarterly return by employer of taxes withheld during preceding quarter plus employer and employee Social Security Taxes.
	31	Quarterly return by employer of State Unemployment Taxes.
	31	Form 940 - annual return by employer of one or more employees.
Feb.	15	Farmers may file a final return.
	28	Forms 1096 and 1099 - annual information return of dividends, salaries and other payments.
Apr.	15	Form 1040 - individual income tax return for prior calendar year.
	15	Form 1065 - partnership return due for those on a calendar year basis.
	15	Form 1040ES - declaration return and payment of one quarter of current year's estimated tax due.
	30	Form 941 - quarterly return by employer of taxes withheld during preceding quarter plus employer and employee Social Security taxes.
	30	Quarterly return by employer of state unemployment taxes.
Jun.	15	Payment due of one quarter of current year's estimated tax.
	15	1040ES - amended declaration return may be filed.
Jul.	31	Form 941 - see above.
	31	Quarterly state return - see above.
Sep.	15	Payment due of one quarter of current year's estimated tax.
	15	1040ES - see above.
Oct.	15	Form 941 - see above.
	15	Quarterly state return - see above.

Notes

- The list above does not include the dates for every tax - principal omissions are Federal Excise taxes and State Sales taxes.
- The penalty for filing late U.S. tax returns is 5% per month of the tax due, up to a maximum of 25%. Even if you do not have the funds, making the tax return itself on time will save the penalty.
- When the due date falls on a Saturday, Sunday, or legal holiday, the return is due on the next business day.

3.3 TAX FORMS

A more complete list of the various Federal tax forms is provided below (taken from "Tax Guide for Small Business" - U. S. Government Printing Office).

	BUSINESS ACTIVITY	LIABILITY	FORM
A)	Do business as:		
	• Corporation, association	Income tax	1120
	• Subchapter S Corporation	Income Tax	1120S
	• Partnership	Information Return	1065
	• Sole Proprietor (or partner)	Income Tax	1040
		Estimated Tax	1040-ES
		Self-Employment Tax	1040

3/Tax Aspects

BUSINESS ACTIVITY	LIABILITY	FORM
B) Employ:		
• 1 or more persons	Income Tax Withholding	941
	FICA	941
• 1 or more persons	FUTA Tax	940
C) Furnish Facilities for:		
• Local and toll telephone teletypewriter exchange	Excise Tax	
• Air transportation Persons and Property	On Facilities	720
D) Import:		
• Adulterated or process butter	Stamp Tax	923
• Filled cheese		
• Firearms	Occupational Tax	11
E) Issue:		
• Insurance policies (if you are a foreign insurer)	Excise Tax	720
F) Maintain for use:		
• Slot machines	Occupational Tax	11-B
• Punchboards	Occupational Tax	11-C
	Wagering Tax	730
G) Manufacture:		
• Adulterated or process butter	Occupational Tax	11
	Stamp Act	218
• Automobiles, trucks, buses, or trailers	Mfg. Excise Tax	720
• Beer	Excise Tax	2034
• Cigars, cigarettes, cigarette paper or tubes	Excise Tax	2137, 2617, 3071
• Distilled spirits	Excise tax	2521, 2522, 4077
	Occupational Tax	11
• Filled cheese	Stamp Tax	218
• Firearms (licensed	Occupational Tax	720
J) Sell Firearms:		
• Retail & wholesale under National Firearms Act of 1968	Occupational tax	11
K) Transfer (or otherwise dispose of):		
• Firearms classified under National Firearms Act	Stamp tax (adhesive)	4 (Firearms)

3.4 RECORD KEEPING FOR TAX PURPOSES

The U. S. Treasury Department requires you to keep such records that the accuracy of your income statement can be verified. You are required to keep records for as long as you are subject to tax violation, that is three years after

69

you file a given return. However, there is no time limit on fraud.

You are required to keep your records of Federal employee income tax withholding, Social Security and unemployment taxes for at least four years after you filed your return and paid these taxes.

The Payroll Tax Record Book published by Dome Publishing Company should be adequate for all your recordkeeping needs. If you have any further questions the Government Printing Office provides a booklet entitled "Guide to Record Retention Requirements".

3.5 TAX ASPECTS OF BUSINESS FORMATION - CORPORATIONS

Some of the major tax aspects involved in the various business entities were discussed in Chapter Two. It was pointed out that in addition to the aspect of limited liability, the corporate form also offered the benefit of the most flexible structure for tax avoidance. However, many of the tax benefits of the corporate form must be captured at the very moment of corporate formation.

Note - In the following paragraphs reference will be made to Section 351, Section 1244, etc. These are references to the various provisions given under those section numbers in the Internal Revenue Code.

3.5.1 Section 351 Exchange

You will of course, want to exchange some of your assets for corporate stock when you form your corporation. Section 351 allows you to make this exchange without incurring any tax penalty. This is useful, since it may enable the taxpayer to avoid recognition of a "gain" when he exchanges a property, which has markedly increased in value for corporate stock. On the other hand, the owner of property that had declined in value might prefer to "sell" it to the corporation and deduct his "loss". In the latter instance, the property is still in the owner's control.

It may also be possible to convert the sale of non-capital assets to give the appearance of capital assets by use of the corporate entity. The difference being, of course, that the sale of non-capital assets results in ordinary income whereas the sale of capital assets results in capital gain income, which is taxed at a much lower rate. The procedure to follow would be a tax-free exchange of the non-capital asset to the corporation in exchange for corporate stock. After a suitable time period a buyer may be found who would purchase corporate stock for the appreciated value of the asset. The gain from the sale of corporate stock would constitute a capital gain unless a hasty transaction leads the I.R.S. to view the action as a transparent vehicle.

Note - Capital assets are defined by the Internal Revenue Code as all assets except:

1) Inventory or "property held by the taxpayer primarily for sale to customers"
2) Real or depreciable property used in trade or business.
3) A copyright, a literary, musical or artistic composition.

The tax treatment of item 2 (real or depreciable property) is governed by Section 1231, which states that judgement on the tax aspects of the sale

3/Tax Aspects

of these items is deferred until the year's end. If, at year's end, the net result of all Section 1231 transactions is a loss, each of the items is treated as a non capital asset, whereas if the net result is a gain, each item is treated as a long-term capital asset.

3.5.2 Section 1244 Stock

The benefits of an initial issue of 1244 stock were described in paragraph 2.2.4, since this stock can be used to convert a capital loss into an ordinary income loss, which, of course, has far greater tax deductibility.

3.5.3 Preferred Stock

The benefits of an initial issue of preferred stock were also described in paragraph 2.2.4. In this instance corporate income can be extracted as a capital gain where amounts of preferred stock are sold in disproportionate amount, relative to each stockholder's holding, to an external financial agency only to be repurchased later, at a slight premium, by the corporation.

NOTE - The benefits of a Subchapter S corporation are somewhat negated because of the stipulation that only one class of stock can be outstanding in a Subchapter S corporation. You would, of course, like to have an initial issue of 1244 stock, some preferred stock, and some common stock for the reasons given above.

3.5.4 Tax Aspects Of Buying A Corporation

A business, which is incorporated, may be acquired by outright purchase of its assets or by purchase of its stock. An important difference between these two methods of purchase lies in how the buyer can depreciate the fixed assets he has acquired. If, for example, the business acquired by outright purchase has $50,000 worth (fair market value) of depreciable fixed assets (buildings, cars, trucks, fitments, furniture and so on), they may be depreciated using the $50,000 as a starting point or basis. Alternatively, if the stock is purchased, the depreciable basis of the assets is the same as that of the prior owners. That is to say the prior owner may have used accelerated depreciation techniques (to be discussed later) and depreciated the assets down to a basis of only $10,000. Under these circumstances, the $10,000 becomes the depreciable basis for the new owner. Since depreciation is a valuable factor in offsetting current income for tax purposes, $40,000 worth of tax offsetting depreciation expense has been lost in this method of acquisition.

A reverse situation occurs when the depreciable basis of the assets is above the fair market value of these same assets. In this situation it would be to the new owner's advantage to buy the corporation's stock rather than the assets directly. Indeed, the depreciable basis may be well above the price he pays for the stock. Thus, he is, in effect, buying a built in tax-shelter with his new business.

It is important for the buyer of the assets of a business to realise that the allocation of the total purchase price to each specific asset is critical for future tax purposes. Often, the interests of buyer and seller are opposite.

If, however, through ignorance of one of the parties, the allocation is lopsided, the I.R.S. may choose to reallocate and thus remove some hoped for tax advantage. From the buyer's viewpoint, the order of preference in allocating the value of business assets would be:

1) Items such as inventory that can be deducted in full from income.
2) Items such as depreciable equipment, where depreciating value can be deducated from income.
3) Non-depreciable items, such as land, that have no effect on income.

NOTE: "Goodwill" is a category three item, since it cannot be depreciated. A "Covenant not to compete", where the seller agrees not to compete with the purchaser for a given number of years in a given geographical area, is a category 2 item.

3.5.5 Lease Versus Ownership Of Fixed Assets

The new businessman may have sufficient capital that he can choose between leasing or buying a fixed asset. For example, he can purchase or lease his premises or his delivery trucks. The choice to be made depends very greatly on the tax benefits of each course of action. If an asset is purchased the factors to be considered are:

- the amount of investment tax credit currently permitted (10% of purchase price in 1979)
- the amount of depreciation
- the interest foregone by purchase of the asset instead of investment

If the asset is leased the factors to be considered are:

- the annual lease payment and conditions of the lease
- the tax reduction created by the operating deduction

The two choices, lease versus rent, can only be correctly made by using present value calculations. Such techniques are not difficult, but are beyond the scope of this book. The reader should consult such excellent texts as: "Engineering Economy" by Grant and Ireson published by Ronald Press Company.

3.5.6 Election Of Accounting Method And Fiscal Year

The tax effects of choice of accounting method and the fiscal year elected were discussed in Chapter One. It is preferable to use a cash basis for your accounting system, where this is permitted, so that you can advance or delay cash receipt or payment to fall in a specific tax year. Tax obligations may be delayed for up to a whole year by such maneuvers. A corporate form of business is also able to choose the period of its fiscal year. The advantages of arranging that the corporation's fiscal year does not coincide with the taxpayers tax year were explained in Section 1.2.

These two elections (accounting method and fiscal year) must usually be made very early in the company's life and cannot easily be changed. It is vital, therefore, that competent taxation advice is obtained in these matters.

3/Tax Aspects

When a new business is started there are, almost certainly, large nonrecurring start up expenses or losses. These most often occur during the first six months or so of a business' life. If the company is started mid way through the year it would be advisable to extend the fiscal year well beyond the calendar to shield as must income as possible behind the start up expenses.

Conversely, if, for example, an on-going business is purchased just before the Christmas selling season when sales are highest, the tax year should also be extended to balance the initial high profit months against the low or negative profit months of the summer period.

3.5.7 Loss Carryover

An acquired corporation may have a current or accumulated net operating loss or some current capital losses. The law severely restricts the carryover of these losses into the acquired corporation even though it is the same corporate entity. The carryovers involved are:

- net operating loss carryover
- investment credit carryover
- work incentive program credit carryover
- foreign tax credit carry over
- capital loss carryover

Where 50% or more of the corporation's stock is acquired by 10 or fewer persons no carryover is permitted.

A new corporation is permitted to carry over any net operating loss (defined as the excess of gross income less all allowable deductions) for a period up to seven years.

The advantage of a Subchapter S corporation is that the corporation's net income loss can "flow through" directly to the shareholder and offset his taxable income in the year of loss. The disadvantages of Subchapter S election have been described previously. Thus, the choice of Subchapter S election depends very much on the projected financial future of the business. If the business may eventually have a huge gain or a hugh loss, then Subchapter S election is inadvisable, since Subchapter S election prevents the concurrent issue of preferred stock and 1244 stock. Preferred stock would be of use, in extracting any gain with the minimum tax penalty. 1244 stock would enable the stockholder to convert a capital loss into an income loss (with greater tax benefits) in the event of a business failure. Alternatively, if the business is projected as one that will have moderate early losses and moderate later gains, then the election of Subchapter S corporation for the early loss year or so is probably a wise choice.

3.5.8 Purchase Of A Corporation With Borrowed Money

Occassionally, the purchaser of a corporation does not have sufficient funds of his own to purchase all of the outstanding stock. He might arrange to borrow the amount outstanding and pay off that loan with profits provided by the corporation. However, one disadvantage is that corporate income taxes will have to be paid on the loan payment prior to transfer to the purchaser.

Another approach is for the purchaser to buy only that portion of the outstanding stock he can with his initial funds. The balance of the stock is redeemed by the corporation, the corporation then being able to deduct interest paid on the loan and reduce corporate taxes.

3.6 TAX ASPECTS OF BUSINESS PURCHASE - SUBCHAPTER S CORPORATIONS

The purchaser of a Subchapter S corporation has the option of buying its stock or its assets. If the stock is acquired he also has the option of whether or not to continue the Subchapter S election. If he does not wish to continue the election he has 60 days, after the stock acquisition, in which to terminate the election.

Note, the purchaser of shares of a Subchapter S corporation should be aware that:

- Corporate income that is undistributed at the end of the fiscal year is attributed to the new shareholder as if he were a shareholder for the entire year.
- Any net operating loss, on the other hand, is only attributable to the purchaser from the moment a stock acquisition, and thus must be allocated with the seller.
- The rights to any nondividend distribution are attributed to a specific individual and do not transfer with stock ownership.

The tax aspects of Subchapter S election with respect to loss flow through the income withdrawal were discussed in the previous section.

3.7 TAX ASPECTS OF BUSINESS PURCHASE - PARTNERSHIPS

For taxation purposes the value of each partner's interest in a partnership is known as his "basis". The basis is his original capital contribution plus any further contributions, less any distributions that have been made to him. Because of the non-cash effects of depreciaiton, etc. the basis is usually not equal to the partner's share of the net worth of the partnership. The purchase of a partnership interest does not affect the basis of the partnership. Thus, a purchasing partner may face the possibility of being charged capital gains tax if the partnership sells an appreciated asset above its basis value at a later date, although he himself has not benefited by that capital gain (he may have bought in at the appreciated value).

The purchasing partner may avoid such problems by making use of Section 754 of the Internal Revenue Code, which adjusts the value of the basis that the purchasing partner has in a particular asset to reflect its purchase price. However, the partnership must agree to make this election.

3.8 TAX ASPECTS OF BUSINESS PURCHASE - SOLE PROPRIETORSHIPS

From a tax viewpoint a proprietorship is not a single entity and cannot be purchased as such - each asset must be separately valued. A purchaser usually views the allocation process with the same degree of caution as he would the allocation of assets of any other form of business entity. His interests are the same as those described in Section 3.5.4.

3/Tax Aspects

METHODS OF REDUCING CORPORATE INCOME TAX

One obvious method, of course, is to elect to operate as a Subchapter S corporation. If this is not possible, then almost the same result can be achieved by splitting off a portion of corporate activities in such a way that a legitimate proprietorship or partnership is formed.

3.9.1 Collapsible Corporations

One method of avoiding ordinary income tax for the owner-shareholder is to accumulate corporate earnings and then liquidate the corporation at an appropriate moment. In the event that the liquidation results in excessive income such that both accumulated earnings tax and corporate income tax has to be paid, a tax saving to the shareholder may still result since his distribution is a capital gain rather than ordinary income (only 40% of a capital gain is recognised as income). Clearly, both corporate taxes and accumulated earning tax are avoided if the liquidated property is distributed directly to the shareholder at liquidation. The shareholder would be subject only to capital gains tax. Such a situation results in a "collapsible corporation" and such tax savings are governed by Section 341, which in many cases make the results of the sale of a "collapsible corporation" ordinary income.

The status of a "collapsible corporation" can be avoided in several ways. One way is to hold the corporate property, which could be a building, for three years before selling it. Another method is to use Section 341(f) to shift the status of collapsibility from the seller to the buyer. Here the buyer agrees to the loss of non-recognition of gain benefits when he ultimately disposes of the property. The seller, however, can use Section 341(f) to sell his corporate stock and recognize a capital gain.

"Collapsible Corporations" occur most frequently where a corporation is formed to develop and sell a property.

3.9.2 Purchase Of A Loss Corporation

A profitable corporation often used to acquire a loss corporation and use that corporation's accumulated deficit to offset its profits. Section 382 severely limits this possibility by restricting the amount of net income loss carryover available. If the change in stock ownership is more than 60%, each percentage point over 60% and up to 80% will reduce the loss carryover by 3.5%. Each percentage point above 80% will produce a 1.5% reduction in net income loss carryover. Clearly, a 100% takeover would result in zero carryover.

3.9.3 "Thin Corporations"

Thin corporations, which have been discussed previously, occur when the equity of corporate formation is small and the debt high. The founders provide both debt and equity, and are paid interest on the debt. The corporation can deduct the interest as an expense. How "thin" can a corporation be? In fact, ratios of debt-to-equity of 9:1 have been allowed whereas 11:1 disallowed. However, the I.R.S decision may turn on other factors.

Another advantage of a high debt-to-equity ratio is in the event of business failure. Here, the loss of the debt may be classified as a nonbusiness bad debt and be a capital loss (Section 166(d). Alternatively, it may be a business bad debt and be deductible in full (Section 166(a). Ordinarily, the loss of equity capital is subject to capital loss restrictions.

3.9.4 Corporate Leasing From Shareholders

When a corporation is formed it is not necessary to transfer all fixed assets to the corporation. The shareholder may lease the asset to the corporation, the corporation then being entitled to deduct the rent or lease payment from its income. However, the amount of the lease must be in line with current prevailing values determined in fair "arms-length" transactions.

3.9.5 Use Of A Loss Corporation As A Tax-Shelter

The owner-shareholder of a loss corporation can transfer income producing securities to the loss corporation, the net-income loss shielding the income from the securities. In addition, the corporate may be able to receive 85% of the dividends from the securities tax-free. This benefit is not available to the owner himself.

3.9.6 Personal Holding Company Tax

Tax code Sections 541 through 547 contain provisions to limit the benefits of "incorporated pocket books", "incorporated talents" or "incorporated pleasure facilities". These incorporations seek to obtain the tax benefits of the corporate form unobtainable as an individual.

The tax penalty imposed on personal holding companies, as they are known, is a 70% tax on income that remains undistributed at the end of the tax year. Two methods of avoiding the tax penalty are:

- avoid classification as a personal holding company
- retain no personal holding company income at year end.

A corporation will be classified as a personal holding company if five of the largest stockholders own more than 50 percent of the value of the outstanding stock. Personal holding company income is either (a) passive income - dividends, royalities, etc. or (b) personal talent income - actors, sportsmen, authors, etc. However, if less than 60% of a corporation's income is personal holding company income, the corporation will not be a personal holding company.

The trick, therefore, is to combine personal holding company income producing assets with other assets to form a normal corporation. Alternatively, a corporation formed by 11 individual taxpayers owning equal shares in a corporation with nothing but passive income, would also avoid personal holding company tax.

3.9.7 ESOTS

Employee Stock Ownership Trusts were officially recognized by the "Employee Retirement Income Security Act" of 1974. An ESOT enables a company to make tax-deductible contributions to the trust in the form of corporate stock. The amount contributed is generally limited to 15% of the payroll of the employees, but under certain special circumstances can be as high as 25%. Thus, at no current cash cost, the ESOT provides retirement security for employees and tax-deductible benefit for the corporation. The corporation may be either publically or privately owned. There are many other advantages of the ESOT, and relatively small companies can enjoy the benefits. More information is provided in: "The Magic of ESOT" by Robert A. Frisch published by Farnsworth Publishing Company, Inc.

INCOME SPLITTING TO REDUCE PERSONAL INCOME TAX

A family partnership can be used to reduce the overall income tax of the family. However, this cannot be done by merely assigning business income to various family members. What has to be done is to assign income producing property to each family member - thus the income from a single apartment building can be legitmately allocated among several family members.

A corporation can also be used to split income, where the shares are split between various family members. It is difficult, but not impossible, to incorporate a professional business (doctor, lawyer, etc.) to achieve income splitting.

3.10.1 Family Trusts

Deductible business expenses can also be paid to a family trust. The family trust would have to be set up in such a way that its income does not result in taxpayer liability. A trust-leaseback situation can result in substantial tax savings over a number of years. A simple example is the case of a taxpayer owning his business premises, which has a rental value of $15,000 per year and a depreciation deduction of $5,000 per year. Currently, therefore, he can only deduct the $5,000 depreciation as a business expense. If he now transfers the property to the trust (and meets the requirements of Sections 671-678) he can lease it back from the trust at $15,000 per year. Of course, the $5,000 depreciation deduction is lost, but he can now deduct $15,000 thus increasing his deductible tax savings by $10,000 a year. Family trusts, per se, are outside the scope of this book, but should be investigated by anyone interested in tax savings.

METHODS OF EXTRACTING CORPORATE INCOME

There are six general methods by which accumulated retained corporate income can be extracted by its shareholders. The methods involving no tax liability would obviously be most preferable, with capital gain income having next preference and ordinary income the least preference. The various methods of income extraction in order of preference are:

1. Repayment of Debt

    If some of the initial capital used to form the corporation is designated as a loan, then the loan may be repaid by the corporation at a later date completely tax free. However, the I.R.S will not permit distributions from "thin corporations", i.e. those with a very high debt to equity ratio, to be entirely tax free. A debt-to-equity ratio of no higher than 3:1 would probably withstand I.R.S. scrutiny.

2. Complete Liquidation

   This method requires the termination of the business and the distribution of the proceeds from the sale of corporate assets to the shareholders. The distribution of the proceeds would result in a capital gain for the shareholders.

3. Partial Liquidation

   A less drastic step than complete liquidation is a partial liquidation of the corporation's assets, which results in a "significant corporate contraction". The proceeds ensuing from the partial liquidation would be entitled to capital gains classification.

4. Stock Redemption

   This method involves the shareholder surrendering part or all of his shares to the corporation in return for a specific payment. This payment may be treated as ordinary income or capital gain depending on the type of stock redemption made. If the stock redemption is made to a sole shareholder or is made pro rata amongst the shareholders, the effect on corporate ownership is nill and this distribution would be regarded by the I.R.S. as ordinary income. If, however, a disproportionate distribution were made that significantly redistributed corporate ownership, the distribution stands a good change of being regarded as a capital gain.

5. Dividend

   Dividend payment is the usual method by which a corporation makes a uniform distribution of part of its profits to its shareholders. Dividends are always regarded as ordinary income, but the first $100 per individual is exempt from taxation.

6. Salary, Interest, Etc.

   These are, of course, treated as ordinary income to the shareholder.

3.12 TAX-DEDUCTIBLE BENEFITS

Just about the only tax-deductible benefit available to a sole proprietor or partner is a self-employed persons' retirement plan, sometimes called an H.R.10 or Keogh Plan. This plan enables the self employed owner to set aside 15 percent of $7,500 of his income (which ever is the lower) to build a fund for retirement. The amount set aside is deductible from gross income for that year.

There are many tax-deductible benefits available to the owner-shareholder of an incorporated business.

3.12.1 Group Health Insurance

A group medical and dental plan can be set up, the cost of which is tax-deductible. The basic Blue Cross/Blue Shield benefits can be provided to all with, perhaps, a Major Medical Plan covering key employees.

3.12.2 Accidental Death And Life Insurance

Group life insurance is tax-deductible if it provides $50,000 or less per employee. Even a single employee corporation (the owner) may qualify

3/Tax Aspects

for a tax-deductible life insurance plan.

Accidental death coverage is also deductible and covers the owner and key employees who are required to travel frequently.

12.3 Pension Benefits/Profit Sharing Plans

A variety of tax-deductible plans are available. These can be funded on the last day of the corporation's fiscal year and still qualify as deductible.

Profit sharing plans are somewhat different but also qualify as tax-deductible.

TAX CREDITS

A tax credit directly reduces income tax due, whereas a tax deduction reduces the income that is liable for taxation. Thus a tax credit is much more valuable than a tax deduction. The most important credit available to a small businessman is the investment tax credit for all tangible depreciable property (except your building). The value of the credit is 10% of the basis of the depreciable asset. The credit is available at the end of the year in which you bought the asset and is in <u>addition</u> to any depreciation you are allowed. The maximum investment tax credit allowed in any one year is $100,000. Any unused credit may be carried back three years or foreward seven years to offset past then future income.

TAX DEDUCTIONS

Tax deductions are the various legitimate expenses that can be charged by a business and, thereby, reduces the net taxable income. Some of the deductions are purely dependent upon ongoing expenses, such as interest on loans. Other deductions can be adjusted to suit your needs. Such deductions are very useful in the early days of the business, since they can be maximized to reduce taxation thus making more money available for reinvestment in the business. Conversely, when you come to sell a business, you will want to minimize the deductions and show maximum net income.

4.1 Depreciation

The deduction for depreciation allows the wear and tear of a fixed asset, such as an automobile, to be charged off as a business expense. The most common depreciation methods are (1) straight-line depreciation, (2) sum-of-the-years-digits method and (3) declining balance method. No asset may be depreciated below its salvage value under any of the three methods.

- Straight-Line Depreciation

    As its name implies, this method depreciates an asset by equal amounts over each year of its life until zero value remains at the end of the last year of its life. Thus, an asset worth $10,000 and having a 10 year life would be depreciated by $1000 each year. The effects of salvage value, if any, are ignored in these calculations if less than 10% of the assets initial value.

    The I.R.S. publishes a table of guideline lives over which assets may be depreciated. Typically, each asset class is given a life range (ADR) which is plus or minus 20 percent of a specific value.

- The Sum-Of-The-Years'-Digits Method

    This method is an accelerated depreciation method and provides faster depreciation in the early years. Again, the taxpayer must establish the initial value of the asset and its life. Next the sum of the years of the life of the asset are calculated. For example, a $6,000 automobile having a life of three years has a sum-of-years of $3 + 2 + 1 = 6$. Thus the depreciation is:

First year:	3/6 x 6,000 =	$3,000
Second year:	2/6 x 6,000 =	$2,000
Third year:	1/6 x 6,000 =	$1,000

- The Declining Balance Method

    This is another accelerated method of depreciation. Again, you must establish the asset's initial value and life. Salvage value can be ignored in the depreciation calculation. The first step in the calculation is to determine the straight line depreciation percentage, which on an asset with a 10 year life is 1/10 or 10%. Next, the declining percentage multiplier is chosen depending on the type of property being depreciated. Three multipliers are allowed; 2 times, $1\frac{1}{2}$ times and $1\frac{1}{4}$ times. If the 2 times multiplier is permitted, then a $10,000 asset with a ten year life would be depreciated as follows:

First year depreciation:	$10,000x20% =	$2,000
Second year depreciation:	$ 8,000x20% =	$1,600
Third year depreciation:	$ 6,400x20% =	$1,280

    Note, that the constant depreciation percentage is applied to the declining value or balance of the asset each year in calculating that year's depreciation deduction.

- Comparison Of The Three Methods

    The fastest depreciation method over the first year and the second year is the double declining (2X multiplier) balance method (DDB). The sum-of-years'-digits method accumulates the most depreciation from the third year onwards. One can switch from an accelerated method to the straight line method at anytime, but not vice-versa. It becomes advantageous, if the DDB method is used, to make the change to the straight-line method at a certain point.

- First-Year Depreciation Deduction

    Additional first-year depreciation can be claimed for machinery, equipment, and other types of tangible personal property (non-realty) that have a useful life of at least six years. 20% of the cost of qualifying property (up to specific limits) can be deducted as additional first-year depreciation in addition to the regular depreciation.

    The cost of property is limited to $10,000 in a separate return and

$20,000 for a joint return. This applies directly for a sole proprietor. The amount of extra depreciation that a partnership can pass through to all of its partners is limited to $2,000 a year (20% of $10,000). A corporation or members of a group of controlled corporations are treated as one tax payer ($2,000 a year maximum deduction) for the purposes of determining the additional first year depreciation.

3.14.2 Deductible Business Expenses

- Travel And Entertainment Expenses

    Legitimate business related expenses can be deducted as a business cost, whatever business form is employed. In any case, accurate records must be kept to substantiate any deduction made.

    Generally speaking, you must be away from home overnight for travel expenses to be a deductible business expense.

    In terms of transportation expense, overnight transportation to a business destination is, of course deductible, as is the cost of operating an automobile for business expenses. In the latter case, you may not deduct the proportionate amount used for family purposes.

    Over the years individual abuses on entertainment expenses and extravagant facilities have caused the I.R.S. to tighten up on this type of deduction. For example, the Revenue Act of 1978 eliminated deductions for yachts, hunting lodges and fishing camps, but country club dues are still deductible. Clearly, this is an area where the latest tax advice is required.

- Salaries, wages (including the owner's - if the business is incorporated).

- Rental Expenses (included that paid to a shareholder if arrived at by "arms-length negotiations").

- Bad Debts - a distinction is made between business and non-business bad debts. A business debt is one that is created in the course of normal business operations; sales, services rendered, unpaid rents and so on. Non-business debt relates to losses on capital items such as buildings, equipment or business loans. All bad debts of a corporation are business bad debts. Non-business bad debts, applicable to sole proprietorships and corporations, must be treated as short term capital losses and not be deducted from gross income as bad debts.

- Interest - you may deduct all interest paid or accrued during the tax year. Alternatively, you may elect to capitalize interest incurred in connection with certain real and personal property.

- Insurance - business insurance to protect against normal business hazards is deductible. Life insurance premiums are deductible under the rules discussed earlier.

- Taxes – you may deduct various Federal, State, Local and Foreign Government imposed taxes. Federal income, estate and gift taxes and State inhertitance, legacy, and succession taxes are never deductible.

    The various tax categories are:
    1. Real property tax – may be deducted if part of business, but <u>must</u> be capitalized if local taxes add to your property values, for example by street construction, sidewalks, etc.
    2. State taxes imposed on businesses are deductible; those imposed on individuals are not deductible as business expenses but may be deducted in computing the individual's income tax bill provided the standard deduction is not claimed.
    3. Other taxes – any personal property tax imposed on business property is deductible as are State Registration Fees, sales Taxes and Corporate Franchise Taxes.
    4. Employment taxes – these have been discussed in detail earlier and are fully deductible.

- Other Deductible Business Expenses

    All necessary business expenses you pay or incur: heat, light, power, incidental supplies and material, professional expenses, advertising, licenses and regulatory fees, penalties for non performance of contract, charitable contributions, donations to business organizations, franchise, trademarks, trade name expenses, certain educational expenses, commitment fees, and losses. Contested liabilities may or may not be deductible and fines and penalties for violation of Federal or State laws are never deductible.

3.15 CAUTION

1. The guidance provided in this chapter is current at publication, but taxation law is a living, ever changing subject and the latest guidance must be obtained when any crucial decision must be made. However, the laws change slowly over the years, so that general principals remain true.
2. Taxation can become a criminal matter if tax evasion is suspected. If you ever have dealings with an I.R.S. offical, <u>first</u> ask him to identify himself by showing you his badge. If the words "SPECIAL AGENT" are printed in large letters across the lower half of the badge, he is not at all interested in collecting taxes from you – he is interested only in your criminal prosecution. At that point, you should politely excuse yourself and retain the service of the best tax-attorney you can find!
3. Even though you have by accident or design failed to pay certain taxes that you should, a competent tax-attorney might be able, by various strategems, to reduce the amount of tax assessed against you. Thus, all is never lost in the tax world and, like the rest of the legal world, a competent legal advisor can work wonders.
4. Tax law itself is merely a specialized branch of Federal laws, the basis of

which are the precedents created by various Federal and State courts. The application and interpretation of any tax law must be discovered from examining the records of the various tax courts. Thus, if an I.R.S. agent showes the I.R.S. code to you and proclaims that it is the law, he is mistaken.

There are a series of mechanisms for settling disputes between the individual or corporation and the I.R.S. The taxpayer should <u>never</u> ignor letters or calls from the I.R.S. He should always reply in writing and, if he wishes to obtain more time to gather his wits and information, he can always respectfully request the I.R.S. to provide him with more specifics as to its request and so on.

Briefly, the income tax appeal procedure is as follows. When agreement cannot be reached with the first I.R.S. auditing agent, a district level conference is convened with a specially trained agent, who is independent of the first auditing agent. If this does not resolve the dispute, a regional level conference is convened at one of the seven appellate division offices. If this does not reach a satisfactory agreement, the taxpayer will go to tax court. Above the regular tax court is the Court of Appeals and, finally, the U.S. Supreme Court. A review of the statistics reveals that the taxpayer has a higher chance of victory the higher the court his case reaches. However, court cases should normally be avoided if possible, and the I.R.S. will normally agree to accept less than the disputed tax deficiency rather than proceed into a court battle. This "plea bargaining" results from an I.R.S. desire to use their resources most efficiently from a tax collected versus time expended viewpoint.

6 SOURCES OF TAX INFORMATION

- I.R.S.

    As might be expected, the I.R.S. provides a wealth of information. The following can be obtained from the U.S. Government Printing Office.

    - Tax Guide for Small Business. I.R.S. publication 344(75¢), which is a 260-page manual defining tax terminology showing how to complete various tax forms.

    - Your Business Tax Kit. I.R.S. publication 454 provides simplified instructions on complying with the Federal tax laws.

    - Employers' Tax Guide - Circular E. This provides information on social security and income tax withholding.

The following is an abridged list of I.R.S publication on specialized topics and can be obtained free of charge from your local I.R.S. office:

INTERNAL REVENUE SERVICE PUBLICATIONS

Title	Publication Number
Farmer's Tax Guide	225
Travel, Entertainment, and Gift Expenses	463
Tax Withholding and Declaration of Estimated Tax	505
Computing Your Tax Under the Income Averaging Method	506
Tax Calendar and Check List for 19XX	509

Title	Publication Number
Information on Excise Taxes for 19XX	510
Credit Sales by Dealers in Personal Property	512
Adjustments to Income for Sick Pay	522
Taxable Income and Nontaxable Income	525
Income Tax Deduction for Contributions	526
Rental Income and Royalty Income	527
Miscellaneous Deductions and Credits	529
Reporting Your Tips for Federal Tax Purposes	531
Information on Self-Employment Tax	533
Tax Information on Depreciation	534
Tax Information on Business Expenses	535
Losses from Operation of a Business	536
Installment and Deferred-Payment Sales	537
Tax Information on Accounting Periods and Methods	538
Withholding Taxes from Your Employee's Wages	539
Tax Information on Repairs, Replacements, and Improvements	540
Tax Information on Partnership Income and Losses	541
Corporations and the Federal Income Tax	542
Sales or Other Disposition of a Business or Business Interest	543
Sales and Other Dispositions of Assets	544
Income Tax Deduction for Interest Expense	545
Income Tax Deduction for Taxes	546
Tax Information on Disasters, Casualty Losses, and Thefts	547
Tax Information on Deductions for Bad Debts	548
Condemnations of Private Property for Public Use	549
Tax Information on Investment Income and Expenses	550
Recordkeeping Requirements and a Guide to Tax Publications	552
Audit of Returns, Appeal Rights, and Claims for Refund	556
How to Apply for Recognition of Exemption for an Organization	557
Federal Tax Guide for Survivors, Executors, and Administrators	559
Valuation of Donated Property	561
Tax Information on Mutual Fund Distributions	564
Tax Information on Investment Credit	572
Tax Information on Pension and Annuity Income	575
Tax Information on United States Savings Bonds	576
Amortization of Pollution Control Facilities	577
Tax Information for Private Foundations and Foundation Managers	578
Tax Information for Manufacturers of Firearms, Shells, and Cartridges	580
Questions and Answers Regarding Original Issue Discount on Savings Deposit Arrangements	581
Federal Use Tax on Civil Aircraft	582
Recordkeeping for a Small Business	583
Workbook for Determining Your Disaster Loss	584
The Collection Process	586
Tax Information on Operating a Business in Your Home	587
Tax Information on Condominiums and Cooperative Apartments	588
Tax Information on Subchapter S Corporations	589
Tax Information on Individual Retirement Savings Programs	590
The Federal Gift Tax	592
Tax Guide for Commercial Fishermen	595

- **Non-IRS Information Sources**
    1. J. K. Lassers - Your Income Taxes published by Simon and Schuster. This tax guide primarily covers personal income taxes.
    2. The Dow Jones - Irwin Guide to Tax Planning by R. Summerfeld, published by Dow Jones. This guide deals with tax planning problems related to individuals or business.
    3. Federal Income Taxation of Corporation and Shareholders by B. I. Bittker and J. S. Eustice, published by Warren, Gorham and Lamont. This book is a scholarly tome giving detailed interpretation of the I.R.S. code and Treasury Regulations and Rulings.
    4. 19XX United States Master Tax Guide published annually by Commerce Clearing House. This guide interprets the latest version of the I.R.S. code in everyday language.
    5. 19XX Internal Revenue Code published by Commerce Clearing House. This, of course, contains the tax codes as provided by various acts of Congress. Unfortunately, it is almost incomprehensible to most readers.
    6. There are two taxation "encyclopedias" published that provide an answer to almost every tax question. These are written in straight forward English and enable the inquirer to proceed to any depth he requires. They do, for example, quote tax court rulings, I.R.S. code, Treasury regulations and rulings. These encyclopedias are published and updated annually:
        - "Standard Federal Tax Reporter" published by Commerce Clearing House (CCH). This 15 volume set covers every aspect of taxation and contains a single volume topical index, which references each tax topic by paragraph. CCH publishes a small booklet entitled "Finding the Answers to Federal Tax Questions", which shows you how to use its guide.
        - Prentice-Hall Federal Taxes is a similar tax encyclopedia published by Prentice-Hall and is composed of 14 volumes. The first volume being the index. The P. H. guide booklet is entitled "Research in Federal Taxation".
    7. "The Institute of Federal Taxation" now published annually in two volumes by Matthew Bender for New York University. This publication contains long, easy to understand articles on current tax matters. For example, in Section 5-1, 1979 is a 108 page article on "Sale of a Business".

4

Business Advice

4.0   Most business advice does not come cheaply. A good attorney, for example, can charge over $100 per hour. Your accountant or CPA will also charge you for his consulting time. However, there are several sources of good advice that are almost free of charge. Your insurance agent, for example, can provide valuable business insights as well, of course, as selling you insurance. Get to know all your professional advisers, their help will certainly be needed. Deal only with local individuals who can be readily contacted when needed.

4.1   THE SMALL BUSINESS ADMINISTRATION (SBA)

The SBA is an independent government agency that has field offices in 98 major cities across America. It offers a variety of services to the small business - from advice to an SBA-backed business loan - all of which are free. To qualify as a small business in the eyes of the SBA, you must meet the following criteria:

- Number of employees - depends on type of industry. A manufacturing company is small if it employs less than 250 to 1,500 people. However, American Motors has been classified as small, even though it employs 25,000 people, because it has a market share of less than 5%.
- Dollar annual sales volume - again, dependent on the type of industry; below $2-7.5 million for retail, below $2-8 million for a service operation, $9.5-22 million for wholesale and under $9.5 million for construction.

Thus, most of you fall well within the province of the SBA. In fact, 97% of all business enterprises are included, and they provide 52% of all private employment, 43% of U.S. output and one-third of the gross national product.

The SBA provides three categories of service:

1. Management and technical help
2. Procurement assistance
3. Financial assistance

4.1.1 Management Assistance

Even if you do not immediately require financial help, you should make use of the management assistance provided. There are several kinds of management assistance:

- SCORE - The Service Core of Retired Executives
  One-on-one consulting is provided by retired executives, who gen-

erally have a reasonable amount of time to devote to this type of program. There are about 12,000 SCORE/ACE volunteers around the country; far more than the 4,400 total employees of the SBA itself. The SCORE volunteers are organized on a local basis and can be contacted through the local SBA office.

- ACE - Active Core of Executives

    This group is similar to SCORE, but is composed of individuals who are themselves still active in the business world, but who want to help small businesses. ACE is not quite as large or as active as SCORE, probably because the individuals are unable to devote as much time to this volunteer activity.

- SBI - The Small Business Institute

    This involves a small team of college students (typically working on MBA degrees), who provide an in-depth study of one particular business. The particular study is determined by discussions between the faculty member and the businessman. Since many of the students are mature individuals with commercial and industry backgrounds, they are able to provide a multifaceted approach to a particular business problem.

- UBDC's - University Business Development Centers

    This is a new program (1976) designed to coordinate the activities of both university faculty and students in small business studies.

- SBA Consultation

    Management assistance officers from the local Business Administration offices are available for one-on-one consultation.

- SBA/Chamber of Commerce Resource Center

    This is the newest program - a pilot program was launched in Colorado in June, 1977. It is an outreach program to intensify efforts to assist the small business community at the local level. In addition to the regular SBA service referrals, the Chamber of Commerce has many contacts with local banks and financial institutions that can assist the businessman in his search for financial aid.

Education

The SBA conducts a variety of educational courses designed to help the small business. For example, it conducts one day pre-business workshops designed to prepare anyone going into business. Questions are answered, and participants can learn to avoid the pitfalls that can wreck a newly established business. Conferences are organized, usually on a one-day basis that discuss specific business subjects, such as taxes, crime prevention, credit and collection. The SBA also sponsors courses, usually at local colleges, on a variety of business topics. These courses run from a few weeks to a full semester.

Technical Assistance

The SBA has an ongoing program of mailing SBA Technology

Assistance Flyers to small businesses. These flyers offer the opportunity to take advantage of the benefits of more than $150 billion worth of government research and development studies.

4.1.2 Procurement Assistance

In 1978, the Federal Government procured $77 billions worth of goods and services. The amount awarded to small businesses was $17 billion. The SBA has a special section devoted to assisting small companies in securing government "set-asides" on major defence contracts. In 1978 small business "set asides" were worth $5 billion. Thus, about 29% of the value of prime defense contracts were specifically awarded to small businesses in order to stimulate small business activity. There is also a program, known as the Joint Determination Program, which permits more than one small firm to link up to form a mini-corporation to handle large contracts.

The SBA will contact various government agencies and installations, such as defense bases, to alert them that you are an approved vendor for a particular type of product. In addition, certain SBA offices have individuals who can actively solicit government contracts on your behalf - thus acting almost as an extension of your own company's sales force.

Special assistance is available to award contracts to firms owned and controlled by socially and economically disadvantaged persons. Minority small businesses are helped by the Minority Business Opportunity Committee (MBOC) and the office of Minority Business Enterprise (OMBE), which were established by the Department of Commerce.

Women, too, are receiving increasing attention from the SBA and in 1978 55,800 received SBA counseling, up sharply from 19,800 in 1977.

Property sales assistance is also a feature of SBA services. In 1978, 5.8 billion board feet of timber was purchased from the Federally owned forests by small businesses.

4.1.3 Financial Assistance

The SBA provides two types of financial assistance to small business.

- SBA Guaranteed Loans - debt financing - where the SBA cosigns the bank note with the small businessman. Thus, the SBA does not, in this case, make direct use of its own small loan fund but rather guarantees the loan made by another financial source. The SBA guarantees these loans when the businessman has been refused a loan by several banks and then turns to the SBA for help. The loan may then be obtainable when the SBA cosigns the note and thereby becomes responsible for it in case of default. In this case, the SBA guarantees to pay between 50-90% of the defaulted loan. In fact, the cumulative loss rate on all disbursed business loans since SBA was formed is 4.18%, which is remarkably low.

    The SBA sets maximum allowable interest rates on guaranteed loans that are based on prevailing market conditions as determined by SBA field personnel. Typically, the SBA manages to obtain a better interest rate for the entrepreneur, which is usually 2 to 3 percentage points above the prime rate.

1. The 7A Term Loan Guarantee

    This is an SBA guaranteed load of up to $350,000, or 80% of the bank loan, whichever is the smaller. Typically, the entrepreneur is required to put up about 50% of the total capital requirements to fund his business venture. Various assets, such as inventory and real estate, are used as collateral for the loan. The term of the loan granted depends upon the use of the loan — six years for working capital, ten years for buying fixed assets and 15 years for contruction purposes.

2. The OBM Program

    This program is aimed specifically at econonomically or socially disadvantaged minorities and has the same terms as the 7A Term Loan program. However, it does permit minorities to borrow up to 80% of their funding requirements, again pledging their business assets as collateral.

3. The EDL Program

    This program assists entrepreneurs who can provide only 20% of their capital requirements. The borrowers must be economically disadvantaged regardless of race, such as the physically handicapped. The maximum loan ceiling is $50,000 and the maximum term is 10 years.

4. Line Of Credit Guarantees

    A line of credit is an absolute must in certain types of industry; for example, an industry that sells merchandise but does not receive payment for 60 to 190 days. In this case, a line of credit is required to finance new inventory while waiting for payment on the goods previously sold. The collateral for the line of credit is the specific accounts receivable for the goods, service or construction that has been sold. The amount of credit available is up to $350,000 or 90% of the bank line of credit, whichever is the smaller. The line of credit is available for one year but may be extended by negotiation.

In the situation where the SBA guarantees the loan, the loan itself must have been reviewed and turned down by several banks. The SBA will then review the loan request using very much the same criteria that a bank would use. The various ratios and profit projections will be discussed in the section on business evaluation. The current (1978) average size of a guaranteed business loan is $85,000.

- Direct SBA Loans - Equity Financing

In certain limited situations, the SBA will lend its own funds directly to a small business. In this case it is a specific division of the SBA, the Small Business Investment Corporation (SBIC), that makes the loan. The SBIC investigates the borrower and then supervises the loan. There are about 300 SBIC across the U.S., and they are typically affiliated with a bank or other financial institution. Loans are granted to individuals, such as the physically handicapped, who are unable to obtain a loan by any other means. The interest rate is very attractive - usually two to three points below the current prime rate. At the end of 1977, the outstanding SBIC loans and investments totalled $622 million.

The MESBIC, Minority Enterprise Small Business Investment Company, was started in 1969 in order to provide funding for minority owned business enterprises.

4.1.4 SBA Loan Ineligibility

The SBA will not provide you with either debt or equity financing in the following situations:

- If the company can get money on reasonable terms:
  (1) From a financial institution
  (2) By selling assets that it does not need in order to grow.
  (3) By the owner's using, without undue personal hardship, his personal credit or resources of his partners or principal stockholders.
  (4) By selling a portion of ownership in the company through a public offering or a private placing of its securities.
  (5) From other Government agencies which provide credit specifically for the applicant's type of business or for the purpose of the required financing.
  (6) From other known sources of credit.

- If the direct or indirect purpose or result of granting a loan would be to:
  (1) Pay off a creditor or creditors of the applicant who are inadequately secured and in a position to sustain a loss.
  (2) Provide funds for distribution or payment to the owner, partners, or shareholders.
  (3) Replenish working capital funds previously used to pay the owner, partners, or shareholders.

- If the applicant's purpose in applying for a loan is to effect a change in ownership of the business; however, under certain circumstances, loans may be authorized for this purpose, if the result would be to aid in the sound development of a small business or to keep it in operation.

- If the loan would provide or free funds for speculation in any kind of property, real or personal, tangible or intangible.

- If the applicant is a charitable organization, social agency, society, or other nonprofit enterprise; however, a loan may be considered for a cooperative if it carries on a business activity and the purpose of the activity is to obtain financial benefit for its members in the operation of their otherwise eligible small business concerns.

- If the purpose of the loan is to finance the construction, acquisition, conversion, or operation of recreational or amusement facilities, unless the facilities contribute to the health or general well-being of the public.
- If the applicant is a newspaper, magazine, radio broadcasting or television broadcasting company, or similar enterprise.
- If any of the gross income of the applicant (or of any of its principal owners) is derived from gambling activities.
- If the loan is to provide funds to an enterprise primarily engaged in the business of lending or investments or to provide funds to any otherwise eligible enterprise for the purpose of financing investments not related or essential to the enterprise.
- If the purpose of the loan is to finance the acquisition, construction, improvement, or operation of real property that is, or is to be, held primarily for sale or investment.
- If the effect of granting of the financial assistance will be to encourage monopoly or will be inconsistent with the accepted standards of the American system of free competitive enterprise.
- If the loan would be used to relocate a business for other than sound business purposes.

4.1.5 SBA Publications

The SBA publishes a variety of literature of interest to the small businessman.

- Counseling Notes - available free of charge.

    As of October 1978, there were 25 different counseling notes on a variety of small businesses from Radio-Television Repair Shop (CN104) to Apparel Store (CN122)

- Management Assistance Publications - free.

    There are three series of these publications:

    1. Management Aids - dealing with functional problems in small manufacturing plants and concentrating on subjects of interest to administrators. Examples include: #193 "What is the Best Selling Price?" and #235 "A Venture Capital Primer for Small Business".
    2. Small Marketers Aids - marketing suggestions for small retail, wholesale and service firms. Examples include: #111 "Interior Display - A Way to Increase Sales" and #143 "Factors in Considering a Shopping Center Location".
    3. Small Business Bibliographies - these leaflets furnish reference sources for individual types of business. For example: #42 Bookstores and #78 Recreation Vehicles.

A complete list of leaflets, which are available free of charge, can be obtained from your local SBA office.

- For-Sale SBA Booklets - these are published by the SBA, but can only be obtained from the Government Printing Office.

  1. Small Business Management Series. These booklets cost from about $1.50 to $3.00 each and are well written discussions of special management problems in small companies. For example; "Handbook of Small Business Finance", 68 pages, $1.80.

  2. Starting and Managing Series. - this series deals with the problems of a specific business. For example; "Starting and Managing a Small Shoestore", 104 pages, $1.35.

  3. Non-Series Publications

     - Export Marketing for Smaller Firms, 84 pages, $2.20.
     - U.S. Government Purchasing and Sales Directory, 169 pages, $4.00.
     - Managing for Profits, 170 pages, $2.75.
     - Buying and Selling a Small Business, 122 pages, $2.30.
     - Strengthening Small Business Management", 158 pages, $2.75.

Again, the full list of booklets available for sale can be obtained from your local SBA office.

4.1.6 Comment On SBA

The SBA should not be shrugged off as just another incompetent government agency. Yes, the SBA does have its rules and procedures, and if you want to obtain a loan through them, you will have to submit yourself to a moderate amount of paperwork and red tape. However, this is true if you deal with your local bank. Experience in dealing with the SBA suggests that this agency has built up a reservoir of experience that the entrepreneur can ignor at his own risk. If you are willing to be helped and guided, and many new businessman are not, then the SBA provides a valuable service. Best of all, it is largely free of charge.

4.2 BANK OF AMERICA PUBLICATIONS

The Bank of America publishes a series of "Business Profiles" for 29 specific businesses. The series itself is called "Small Business Reporter". In California, the booklets are available free from any local Bank of America office. Otherwise, you can obtain any specific publication for $1.00 each from Bank of America, Dept. 3120, P.O. Box 37000, San Fransisco, California, 94137.

The current list of "Business Profiles" is:

Vol.	No.	
9	5	Small Job Printing
9	12	Drug Stores
10	3	Apparel Manufacturing
10	6	Equipment Rental Business

Vol.	No.	
10	8	The Handcraft Business
10	9	Repair Services
10	11	Sporting Goods Stores
11	1	Home Furnishing Stores
11	2	Health Food Stores
11	4	Liquor Stores
11	6	Bookstores
11	7	Mail Order Enterprises
11	8	Day Care
11	9	Bars and Cocktail Lounges
11	10	Sewing and Needlecraft Centers
12	1	Bicycle Stores
12	2	Apparel Stores
12	3	Building Maintenance Services
12	4	Plant Shops
12	5	Shoe Stores
12	7	Camera Shops
12	8	Restaurants and Food Services
12	9	Hairgrooming/Beauty Salons
12	10	Toy and Hobby/Craft Stores
13	2	Dry Cleaning Services
13	3	Consumer Electronics Centers
13	4	Gift Stores
13	5	Auto Supply Stores
13	6	Mobilehome Parks

4.3 GENERAL ADVICE

The following is a list of books and publications that provide general information on business conditions, references and start-up advice:

1. "How to Form Your Own Corporation Without a Lawyer for Under $150.00" by Ted Nicholas. Available from:

   Enterprise Publishing Company
   1300 Market street
   Wilmington, Delaware, 19801

2. "The 33 Most Profitable Small Companies" from W. H. Wise and Co., Inc. 336 Mountain Rd. Union City, New Jersey, 07087. Contains advice on initial investment requirements, number of employees required, and location finding.

3. "How to Organize and Operate a Small Business" by Baumback, Lawyer and Kelley, published by Prentice-Hall. This is an excellent textbook on the subject.

4. "The Entrepreneur's Handbook", by J. Mancuso. It comprises two volumes of references for small business activities.

5. "How to Start and Manage Your Own Business" from W. H. Wise and Co., Inc. (address above). Excellent book on starting a small to medium business.

6. Donald Dible has written several books:
   - "Up Your Own Organization"
   - "Winning The Money Game"
   - "The Pure Joy of Making Money"

   These books have excellent appendixes for business information. More details can be obtained from:

   > The Entrepreneur Press
   > Mission Station Drawer 2759V
   > Santa Clara, California 95051

7. E. Joseph Cossman provides an audio cassette course, which he gave at Pepperdyne University, on Small Business Management. Details from:

   > E. Joseph Cossman
   > 1838 Barona Road
   > Palm Springs, California

8. "Quarterly Economic Report for Small Business". This is a series of economic reports published quarterly by the National Federation of Independent Businesses. It is a compilation of data on business conditions. Write to: NFIB, 150 West 20th Avenue, San Mateo, California, 94402.

9. Dun and Bradstreet, the business publishers, have an excellent 50 page booklet that lists articles and books on small business. Specific business and opportunities are also listed. Write:

   > Dun and Bradstreet
   > 99 Church Street
   > New York, N.Y. 10007

10. Journal of Small Business. This is a journal that is published quarterly with articles of special interest to small businesses. Write:

    > Editor,
    > Bureau of Small Business Research
    > West Virginia University
    > Morgantown, W.V. 26506

4.4 BUSINESS OPERATING GUIDES AND HANDBOOKS

1. "Apollo Handbook of Practical Public Relations" by Alexander B. Adams, 1970. Published by Apollo Editions, 201 Park Avenue South, New York, N.Y. 10003. Guide for preparing news releases, making speeches, and other aspects of communication.

2. "Credit Research Foundation, 2nd Ed.," 1965. Published by R. D. Irwin Inc., 1818 Ridge Road, Homewood, Ill. 60430. How to use credit agencies, collect overdue accounts, and organize a credit department.

3. "Foreign Commerce Handbook (3813) 17th Edition" 1975, $4, Chamber of Commerce of the United States. 1615 H Street, NW, Washington, D.C. 20006. A guide to services of information and services for exporters and importers.

4. "Marketing Handbook". Frey, A.W., Editor. Ronald Press Company, 79

Madison Avenue, New York, NY 10016. Excellent reference book for marketing goods and services.

5. "Office Management Handbook". Wylie, H. L., Editor. Ronald Press Company. Gives principles of running an efficient small office.
6. "Production Handbook". Carson, G. B., Editor. Ronald Press Company. Gives information about every aspect of the manufacturing process, including quality control.
7. "Purchasing Handbook". Aljian, G.W. Editor. McGraw-Hill Book Company, Inc. Avenue of the Americas, New York, NY 10020. Gives information about every aspect of the purchasing department.

4.5 DIRECTORIES

The most obvious source of information is the classified section of the telephone directory. Local libraries stock out-of-town directories. Other sources are:

1. "Guide to American Directories". 9th edition, 1975, B. Klein Publications Inc, 11 Third St., Rye, New York 10580. Directory information is listed, classified by industry, by profession and by function. Useful for locating new markets or sources of supply.
2. Business Information; "How to Find it and How to Use it", published by the MIT Press. Write MIT Press, Cambridge, Mass, 02139.

Directories that serve specific sections of the business community are listed below under six group headings: Associations, Financial, Government, Individuals, Manufacturers and World Trade.

Associations

"Directory of National And International Labor Unions in the United States", 1973. U.S. Department of Labor, Biennial. GOP. Gives facts about the structure and membership of national and international labor unions.

"Encyclopedia of Associations, Vol. I., National Organizations of the United States". Biennial. Gale Research Company, Book Tower, Detroit, Mich. 48226. Lists trade, business, professional, labor, scientific, educational, fraternal, and social organizations of the United States, includes historical data.

"National Trade and Professional Associations of the United States & Canada & Labor Unions'. Annual. 1975. $20. Columbia Books Publisher, 934 Fifteenth Street, NW, Washington, D.C. 20005. Lists the name, telephone number, address, chief executive officer, size of staff and membership, and year formed of more than 4,000 national business and professional associations.

Financial

"Dun & Bradstreet Reference Book". Six times a year. Contains the names and ratings of nearly 3 million businesses of all types located throughout the United States and Canada. (Dun & Bradstreet also publish other specialized reference books and directories, for example, "Apparel Trades Book and Metalworking Marketing Directory".

"Moody's Banks and Finance". Annual with twice-weekly supplements. $175

Moody's Investor Service, 99 Church Street, New York, NY 10007. Indexes more than 9,700 American banks and financial institutions, listing their officers, directors, and other top-level personnel.

"Rand-McNally International Bankers' Directory". Semiannually. $50. Rand-McNally & Company, Box 7600, Chicago, Ill. 60680. Lists over 37,000 banks and branches, giving their officials, and statement figures. It also includes the American Banking Association's check routing numbers for all U.S. banks, and a digest of U.S. banking laws.

Government

The following references include directories of municipal, State, and Federal agencies, their personnel and functions.

"Municipal Year Book". Annual. $19.50. International City Management Association, 1140 Connecticut Avenue, NW., Washington, D.C. 20036.

"Book of the States". Biennial. Council of State Governments, Iron Works. Pike, Lexington, Ky. 40511. $13.50 alone, $19.50 with two supplements.

"State Bluebooks and Reference Publications". Council of State Governments, Iron Works. Pike, Lexington, Ky 40505 $3 A selected bibliography of bluebooks, reports, directories and other reference publications produced by various departments of each State.

"Congressional Directory". Annual. Joint Committee on Printing. 1975. GPO. Biographical data on Members of Congress, membership and staff of Congressional Committees; directory of the Executive and Judiciary, Diplomatic Corps; and other useful information of Federal and State agencies.

"Directory of Post Offices". Annual. U.S. Post Office Department. 1974. GPO. List of post offices by State, alphabetical list, and post office addresses for Army and Air Force installations.

"Sources of State Information and State Industrial Directories". Triennial. 40 cents. Chamber of Commerce of the United States, 1615 H Street, NW., Washington, D.C. 20006. Contains names and addresses of private and public agencies which furnish information about their States. Also listed, under each State, are industrial directories and directories of manufacturers published by State and private organizations. Some regional directories are included.

"United States Government Organization Manual". Annual. National Archives and Records Service. 1974-75. GPO. The official organization handbook of the Federal Government containing descriptive information on the agencies in the legislative, judicial, and executive branches. Abolished or transferred agencies are listed in an appendix.

Individuals

The following lists only the most general works. Who's Who directories are also available for specific occupations and locations.

"Current Biography". Monthly. $14 a year. H.W. Wilson Company, 950 University Avenue, New York, NY 10452. Extensive biographical data on prominent contemporary personalities.

"Standard & Poor's Register of Corporations, Directors and Executies". Annual.

3 vols. Standard & Poor's Corporation, 345 Hudson Street, New York, NY 10014.

"Who's Who in America". Biennial. $69.50 Marquis - Who's Who, Inc., 200 East Ohio Street, Chicago, Ill. 60611.

"Who's Who of American Women". Biennial. $44.50 Marquis - Who's Who, Inc., 200 East Ohio street, Chicago, Ill. 60611.

"World's Who's Who in Finance and Industry". $44.50 Marquis - Who's Who, Inc., 200 East Ohio Street, chicago, Ill. 60611. Biographical information of men and women prominent in finance, industry, and trade.

Manufacturers

In addition to the directories listed, there are available many State manufacturer's and industrial directories. These are too numerous to list here. Ask your librarian if such a directory is published for the State in which you are interested.

"U.S. Industrial Directory". Annual, $35. 3 vol. set. Cahners Publishing Company, 89 Franklin St., Boston, Mass. 02110. Alphabetical listing of manufacturers showing product lines, code for number of employees, addresses, and telephone numbers. Classified section lists products with names and addresses of manufacturers. Special chemical and mechanical sections, and trademark and trade name identification.

"MacRae's Blue Book". Annual. 5 vols. $47.50. MacRae's Blue Book Company, 100 Shore Drive, Hinsdale, Ill. 60521. Lists sources of industrial equipment, products and materials; alphabetically arranged by product headings. Separate alphabetical listing of company names and trade names.

"Thomas' Register of American Manufacturers". Annual. 11 vols. Thomas Publishing Company, One Penn Plaza, New York, NY 10001. Purchasing guide listing names of manufacturers, producers, and similar sources of supply in all lines.

World Trade

"International Yellow Pages". The Reuben H. Donnelley Corporation, 235 East 45th Street, New York, NY 10017. Lists business and professional firms and individuals from 150 countries throughout the world under headings which are descriptive of the products and services they have to offer in worldwide trade.

5

Financial Sources

5.0 You will be extremely lucky if you do not, at some point in the life of your business, need to raise some funds. Of course, you may need extra capital to start or buy a new business. Perhaps, you will need funds for expansion, or establishing a line of credit to finance inventories. Thus, the question becomes - where does the entrepreneur go for funds and how does he present his case?

The five most common situations where funds are required will be discussed: 1) Business Start-Up, 2) Working Capital, 3) Seasonal Peak, 4) Equipment or Facilities Aquisition, 5) Rapid Growth.

5.1 MOST COMMON SITUATIONS WHERE FUNDS ARE REQUIRED

5.1.1 Capital For Business Aquisition/Start-Up

Whether a business is aquired as an existing concern or started up from scratch, capital is required first to buy its fixed assets, and then further capital is required to pay for ongoing operations. The latter funds being known as working capital.

There are two categories of capital that usually make up to total required funds:

- Equity Capital - provided by the owner(s) of the business
- Debt Capital - provided by lenders under specific terms of repayment.

Equity funding is provided by those who want to have an ownership interest in the business. Equity can be provided by:

1. A sole proprietor
2. A partnership
3. Shareholders via a stock issue to a small inside group, a stock issue to a venture capitalist or a stock issue to a SBIC/MESBIC.

Debt funding for business start up can be obtained from the following sources:

1. Bank - via a real estate loan, an equipment leasing loan, an equipment loan or an unsecured term loan.
2. Commercial Finance Company - via a real estate loan, an equipment leasing loan, or an equipment loan.
3. Savings and Loan Company - via a real estate loan
4. Leasing Company - equipment leasing loan

5. Consumer Finance Company - personal property, term loan
6. SBA - term loan
7. SBIC/MESBIC - term loan
8. Prior Owner - term loan - for small business this source is surprisingly common.

5.1.2 Working Capital

Working capital is usually provided by long-term debt instruments. The same sources of finance, numbered 1 through 8 above, are available to provide working capital funds.

5.1.3 Seasonal Peak Capital

Seasonal peaks are financed by short-term debt instruments and by lines of credit. The sources of such finance are:
1. Suppliers - trade credit is extended, usually for 30 days, but with risk can be stretched to 60 or even 90 days.
2. Bank - via a commercial loan, accounts receivable financing, inventory financing, flooring (financing floor stock), and an unsecured line of credit.
3. Factor - via a factoring operation where a factor purchases the accounts receivable at a discount price.
4. Commercial Finance Company - via accounts receivable financing, inventory financing or factoring.
5. Consumer Finance Company - via a personal property loan
6. SBA - via a credit guarantee

5.1.4 Equipment Or Facilities Requisition Financing

This type of long-term debt is financed from the same debt sources as working capital.

5.1.5 Financing Rapid Growth

If you have genuine growth that is readily apparent, then, of course, your task of obtaining financing is easier. You can increase your equity funding via fresh owner equity, such as a further stock offering. Or you can increase your debt burden by going back to your supplier of long-term credit. Help can also be obtained by increasing your line of credit from seasonal peak sources.

5.2 EQUITY FINANCING

The amount of capital required, either to buy or to start up a business will very often determine the type of equity financing needed. The equity portion of the of the funds is provided by the owner(s) of the business, the rest being provided by various lenders.

The proportion of equity required, sometimes called the debt-to-equity ratio, is often determined by lenders. This is because the lenders do not feel comfortable with high debt-to-equity ratios, which give rise to large, sometimes unmanageable, loan repayment schedules. In general, most lenders will not go above a 1:1 debt-to-equity ratio and prefer to see a 1:2 ratio. Thus, a small businessman needing a total of $60,000 to start a business must expect to provide at least $30,000 of his own money. An exception to this is the quite common case where the seller, who is anxious to unload his business, might accept a 20% down payment and grant loan repayment terms for the rest. The debt-to-equity ratio in the latter case being 4:1.

Where an individual can provide the entire equity required, a sole proprietorship is formed. A partnership is formed where greater equity is required or where two or more individuals decide to share the management responsibility. In large partnerships, there will usually be both general and limited partners. The general partners provide both capital and management capabilities, and are responsible for all business debts. The limited partners provide capital without any management responsibility and are not responsible for business debt beyond their capital contribution.

A corporation can be formed with very small numbers of stockholders, who will enjoy the legal and tax advantages. Most small businesses have a very limited number of stockholders who are usually friends or professional associates. Stock offerings to the general public are reserved for reasonably large and offering.

The following financial instruments can be used in forming a corporation:

1. Common Stock - provides for business control, via voting priviledges, and maximum return on investment via payment of dividends.
2. Preferred Stock - usually provides no voting priviledges or control but does provide a fixed rate of annual dividend payment. The preferred stockholders will be paid dividends ahead of anything paid to common stockholders.
3. Convertible Debentures and Warrants - these are really long-term debt instruments rather than straight equity but being convertible may be converted into equity at a later date.

A legal adviser must be employed to create proper financial instruments for equity financing.

5.2.1 Non-Professional Equity Financing

When extra equity funding is required beyond that immediately obtainable, the first place to look is to non-professional sources who may wish to buy a share of the ownership of the business. Likely sources are: Relatives, friends, business clients, suppliers, and wealthy individuals. The latter can often be contacted through your professional advisers such as attorneys, accountants, bankers, or insurance agents. Various IRS provisions make it attractive for the wealthy to invest in small businesses as tax-shelters.

1. Issue of Section 1244 stock provides the investor with the opportunity to deduct any losses as ordinary income losses rather than capital losses (see Section 2.2.4) with proportionate tax savings.
2. A Subchapter S corporation with 15 or fewer shareholders can elect to be taxed as a partnership and avoid the "double" taxation of a corporation.
3. A limited partner may deduct any partnership loss as an ordinary income loss, but have no liability beyond his initial investment.

5.2.2 Professional Equity Financing–Venture Capital

Professional funding may be the only answer where large equity financing is required. This is especially true in a business project that is relatively risky, but offers large returns if successful. Venture capital may be available in this case.

Venture or high risk capital may be obtained from a variety of sources – corporations, banks, insurance companies, or a small group of wealthy investors. There are often minimum rather than maximum equity investment limits set by these venture capital groups. This limit may be as small as $20,000 to $500,000 depending on the size of the company. Often, the size of the equity investment is such that the venture group owns more than 50% of the company. However, this should not concern the entrepreneur since the company could grow quickly and even a small equity share be extremely valuable. In addition, members of the venture capital group will often be available to sit on the board of directors and provide management guidance.

Usually though, venture capitalist do not enter at the point of initial business start up but prefer to wait until the small company has its first product or has developed its initial business management. At that stage, just before rapid expansion, the venture capitalist can buy stock cheaply and provide the funds required for that expansion.

Venture capitalists often prefer a particular type of industry or business location, but will certainly look extremely closely at a business plan that describes the investment opportunity. If the venture capitalist is at all interested in the business proposal, his investigation and negotiation can last several months. The key points that attract the venture capitalist are:

1. Is the product in a growth industry?
2. Is the product new or revolutionary such that it has very limited immediate competition?
3. Is the quality of the management such that it will be successful with a new enterprise?

5.2.3 SBICS/MESBICS

These were covered somewhat in the previous chapter but are investment companies set up by the government to provide small business capital. These institutions are more conservative than venture institutions and look for more normal businesses in healthy condition. Again, a sound business proposal is a must when dealing with these institutions.

5.3 DEBT FINANCING

There are far more sources of debt financing available than equity financing. Again, key considerations to the lender are the debt-to-equity ratio, the risk, and the quality of the borrower himself.

Large corporations are able to borrow at close to the prime rate of interest. However, the average small business has to pay two or three points above the prime rate. Thus, the prevailing prime rate itself is a key factor in the cost of capital – during 1979 the prime rate reached an all-time high of over 15 3/4%.

As previously discussed, the lender very often controls the total amount of financing (including the equity portion) available to the small businessman by his debt-to-equity ratio preference. The various sources of debt capital are:

5.3.1 Banks

Banks are by far the most common commercial lenders and are generalists in the sense that they are prepared to consider a loan on almost any type of business. Other lenders are available but they are often more specialized in the type of business loan they offer. The following considerations apply when dealing with a bank:

A) Credit Worthiness - in most cases the banker accepts token collateral on any loan and does, in fact, provide the loan on the basis of the lenders ability to repay the loan. The loan officer will look at the following factors:

1. Character - do you have a record of repaying loans? Are you essentially honest? Your management ability is also scrutinized, so if you can provide evidence of management experience or training it will count in your favor.

2. Loan Useage - this will determine what type of loan will be made - short or long-term. Money to be used for the purchase of seasonal inventory will be capable of quicker repayment than money used to buy fixed assets.

3. Repayment Capability - a financial schedule must be provided showing where the money is generated to repay the loan.

4. Loan Size - often the banker will provide a larger loan than requested because he feels that the MUF factor (mess-up factor) has been ignored. After all, a reasonable cushion will be required to see you through unforeseen emergencies.

5. Business Outlook - the banker will look at the general business scene and relate it to the propects for your particular business.

A sample loan proposal is discussed in the second section of this book. However, the proposal should contain the following basic data:

1. The balance sheet and profit and loss statements for at least the last five years - if the business is to be purchased. Proforma financial statements will be required for new businesses. The balance sheet provides the banker with an idea of how solvent the business is, whereas the P&L indicates how profitable the business is. Year over year comparisons of these statements determine how stable the business is and its growth potential.

2. General information should be provided that shows that the books and records have been well kept and are up-to-date. The balance of the accumulated notes payable will be scrutinized, as well as the salary of the owner. The insurance coverage is important, as well as the order backlog or sales trend.

3. Accounts receivable is given a special examination. The accounts will be "aged" to determine how many are outstanding beyond specific periods of time. This will provide clues as to their collectibility. The allowance for doubtful accounts reserve will be examined to see if there is enough coverage. The accounts will also be segmented by client to determine any potential exposure by payment default of one or more large clients. The banker will want to know if any of the accounts receivable is pledged to another creditor.

4. Inventories will be examined in detail to discover the degree of obsolete merchandise in hand. The degree of mark down required to sell it will be discussed. A manufacturing organization will be asked to provide information on a) raw material b) work in process and c) finished goods.

5. The condition of the fixed assets will be examined to determine if replacement or repair is needed. Your figures for maintenance of fixed assets must reflect a realistic assessment of their condition.

NOTE: Bankers have reference to the general ratios for any kind of business and will expect that the financial records of your business fall into line. You should make sure that the ratios he looks for do fall into line and that any deviations have a plausible explanation. The source and use of these ratios (Robert Morris Associates) will be described in depth in section two of this book.

B. Type Of Loan Requested

In requests for debt capital there are two basic loan types; short-term loans and term loans. Generally, short term loans are repaid from the selling of current assets, usually inventory, whereas long-term loans are repaid from residual earnings.

- Short Term Bank Loans

    A short-term loan is granted to a small business to finance a short-term business need such as to take advantage of a supplier's discount, or to increase inventory during peak selling seasons, or to pay accrued taxes, and so on. These loans are only granted for short periods and are expected to be fully paid off when the receipts are collected for the increased activity.

    In general, loans can be unsecured or secured. An unsecured loan is granted purely on the creditworthiness of the borrower, with no collateral required. A secured loan involves the use of a specfic asset as collateral for that loan.

    NOTE: Most small business loans, even to corporations are made as personal loans to the businessman himself. Thus, should the business fail the businessman himself is liable for the loan repayment. He cannot, in fact, hide behind the corporate facade to avoid debt repayment.

    Four short-term types of loans are normally available:

1. The commerical loan, to be repaid after 30 or 60 days in a lump sum is the normal short-term loan vehicle. Usually, this type of loan is not for very large sums of money and does not require to be secured. Occasionally, the bank may want to make its loan against the borrower's savings account or pledged C.D.'s. Sometimes, the bank will request that a compensating balance be kept in the bank. This balance is in reality a method of increasing the interest rate on the loan, since the borrower is, in fact, unable to use the amount of money in the "compensating balance" although he has to pay interest on it.

2. Accounts receivable financing is used when a substantial proportion of a firm's current assets is tied up in accounts receivables. The accounts receivables themselves, if known to be collectible, provide the banker with the security he needs. The advantage of this type of financing is that it grows as the accounts receivables grow and does enable a firm to finance its growth. Usually the banker will advance between 60% to 80% of the accounts receivables balance as cash. The receivables are assigned to the bank. The bank then tracks the payments for the goods sold as the checks arrive at the borrower's business account in the bank. The bank deducts principal and interest charges as agreed, and deposits any balance in the borrower's account. This type of financing is really a type of revolving line of credit that is negotiated with the bank on a year by year basis.

3. Inventory financing or commodity loans is also a type of revolving line of credit. The firm's inventory serves as collateral for this type of loan. However, since a company's inventory is less liquid than accounts receivables, its ultimate conversion into cash is less certain. Thus, the bankers will usually only advance up to 50% of the value of the current inventory. Inventory financing is often used in conjunction with receivables financing to finance the extra inventory needed for peak selling seasons such as Christmas. In this case, the inventory loan is paid off with cash advanced via accounts receivables financing. Collection of accounts receivables will eventually pay off the accounts receivables financing.

4. An unsecured line of credit can usually be established at a bank by a customer of known creditworthiness. The line of credit is usually provided for a specific period and up to a specific limit. The bank normally likes a customer to borrow, completely pay off, then borrow again without allowing the amount borrowed to continually increase until the lending limit is reached.

5/Financial Sources

- Long Term Bank Loans

    Any loan for over one year is considered to be a term loan and is normally repayed from the cash flow of the business on a monthly basis. Term loans are used in business acquisition, in start up, in financing the purchase of expensive fixed assets, and in providing working capital. Various types of term loans are available:

    1. Standard term loans - these are most commonly offered in business start-up and, since repaid out of future profit, cause the banker to look at the future prospects of the business venture. The banker will generally seek to protect his loan by inserting clauses, known as covenants, into the loan agreement that will help to increase future cash flow devoted to loan repayment. Generally, the covenant will limit salaries or dividend payout, will limit the indebtedness to other financial institutions, will require adequate insurance coverage, may require periodic reporting of financial statements, will require the maintenance of minimum working capital and will required repaying the loan in accordance with the loan agreement.

        Term loans for small businesses are usually only partially secured by business assets. Usually, personal guarantees are required, which may be backed by stocks, bonds or C.D.'s.

    2. Equipment leasing loans have become more common banking instruments. The businessman has the advantage of obtaining his equipment at reasonable rates since the banks take advantage of the tax breaks that come from owning the equipment. The length of the lease depends on the contract negotiated but the bank may require a minimum of three years. The entrepreneur should always note that leases are future financial obligations that must be paid in the event of business failure.

    3. Equipment loans are somewhat easier to obtain since the equipment itself provides the collateral for the loan. Usually a bank will limit the amount of an equipment loan to between 60% and 80% of the cost of the equipment and arrange financing over a five year period. Equipment loans are, in general, advantageous to the small businessman since he can use the various tax deductions, such as a) investment tax credit, b) extra first-year depreciation, c) regular depreciation and, d) interest paid on the loan. In the event of business failure, the equipment can be sold the amount obtained thereby repaying most of the loan.

    4. A commercial or an industrial mortgage is the normal vehicle used to finance business real estate. Up to 75%

105

of the value of the property can be financed by mortage, with repayment terms extended over 10 to 20 years. Banks do not usually provide second mortgages on business property.

- Special Financing Situations

    Many banks, and especially the larger ones, have been broadening the type of service they offer to the business community.

    1. Factoring - in this situation the bank will purchase your accounts receivables at a suitable discount and take responsibility for credit checking and collection. Thus, the business obtains cash immediately a sale is made, which it can then use to finance inventory build up, business expansion, etc.

        Factoring, per se, is not a loan, but a financial transaction in which the value of the accounts receivable is sold. The factor (bank) will immediately pay between 60% to 80% of the value of the accounts receivable, paying the balance less the factoring charge, when the customers pay. The factoring charge covers the factor's risk since he buys receivables without recourse, that is he is responsible for uncollectible accounts. In addition, the factoring charge covers interest costs. The actual charge varies from 1 to 2% for each invoice, plus a percentage based on the cost of interest.

        Some factors are selective in the receivables they will accept, leaving the poor risk accounts with the business. The total cost of factoring to the small business is well above the cost of comparable commercial loans from banks or other financial institutions. However, the businessman is spared the cost of establishing a credit department and the costs of credit collection.

    2. Floor planning finance is made available by a bank on expensive retail items, such as motor cycles, where the bank holds a security interest in each serial numbered item until it is sold. The bank collects monthly interest on each item and is paid in full when the item is sold.

    3. Installment financing is used when a retail store wishes to sell expensive items to consumers on an installment basis but does not have sufficient funds to finance the installment sales itself. The bank advances between 70% to 80% of the purchase price, which the retailer repays with interest from the cash flow provided by the consumer repaying him.

C. The Amount Of Money Requested

The amount of money you request depends on your specific needs. In the case of business acquisition or new start up, three general categories of funds are required:

5/*Financial Sources*

- Capital to purchase the business or fixed assets
- Working capital to purchase inventory and pay for operating expenses
- Capital reserve (MUF) for unforseen emergencies.

It is vitally important that each of these components be adequately documented and presented to the banker in a credible manner. This aspect is covered in fine detail in the second section of this book.

D. Collateral

You will undoubtedly be asked to provide collateral on any loan request for a new business. Collateral will also be requested for many other loan situations. Collateral can take many forms, the most common are:

- Endorsers, Co-makers, and Guarantors

    Borrowers often get other people to sign a note in order to bolster their own credit. These <u>endorsers</u> are contingently liable for the note they sign. If the borrower fails to pay up, the bank expects the endorser to make the note good. Sometimes, the endorser may be asked to pledge assets or securities that he owns.

    A <u>co-maker</u> is one who creates an obligation jointly with the borrower. In such cases, the bank can collect directly from either the maker or the co-maker.

    A <u>guarantor</u> is one who guarantees the payment of a note by signing a guarantee commitment. Both private and government lenders often require guarantees from officers of corporations in order to assure continuity of effective management. Sometimes, a manufacturer will act as guarantor for one of his customers.

- Assignment of Leases

    The assigned lease as security is similar to the guarantee. It is used, for example, in some franchise situations.

    The bank lends the money on a building and takes a mortgage. Then the lease, which the dealer and the parent franchise company work out, is assigned so that the bank automatically receives the rent payments. In this manner, the bank is guaranteed repayment of the loan.

- Warehouse Receipts

    Banks also take commodities as security by lending money on a warehouse receipt. Such a receipt is usually delivered directly to the bank and shows that the merchandise used as security either has been placed in a public warehouse or has been left on your premises under the control of one of your employees who is bonded (as in field warehousing). Such loans are generally made on staple or standard merchandise which can be readily marketed. The typical warehouse receipt loan is for a percentage of the estimated value of the goods used as security.

- Trust Receipts and Floor Planning

    Merchandise, such as automobiles, appliances, and boats, have to be displayed to be sold. The only way many small marketers can afford such displays is by borrowing money. Such loans are often secured by a note and a trust receipt.

    This trust receipt is the legal paper for floor planning. It is used for serial-numbered merchandise. When you sign one, you (1) acknowledge receipt of the merchandise, (2) agree to keep the merchandise in trust for the bank.

- Chattel Mortages

    If you buy equipment such as a cash register or a delivery truck, you may want to get a chattel mortgage loan. You give the bank a lien on the equipment you are buying.

    The bank also evaluates the present and future market value of the equipment being used to secure the loan. How rapidly will it depreciate? Does the borrower have the necessary fire, theft, property damage and public liability insurance on the equipment? The banker has to be sure that the borrower protects the equipment.

- Real Estate

    Real estate is another form of collateral for long-term loans. When taking a real estate mortgage, the bank finds out: (1) the location of the real estate, (2) its physical condition, (3) its foreclosure value, and (4) the amount of insurance carried on the property.

- Accounts Receivable

    Many banks lend money on accounts receivable. In effect, you are counting on your customers to pay your note.

    The bank may take accounts receivable on a notification or a <u>nonnotification</u> plan. Under the <u>notification</u> plan, the purchaser of the goods is informed by the bank that his account has been assigned to it and he is asked to pay the bank. Under the <u>nonnotification</u> plan, the borrower's customers continue to pay him the sums due on their accounts and he pays the bank.

- Savings Accounts

    Sometimes, you might get a loan by assigning to the bank a savings account. In such cases, the bank gets an assignment from you and keeps your passbook. If you assign an account in another bank as collateral, the lending bank asks the other bank to mark its records to show that the account is held as collateral.

- Life Insurance

    Another kind of collateral is life insurance. Banks will lend up to the cash value of a life insurance policy. You have to assign the policy to the bank.

    If the policy is on the life of an executive of a small corporation, corporate resolutions must be made authorizing the assignment. Most insurance companies allow you to sign the policy back to the original beneficiary when the assignment to the bank ends.

    Some people like to use life insurance as collateral rather than borrow directly from insurance companies. One reason is that a bank loan is often more convenient to obtain and usually may be obtained at a lower interest rate.

- Stocks and Bonds

    If you use stocks and bonds as collateral, they must be marketable. As a protection against market declines and possible expenses of liquidation, banks usually lend no more than 75 percent of the market value of high grade stock. On Federal Government or municipal bonds, they may be willing to lend 90 percent or more of their market value.

    The bank may ask the borrower for additional security or payment whenever the market value of the stocks or bonds drops below the bank's required margin.

E. Interest Rate

No small business should be so anxious to get a loan at any price that he fails to pay close attention to the interest rate. The fact is that at any time different types of loans will carry different interest rates. Some interest rates remain stable, while others move up and down with the prime rate.

In order to understand the interest rate structure you must realise that banking is a business like any other. Banks must obtain their funds from a variety of sources and then make loans at a sufficient margin to make a profit.

Short-term loans are made from short-term deposits, the interest rate of which tends to rapidly fluctuate with market changes. The prime rate is the key factor that determines short-term interest rates. Thus, an applicant for a short term loan should keep a sharp eye on the movement of the prime rate and try, if possible, to time his loan needs to periods when favorable prime rates occur.

Long-term loans are made from funds that remain in the bank for long periods, say one to ten years. Thus, this long term fund remains relatively stable as a loan source and, in turn, interest charged on its use also tends to remain stable, slowly changing from year to year. Thus, timing a loan application is not so critical for long-term loan requirements.

Different types of loans require different administration procedures for the bank and, therefore, different costs. Short term commercial loans cost much less to administer than long term loans.

Risk is another factor which dictates the pricing of the loan. Loans to small, new businesses are more risky than those to large, mature businesses. Larger loans are more risky than small loans; long term loans are more risky than short term loans. Unsecured loans are more risky than secured loans.

In determining the interest rate it will charge you for a specific loan, the bank will weigh the three factors of (1) cost of money from its various sources (2) the cost of administration and (3) the risk factor. This evaluation process is a regular bank procedure, which, of course, is different from one bank to another resulting in slightly different interest rate charges. Thus, it is always wise to shop around for a specific loan.

F. Banker's Rules

In this section, some of the unwritten rules by which bankers make loans will be discussed:

- The time required to process the loan will depend on the type of loan - small, unsecured, short-term commercial loans can be processed much more quickly than large, secured long term loans.

- Bankers require much more information from first time borrowers than established clients.

- Bankers like to lend to individuals with experience in the business venture.

- Partnerships are generally not regarded as being stable in the long-term, since disagreements tend to cause the majority of such associations to dissolve.

- The personal credit record of the lender is thoroughly investigated.

- Bankers place strong emphasis on the ability to repay the loan or to recoup the loan via collateral in the event of a business failure.

G. Tips in Dealing with Bankers

- Go fully informed with the type of loan you require and take a set of neatly packaged information supporting your request - make sure that you understand it!
- Pay particular attention to your personal appearance - bankers are conservative, wear a conservative business suit.
- On a request for start-up capital, deal with one banker at a time. Establish specific times for appointments and set deadlines for his decisions.
- Allow yourself the time to thresh out the terms of the loan. Make a reappointment if necessary to enable you to consult with your advisors or to evaluate your own capability of living with the loan's terms.
- Do not accept less than you require.
- Do not be forced into a quicker payback schedule than you can manage.
- Do not over collateralize the loan - you may need your collateral for future emergencies.
- If your loan is refused, have a series of short questions prepared and do not speak until you have received answers.
    1. I understand you are turning down my loan request?
    2. Which particular aspect of my loan request makes it unbankable?
    3. What would you do in my place?
    4. Should I go to another bank?
    5. Which bank?
    6. Why?
    7. Who should I ask for?
    8. Why?
    9. What should I tell him?
    10. Can I tell him that there has been a policy change at this bank?
    11. What will you tell him when he calls you?

    This list of questions makes maximum use of the first banker's knowledge and prepares the groundwork for a second try at another bank.
- Remember that bankers are in the business of making loans and will make you one, even in bad times, if you persevere.

- Once your loan has been granted, keep your banker informed of your business activities. Good commercial bankers establish good contact with their clients, visiting their premises and offering continuing financial advice. Bankers do not like unpleasant surprises. Learn to project ahead your future financial needs; if you cannot make a future loan payment your banker should be forwarned. He can possibly make alternative loan provisions or make other suggestions.

5.3.2 Commercial Finance Companies

New or even existing companies can be denied credit. When this happens one alternative is to approach a commercial finance company. Such companies provide loans on the basis of good collateral rather than the firm's repayment capability. Sources of collateral are preferred that are highly liquid. Thus, accounts receivables financing is common since these are the most liquid of the current non cash assets. Alternatively, inventory financing can be negotiatiated, and often accounts receivables and inventory financing are used in conjuction with each other where extra financing is required.

Long-term loans are also available, and equipment loans of up to five years are common. Longer term loans of up to ten years are provided where real estate is used as collaterial. Straight mortgage loans are sometimes offered, and where this is the case, second mortgages are available.

Factoring, equipment leasing, equipment sale and lease back transactions are also available from finance companies. Occasionally, finance company loans will exceed the net worth of the borrower - something that most banks would avoid. This is because the finance company is relying on collateral rather than repayment capacity.

Financial companies will require sufficient financial data to establish the value of the collateral offered, but will not require the extensive financial history that banks require. Very often, they will use an industrial appraiser to assess the value of accounts receivables, inventory or real estate.

Since these loans are typically made in higher risk situations than banks permit, and the funds are often obtained from banks, the interest rates charged are higher than bank loans.

5.3.3 Factors

Firms specialising in factoring traditionally operated in the garment industry, although nowadays factors operate in many retail businesses. Factors do not require extensive financial data, but look for:

1. The reliability of the small business owner.
2. The credit rating of the accounts being factored.
3. The degree of concentration with several large customers.

5/Financial Sources

4. The record of the small business in handling complaints, warrantees, and servicing its products.

5.3.4 Life Insurance Companies

- Cash value of policy - loans can be made against the accrued cash value of a life insurance policy. Usually up to 95% of the cash value may be borrowed. Interest is charged, but may be deferred.

- Mortgage loans are made on properties worth more than $150,000. Up to 75% to 80% of the property's appraised value is normally advanced. The loans are amortized over 25 to 30 years, and monthly repayments kept low by the use of a lump or balloon payment that falls due at 10 or 15 years.

- Unsecured term loans are given only to companies with a strong profit history of at least five years. Such loans usually begin at approximately $500,000 and are amortized over 12 to 15 years.

5.3.5 Consumer Finance Companies

When all other sources of debt financing are unavailable, a personal loan may be obtainable from a consumer finance company. Such financing is usually for an expensive item but can be used to finance a small business.

Loans below $10,000 use some form of personal property, such as a boat, car, coin collection, etc., as collateral. Such loans are amortized over periods of up to five years.

Loans above $10,000 are usually secured by a second mortgage on the applicant's house. Such loans are amortized over periods up to 10 years, and are normally limited to $25,000.

Unsecured or "signature loans" are available from some finance companies, usually to individuals with superior credit ratings. These loans are made at interest rates well above prevailing bank rates for similar loans.

5.3.6 Savings And Loan Companies

S and L's are only chartered to make loans for residential or commercial property. Mortgages are available in various amounts up to a prevailing limit dependent on the current money supply. Amortization periods run up to 30 years, at interest rates competitive with banks, finance companies and life insurance companies.

5.3.7 SBA Loans

The SBA was covered in detail in the preceding chapter, but, in general, acts as a guarantor for small business loans that are unbankable without its guarantee. The SBA reduces its risk by setting low loan ceilings and providing management assistance.

A detailed loan application must be made to obtain an SBA loan, rather like that made to a bank. The SBA must be convinced of the long term viability of the business before providing either a loan guarantee or a direct loan.

5.3.8 Local Development Companies

In addition to the Federally funded SBA, the government also helps small business by encouraging communities to form Local Development Corporations (LDCS).

The LDCS solicit SBA and bank loans to fund small business activity. The LDC usually supplies about 10% of a project's cost, relying on banks and the SBA to provide the rest. LDC funds go to provide facilities and cannot be used for working capital.

High risk ventures can be housed via an LDC participation loan. If the venture fails the LDC has to find another tenant to take over the loan.

An LDC loan usually carries a fairly low interest rate. A standard, detailed loan application is required, first to a bank, then the SBA and then to the LDC. A businessman interested in an LDC loan should contact his local SBA office.

5.3.9 Farmers Home Administration (FmHA)

This deceptively titled government agency guarantees and makes direct loans to <u>small, non-farming</u> businesses in rural areas; that is areas where population is no greater than 100 per square mile not adjacent to a large city.

The FmHA, like the SBA, guarantees up to 90% of a bank loan when other financing is not available. Unlike the SBA, the FmHA sets no loan ceilings. The FmHA will guarantee loans to individuals who supply as little as 10% of their captial needs.

The regular SBA loan package is required, but the FmHA requires an additional study to determine if the new business will assist in rural prosperity.

5.4 SELF FINANCING

Self financing is the mechanism by which a small business can generate funds internally to supply its capital needs. This is not the same as equity financing but involves managing the cash flow of the business more astutely.

- Customers - if a business can obtain a deposit, progress payments or even client supplied material, it will reduce its working capital needs.
- Trade credit - a business should obtain as much trade credit as it can, since this credit does replace accounts receivables or inventory financing. The trade cycle required is (1) obtain goods on a credit basis (30 to 90 days), (2) sell the goods and collect payment before the credit payment is due, (3) pay for the goods, and (4) repeat over many cycles, building up sufficient profit to avoid the need for extensive trade credit.
- Real estate - real estate itself is unproductive and small companies do best by renting their premises. If property is owned, cash can be raised by a commercial or industrial mortgage, or by refinancing the property where its value has substantially increased.
- Equipment can be purchased via a loan or leased in order to provide work-

ing capital. Everything from office furniture to heavy construction equipment can be leased from banks, commercial finance companies and the numerous specialized leasing companies.

Sale and lease back transactions can provide a ready source of cash needed for working capital. However, the charges are also high, since the finance company is unable to take advantage of all the tax deductions associated with leasing new equipment. Even a prosperous company should consider lease versus ownership, since lease payments can total less than loan payments especially where the lessor retains the tax benefits of owning the equipment.

EQUITY/DEBT CAPITAL FINDERS

Finding the capital needed to start or expand a business is a perennial problem and specialists have developed to assist businesses find the right loan at the right cost.

- Business Development Organizations (BDOs)

    The BDO offers capital finding services to help minority businesses find capital. However, this government funded organization seldom turns away non-minority applicants. BDO's offer a complete service from establishing the entrepreneurs' needs, preparing a loan proposal, obtaining the loan and providing post-loan assistance.

    The local SBA can direct you to the nearest BDO.

- Finders, Financial Consultants

    Finders are individuals who will, for a 1% to 5% fee find the appropriate source of funds for a client. However, such individuals need to be selected with great care since fraudulent operators are common in this area.

- Investment Bankers

    Investment bankers act as a conduit between an individual and venture capitalists. They analyse the entrepreneur's business proposal and then recommend stock in the business to selected venture capitalists. This private capital placement is performed for a fee, and may involve equity or debt financing.

SOURCES OF FINANCIAL INFORMATION

5.6.1 SBA Leaflets And Books

- "Is Your Cash Supply Adequate" - MA174 - Free
- "Financial Audits: A Tool For Better Management" - NA176 - Free
- "Controlling Cash In Small Retail And Service Firms" - MSA110 - Free
- "Accounting Services For Small Service Firms" - SMA126 - Free
- "Analyse Your Records To Reduce Costs" - SMA130 - Free
- "Handbook Of Small Business Finance" - SBMS No. 15 - $0.70
- "Guides For Profit Planning" - SBMS No. 25 - $0.70

5.6.2 **Organizations**
- Farmers Home Administration
  U.S. Department of Agriculture
  Washington, D.C. 20250
- National Venture Capital Association
  10 South LaSalle Street
  Chicago, IL 60603
- Office Of Minority Business Enterprise
  U.S. Department Of Commerce
  Washington, D.C. 20230
- Small Business Administration
  Washington, D.C. 20416

5.6.3 **Directories**
- Directory Of Members
  Western Association of Venture Capitalists
  244 California Street, Room 500
  San Francisco, CA 94111
- Directory Of Operating Small Business Investment Companies
  U.S. Small Business Administration
  Washington, D.C. 20416

6

Marketing Aspects

Marketing in any business, whether it is wholesale, retail, service or manufacturing, is the sum of those activities that take the goods or service from the business to the customer.

MARKETING PLAN

Marketing should not be a haphazard affair, only dabbled with when the other pressing start-up concerns have been dealt with. Your marketing plan must be evolved before you take over or start your business. You must set aside time and money to think through your marketing plan. The sequence of steps to be followed is as follows:

1. Define your market - the size, complexion and location of your market.
2. Define your marketing program;
   - Define your product line
   - Define your advertising campaign
   - Define your distribution methods
   - Define your pricing strategy
3. Define your marketing objectives;
   - How much money can be spent on advertising
   - How many targeted customers can be reached
   - How many sales can be made per salesperson
   - How much is your overall sales volume
4. Measure your marketing performance;
   - Set up performance standards, and measure your success ratios. Take corrective action in unsatisfactory performance situations.

These four steps will now be discussed in more detail.

6.1.1 Market Definition

This is the process of sitting down and thinking through just who your customer is, how many potential customers for your product or service exist, and just what range of items you can sell. This process is somewhat different for different types of business.

- Retail/Service

   The principles of defining the market for both the retail and the service industry are approximately the same and, therefore, will be discussed together.

The first step is to define the demographics of your customer; that is, age, race, sex, income, family size, religion and position in life cycle (single, married, divorced, senior citizen, etc). There are several methods of defining these demographics:

1. Personal judgement - you may decide from experience, for example, that you wish to sell inexpensive children's clothing, in the age range from 5 to 12, to both sexes, to families in the income range $6,000 to $16,000 per year.

2. Retailers Association - the retailer's association for your particular type of store may have conducted a survey to determine the characteristics of its customers. Information can be obtained from:

- National Trade and Professional Associations of the United States and Canada and Labor Unions. Columbia Books Publisher, 934 Fifteenth Street, NW, Washington, D.C. 20005. This lists contact information on more than 4,000 national business and professional associations.

- Encyclopedia of Business Information Sources, Paul Wasserman, editor, Gale Research Company, Book Tower, Detroit, Michigan 48226. This book will lead you to sources of market information on your business.

- Survey of Buying Power, Sales Management, Inc., 630 Third Ave., NY, NY 10017. This annual publication is a goldmine of information on market and consumer profiles. In its S&MM marketgraph, for instance, it profiles the numbers, ages and incomes of working women.

The three references given above may be found at your local city or university library.

3. Market Survey - You can perform your own version of a market analysis. This can be as simple as selecting a store similar in size and location to the one you are interested in and counting the number, age and sex of its clients. You can even use members of your own family to perform a questionnaire survey near the shop of interest by asking some innocent questions such as "Do you support the creation or expansion of a local recreation facility/park?" - but also inviting the individual to fill in demographic information, without providing a name or address. Anonymous questionnaires solicit more response than if name and address is required. However, you can ask how far the respondent lives from the nearby park, thus obtaining a travel radius to the shopping location.

You can overlay the three techniques just described to build up a composite picture of the typical clientel. You may discover, for instance, that the typical client of a fashionable clothing store is a working woman between the ages of 25 and 45, earning an income of

$10,000 to $18,000 per year.

The second step is to determine the total buying power in the area of your store. This implies identifying the number and buying power of individuals possessing the demographic characteristics that you have identified. There are several sources of information to go to in order to create this information:

1. Survey of Buying Power, S&MM, provides information on the population, income and retail sales estimates for State, County and Metropolitan areas. It provides estimates for the sales volume of certain retail items by area.

2. Survey of Current Business, U.S. Department of Commerce, monthly, Government Printing Office. This carries details of sales and family income spent on specific items.

3. County and City Data Book, Bureau of Census Department of Commerce. 1977, GPO. Provides information on population, retail and wholesale trade, and selected services.

4. Statistics for States and Metropolitan Areas (a preprint from item #3). Presents data for 195 statistical items for the U.S.

5. Statistical Abstracts of the United States. Bureau of Census, Department of Commerce, GPO. This includes many consumer market statistics.

6. A Guide to Consumer Markets, Annual, The Conference Board, Inc., Information Services, 845 Third Ave., NY, NY 10022. Presents a detailed statistical profile of U.S. consumers and the consumer market.

7. E&P Market Guide. Editors & Publisher Company, 575 Lexington Avenue, NY, NY 10022. Tabulates current estimates of population, households, retail sales and income, in nine categories, for States, counties and metropolitan areas.

8. A Guide to Consumer Markets, U.S. Department of Labor, tabulates the amount of family income spent on various items, broken out by family income range.

From the sources above you will be able to build up, by zip code or census tract, the total income of a specific income group. Very often, major spending categories will be broken out - such as the amount spent on clothing, frozen foods, automobiles, etc. Since you have targeted who your customers are and how much they spend on the items you wish to sell, you now know the total sales volume in your area. The next step is to find out how many other local retailers there are who sell a similar line of merchandise. The average potential sales volume per store can be found by dividing the total sales volume by the number of stores. This average can be modified according to the spacing between competing stores. Note, however, that in some retail businesses, such as fast food franchises, stores often group together to form a joint appeal and increase their business volume.

- **Wholesale/Manufacturing**

    With these two business types you are generally selling to other businesses. Where you are selling to consumers, the market analysis described for retailers can be used.

    Two concepts are used in selling to industrial/commercial customers:

    1. Occupany Factor - the ratio of actual clients to potential clients.
    2. Penetration Factor - the amount of your sales to a given client compared with his total purchases of the same item.

    The steps in examining the penetration factor are:

    1. Assign a SIC number (see Section 7.1 for detailed definition of SIC number) to each customer.
    2. Classify all customers in each SIC classification by specific size range categories. Companies of the same size and SIC categories should have very similar needs. Thus, taking insurance companies as an example;
        Size category A -   1-19 employees
        Size category B -   20-49 employees
        Size category C -   50-199 employees
        Etc.
    3. Record your sales volume to every client in a particular size category and plot the distribution (see below)

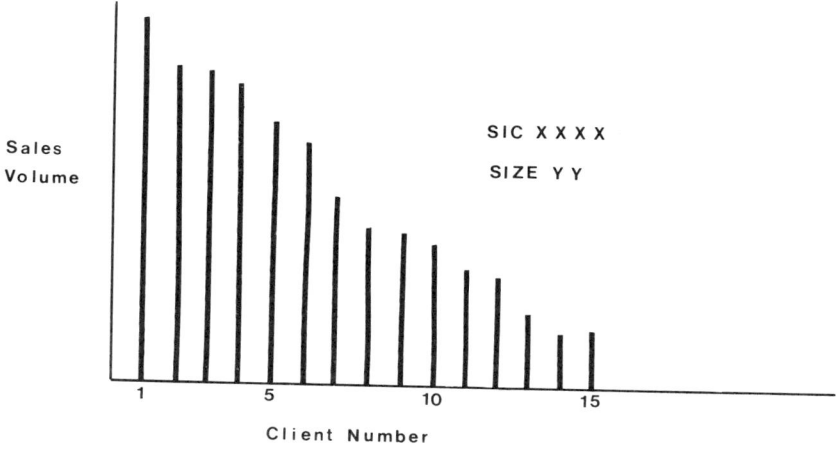

6/Marketing Aspects

It would appear that each client is capable of buying your goods at a quantity that equals, say, the average of the highest three. Thus, you can estimate what your present pentration ratio is and what the maximum potential sales are for each business size category.

4. A composite picture can be built up by evaluating your sales to each SIC category.

The occupany ratio can be found by SIC and size category:

Insurance Industry

Size	Number Of Establishments	Number Of Your Clients	Occupancy
A	16,000	2	0.0001
B	7,200	6	0.0008
C	3,590	24	0.007
D	800	58	0.07
E	300	31	0.1
F	24	14	0.58
G	9	9	1.0
H	1	1	1.0

This data can be plotted in the form of a graph

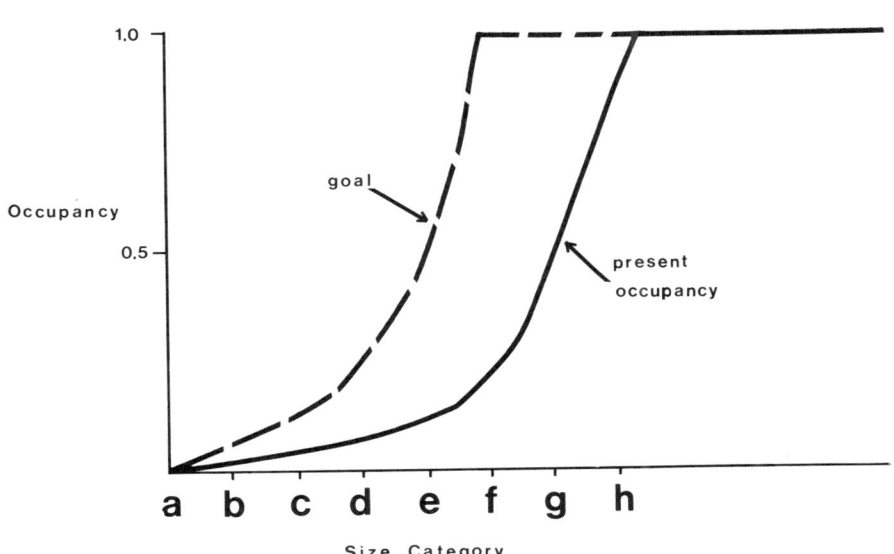

You can determine your strategy for increasing your occupancy factor by targeting on new client companies.

The following are excellent references for industrial/wholesale markets:

1. Bureau of Census, Suitland, MD. 20233
   - Census of Business for 1972: Retail-Area Statistics
   - Census of Manufacturers for 1972
   - Census of Wholesale Trade for 1972
   - Census of Selected Service Industries for 1972
   - Census of Population for 1970
   - Census Tract Manual
   - County Business Patterns
2. Department of Commerce, Washington, D.C. 20230
   - Business Statistics
   - Survey of Current Business
3. Federal Department of Labor, Washington, D.C. 20230
   - Survey of Consumer Expenditure
4. Local Sources
   - Chamber of Commerce
   - Local Libraries and Universities
   - Local City and County Government
   - Research department of local newspapers
   - Field offices of the SBA
   - Field offices of the U.S. Department of Commerce.

A telephone call to a local source will quickly tell you if they have what you need. Almost always the data is available free of charge.

5. SBA Publication - Small Business Bibliography No. 13, "National Directories for use in Marketing".

6.1.2 Estimating New Business Markets

Where your new business is providing well established goods or services it is reasonably easy to estimate, using the methods described in Section 6.1, if there is a large enough market to permit the entry of one more company. For example, if the $500,000 market for cleaning the windows of large office blocks in a small town is shared by five companies, a sixth company could only expect a revenue of $500,000 divided by six, or $83,000. Assuming nominal penetration, it might take the new company one or two years to build up to an equal share of the total available business.

Where an entirely new product is offered, it is difficult to measure the likely market. However, one approach is to evaluate the market for similar products. Another approach might be to evaluate the number of people or businesses who would be potential clients for the product and estimate how much of their income or revenue is likely to be spent on such a product. Where a new product is used in conjunction with an existing product or service, you can estimate two factors; a) the market for the present product, and b) the proportion of your product used with the present product. This latter piece of information can be determined by some form of market research. Take, for example, a new product for use in conjunction with sailing boats. You could canvas the members of a local sailing club concerning their liking for the product at a given price, and so estimate its sales potential.

6.1.3 Market Growth And Forecasting

Any business activity has, of course, seasonal fluctuations in sales and, consequently, in revenues. These season trends are documented for each typical business and will be further discussed in a later section. However, the small businessman should have some idea about the year to year growth prospects for his business. This will depend on whether his business is local, city, regional or nationwide in extent.

- Local Business and City

    1. The local sources given in Section 6.1.1, give excellent information on population and income trends projected over the next five to ten years.

    2. Where your business employs salesmen you can canvas them to provide a projection for each of their sales' areas. Then you can use managerial judgement to build up a composite picture of the overall sales market.

- Regional and Nation Wide

    1. The sales of an existing product are forecast by "Sales Management Magazine" in July of each year. SM&M makes use of a "Buying Power Index" for each product category it forecasts.

    2. The Department of Commerce publishes a survey of buyer intentions in its publication "Survey of Current Business".

    3. Your salesmen can be convased for regional/national forecasts.

    4. Where your product is nationally distributed and depends on the overall economy, then the prediction on the GNP provides a good indicator for the future sales of your product. GNP predictions can be found in numerous publications, including Fortune, Business Week and U.S. News and World Report. Bank letters, such as those published by First National City Bank and Chase Manhattan Bank of New York predict monthly and yearly levels of the economy.

2 THE MARKETING PROGRAM

6.2.1 Product Line

Your product line, that is, the range of goods or service you offer should be carefully analysed for profit contribution to the whole business. It may be that 20 percent of your items contribute 80 percent of your profit. In these circumstances, you should consider pruning your product line down and concentrating on the more profitable items.

Before adding a new product to your line you should perform a financial analysis to determine its degree of profitability. To do this analysis you need to establish; 1) the price, 2) the total costs, including start-up, operating and overhead costs associated with the product, 3) the expected volume of the product, 4) the life of the product. At a minimum you can calculate how long it will take you to break even. More sophisticated financial analysis techniques involve calculating the return on investment (see "Engineering Economy, Grant and Ireson, published by Ronald Publishing Company). You should stack rank several products that might be available for future introduction, one against the other, and see how their paybacks compare. Naturally, where funds are limited you select those products with the shortest payback periods.

It is most important to establish the image of your company and structure your product array to match that image. For example, are you a cut-price, low quality retailer, a medium range retailer, a top quality or specialty retailer? You must decide just what market segment you serve and stay within that segment. If you begin to "contaminate" your product line with superior or inferior lines you may run into trouble by causing customer confusion or resistance. Sears-Robuck for example lost ground by attempting to move "up-market" when it expanded into suburban stores.

6.2.2 Advertising

Advertising is a key ingredient to a "pull" type of product – a pull product being one that is heavily advertised and is pulled through the distribution chain by the buyer demand. This is the opposite of a push product that has to be pushed through the chain using salesmen.

The advertising decision is influenced by the following factors:

- Brand Policy – many products are sold under a brand name. Sometimes these branded products are owned by a manufacturer and sometimes by a wholesale/retailer. It is the responsibility of the brand owner to advertise his product.

- Profit Margin – a low profit margin product is usually heavily advertised since it is the cheapest method of selling. A high profit margin product can be sold through salesmen and dealers.

- Pricing Policy – a cut-price brand as opposed to a branded item is not advertised and relies on its attractive price alone to promote sales volume.

- Advertising Budget – the questions to address are:

    a) How much to spend, and b) what media to use?

    Advertising budget is established by a variety of methods:

    1) Percentage of sales method, which sets the overall advertising budget as a percentage of the overall sales.

    2) Follow the leader method, which establishes how much the industry spends and spend a like amount (see Robert Morris Associates, "Annual Statement Studies", Section 7.1).

3) Objective and task method, which is associated with larger firms who can identify specific advertising targets and work with an advertising agency to reach these targets at a specific cost. The advantage of this method is that it forces the objective evaluation of media effectiveness.

4) All you can afford method, which is whatever is left over after all the non-avoidable costs of doing business have been met.

The advertising media available have a variety of characteristics. The major characteristics to consider for each medium is target audience, characteristics of your product and the cost per exposure.

1) Newspapers - there are two costs to be considered; a) preparation costs, and b) placement costs. Preparation costs equal or exceed placement costs. The preparation involves layout design, production art, typography, photostats and sometimes engraving for photographs. Your cost effectiveness can be improved by establishing a basic format and varying the message within that format. Many manufacturers have camera-ready art for their products at no charge to retailers.

Placement costs in newspapers are priced by the agate line or by the inch. There are 14 agate lines per inch. Thus, if you are running a 3-column by 10 inch ad, the total lineage is 14 x 10 x 3 - 420 lines. Rates are quoted as "open", "contract" or "frequency". Never purchase ad space at the "open" rate. Minimums for the contract rate are well within the retailers' budget. Typical lineage costs run from approximately 16¢ for a small suburban paper to $1.00 per line for a large city paper. In selecting which paper to use consider the advertising area covered and the travelling radius of your potential customers.

The advantages of newspaper advertising lies in its broad exposure, the short closing time necessary before it appears and the fact that you can segment your market appeal by position in the newspaper and choice of newpaper circulation boundaries. The disadvantages of newspaper advertising lie in poor color reproduction, short exposure life and the high cost of national circulation.

2. Yellow Pages Advertising - this is most useful with a service type business but can also be used to show branded product lines, for example Toro lawnmowers or Sony TV's. The rates are normally based on a limited variety of fixed sizes. Typical large city rates run from approximately $4.00 per month for a "Regular Listing" consisting of just your business name, address and telephone number up to about $300 a month for 2 columns wide by five inches high space listing. Significant cost savings can be obtained by using suburban telephone directories rather than the major metropolitan directory if it suits your needs.

3. Direct Mail - this medium offers the best selection for ex-

posure and segmentation. You can purchase mailing lists of particular areas having particular demographic characteristics (see SBA publication #29, National Mailing List Houses). Initially you can use stamped third class piece rate mail, but even so the cost per exposure is high.

4. Magazine - this medium offers good geographic and demographic segmentation (regional editions, age, income, lifestyle, etc). Its life is exceptionally long, providing good color reproduction and reasonable cost. Advertising rates can be found from "Consumer Magazines and Farms Publications" published by Standard Rate & Data Service Inc., 5201 Old Orchard Road, Skokie, Il, 60076.

5. Outdoor Advertising - this medium offers the advantages of repeated exposure to a captive audience, but the message conveyed must be simple. The costs can run anywhere from $40 a month to $50,000 a month depending on the size and location of the sign.

6. Radio - this medium has the advantage of low cost per exposure to a local audience. It can stimulate an immediate response from a particular demographic segment. It has the shortest closing time of any advertising medium. National coverage is expensive but local "spot announcements" on small radio stations can cost as little as $5.00. The "Nielsen Service Report" published by the AC Nielsen Company of Chicago provides demographic data in station audience. The "Standard Rate and Data Service" provides cost information.

7. TV - this medium used to be prohibitively expensive, but nowadays a 10 second spot can cost as little as $20 to $100 depending on the station size and time of day. Indeed, the cost per exposure may be the cheapest of any medium. However, it is difficult to segment the audience and usually a product with mass appeal is most suited to this form of advertising.

- Measuring Advertising Effectiveness

It is important for you to be able to measure the effectiveness of your advertising and change it accordingly. Several methods can be used:

1) Coupons sent in - coupons can request the product or additional information. The number of such coupons received may be sufficient to justify running the ad.

2) Phone or letter requests - these can be tabulated in reference to a specific ad or referral.

3) Split run in newspapers - two different ads with different coupons are run on the same day in a split press run, that is, part of the run has one ad and the rest of the run has the second ad. A relative count of the returned coupons provides an indication of the effectiveness of each ad.

4) Sales of a particular item - when an item is advertised as a

bargain or limited - time offer, you can count the extra sales made over a one, two or three week period after the advertising program.

5) Store traffic count - you will certainly want to build store traffic so that you can expose customers to the complete selection of goods on display. You can employ high school students for a time to count traffic and to ask questions about what brought the client to the store, what goods were purchased and what goods the store should stock.

You can also check the effectiveness of your advertising by measuring the sales of various advertised items over several sales seasons and comparing the sales volumes to the type and amount of advertising used. Thus, you should always log your advertising for later data analysis purposes.

NOTE, you should make a point of asking where customers have heard about your store or your product. You should repeat winning ads, but check for any change in attitude to your store or ad. Try to find out what aspect of a particular ad appeals to customers and delete any aspects that do not appeal.

6.2.3 Distribution Methods

When you are a manufacturer of a product you must decide on the method of its distribution to the consumer. The channel of distribution can be very long. For example, the product can pass from the manufacturer to an agent, then to a wholesaler, next to a retailer, and finally to the consumer.

The first step of this channel of distribution, that is the agent, can be very complex. In fact, there are two types of first line dealer - the agent or the merchant. Merchants typically take title to the merchandise they distribute whereas agents do not. Agents come in a wide variety of types:

- Broker - used especially in the food industry to bring the buyer and the seller together. The broker has no negotiating power, the terms being set by the buyer and the seller.

- Resident buyer - located mostly in New York City in the fashion industry. Each buyer is usually a specialist in a given fashion area and is used by the smaller retailer to determine what is available. Some buyers operate on commission, others on a flat fee.

- Manufacturer's agent or representative - individuals who are independent businessmen but who give the appearance of being part of a manufacturer's sales force. Commission is based on a gross sales basis. The agent has no authority to set price or terms and handles numerous related products from different manufacturers. Agents can work quite well for small manufacturers. Larger concerns, however, usually want to develop their own sales force since agents are limited geographically and are not usually able to sell the manufacturers' full range of products.

- Selling agents - individuals, especially in the textile industry, who serve as the marketing department for a company. These agents are useful to concerns that have no marketing experience. Selling agents do not have control over such items as advertising, pricing or contract terms.

- Petroleum Bulk Companies - these people cater to small service stations selling in rural areas.

Merchants too come in wide variety:

- Commission Merchant - an individual, almost like a broker, but who takes physical possession of the goods and has more flexibility to negotiate price and terms. A commission merchant will usually extend credit.

- Drop Shipper - an individual primarily engaged in selling and risk taking. He will assume title at the production site, normally of bulky merchandise such as coal or lumber, but he never take physical possession of the goods. A drop shipper will find a buyer for the goods and assume the risk during transportation.

- Cash and Carry Wholesaler - this is a wholesaler who sells on a cash and carry basis to small retailers, and is, in reality, a huge supermarket for retailers.

- Wagon Distributor - an individual who sells high priced, specialty merchandise, such as jewelry, directly to a retailer. A wagon distributor does not usually extend credit.

- Rack Jobber - an individual who sells non-grocery items to grocery stores (usually drugs or clothing items). A jobber will price the sales items, stock shelves, count the sales and extend credit.

The second step in the distribution channel is the wholesaler, who exists to warehouse and distribute a mass distribution product out to numerous small retailers taking advantage of an efficient transportation system.

The third step in the distribution channel is the retailer who sells directly to the final consumer. Product control can be focused at any point in the distribution channel. Thus, a product can be originated by a manufacturer, an agent, a wholesaler or even a group of retailers.

In order to select the particular channel of distribution for your product you need to consider these factors:

1) The characteristics of your product.
    - Size - a bulky product will be shipped directly to the buyer.
    - Technical Aspects - a highly technical product requires a more direct sale through a technical sales force.
    - Service Requirements - if service is required you will have to select a middleman who has the capability to provide such service.
    - Unit Value - as the price of the product increases the manufacturing company can afford to absorb the cost of its own salesforce.

2) The characteristics of the market.

6/Marketing Aspects

- Geographic Dispersion - the greater the geographic spread the longer the distribution channel. You can sell directly to concentrated large city markets, but might be forced to use middlemen in thinly populated areas.
- Average Order Size - the larger the individual order size, the more direct the selling method.
- Need - the greater the need for the product, the more intensive and long is the channel of distribution.
- Frequency of Purchase - the higher the frequency of purchase the more middlemen are used.

3) Company characteristics.
- Size and Resources - the larger the company the more it can handle its own distribution system.
- Size of Product Line - a company needs a huge product range to justify the cost of direct selling.
- Expertise of Management - sucessful management of a long channel of distribution requires detailed knowledge of such marketing methods.
- Stage in a company's development - a new company needs more direct selling capability to move an idea, to obtain market exposure and to gain experience.
- Desire for channel control - the best way to control your distribution channel is to sell directly or to obtain a legal contract over the performance of the middleman.

4) Characteristics of the Middleman.
- Availability - is there a middleman who is capable of properly handling your product.
- Nature of the middleman's products - are the products he carries competitive or complementary to yours?
- Quality of the salesforce - are there sufficient men in specific market areas of the right caliber.
- Economics - is the cost of selling through a middleman attractive.

5) Selection of Outlet
- You must define the boundaries covered by each outlet.
- You must select the outlet, determined by its financial status, reputation, sale's volume and geographic market control.

6.2.3 Pricing Strategy

The basic facts required to determine a pricing strategy are 1) competitor's prices, 2) production cost per unit 3) product demand, and 4) objective of your marketing strategy.

Your marketing strategy might be any one of the following: 1) to achieve a given return on investment, 2) to stabilize your market share, 3) to achieve a given target market share, or 4) to prevent competition.

There are five basic pricing strategies for manufacturers.

1) Penetration Pricing (New Products)

In this mode the company sells at a price to cover costs plus a slight

mark-up to achieve a high volume. In order to implement penetration pricing, several conditions must exist:
- The market must be highly sensitive to price
- The market must be large enough to permit economics of scale.
- The price is low enough to discourage competition

2) Skim Pricing (New Products)

In this mode the company sells at a high price and quickly recovers its initial costs. The higher price is charged until competition enters the marketplace. Again, several conditions must exist:
- There must be sufficient buyers at this high price.
- The product must be a high quality product.

3) Intermediate Pricing

In this mode, the price is set midway between penetration and skim pricing to maximize the company's cash flow (but not its overall profits).

4) Variable Cost Pricing

In the manufacture of any product there are the so called fixed costs and the variable costs. The fixed costs are those expenses, such as heat, insurance, machinery that are fixed expenses. The variable costs are items such as raw material and production line labor that make up the underlying cost of the unit. Thus, once a manufacturer has sold enough units to cover his fixed costs, he may want to sell idle production capacity at a cost that would cover only his variable cost. He usually does this by selling the same product under another name.

5. Rate of Return Pricing

This method is used by the large companies, such as GM and Dupont, where they have a good estimate for the demand for a given product. The cost of product at that demand level is then calibrated, say $3.00 per unit for 100,000 units. Thus if a 20% return is required before tax, the sales price per unit is 3 x 1.2 - $3.60. The problem with this pricing method is the huge loss that results if the demand does not materialize.

The situation for retailers is different than the approaches used by manufacturers. There are several pricing methods in use for retailers:

1) Markup Pricing - this is the practice of adding on a given percentage to the wholesale or manufacturer's price for the product. Some shopkeepers define their markup as a percentage of the retail price. In either case, the average markup for each type of retail business is fairly standard and can be found in references given in Section 7.1.

2) Markon Pricing - this method is similar to markup pricing, but makes allowance for so called retail reductions such as markdowns, discounts to employees and stock shortages. The formula for cal-

6/Marketing Aspects

culating markon percentage is:

$$\text{Markon (\%)} = \frac{\text{Gross Margin (\%)} + \text{Retail Reductions (\%)}}{\text{Net Sales (\%)} + \text{Retail Reductions (\%)}}$$

Thus, the markon is higher than the markup to obtain an actual gross margin.

3) Price Lining - where all the merchandise is priced in a small number of price categories, for example, you might sell men's pants at $15, $20, $25, $30 and $35 a pair. This method minimizes the decision making of the customer and facilitates inventory control.

4) Odd Pricing (for example 79¢) - this method was originally used to force an employee to ring up a sale in order to provide change to a customer. In this way, employee stealing was minimized.

5) Bait Pricing - usually a three minute price reduction on a given item designed to keep customers in the store longer.

6) Loss Leader Pricing - where a national branded product, such as Coca-Cola, is sold for a loss in order to generate traffic.

6.3 DEFINING YOUR MARKETING OBJECTIVES

Your marketing objectives are a set of numbers that you should use to guide your marketing efforts.

6.3.1 Advertising Budget

The amounts for each type of medium should be set up at the start of your financial year on a month by month basis, timed to coincide with your peak sales seasons or to enhance clearance sales. You should establish how many consumers in your area have been reached by your advertising program and what proportion remain untapped.

6.3.2 Sales Targets

Sales targets should be set up for each person and each sales territory (if you sell direct). A bonus incentive plan should be set up and published prior to the start of the sales year. If your business is a retail store you must plan your sales targets for each category of merchandise you are intending to offer for sale. In some businesses, for example the fashion trade, your inventory must be selected and ordered up to four months ahead of the selling period.

6.4 MEASURING YOUR MARKETING PERFORMANCE

It is extremely important that you measure and record the results of your marketing program. You should keep track of how much you spend on advertising and how effective it was, season over season. You should also track the performance of your sales people, not only in actual sales but also in intagible items such as courtesy that enable you to obtain repeat business. You should also keep track of the sales of each item of your product line; often some stores need to take inventory on a daily basis to spot sales trends developing.

6.5 SOURCES OF ECONOMIC AND MARKETING INFORMATION

You will need to keep abreast of the changing conditions in your market area. The list given below of current books, booklets and periodicals will provide information in the areas of economics and marketing. Some are private publications and others are compiled by the Federal Government.

<u>Bibliography of 1973 Publications of University Bureaus of Business and Economic Research.</u> $7.50 ea. Association for University Business and Economic Research, University of Colorado, Boulder, Colo.

<u>Business Statistics.</u> Biennial. U.S. Department of Commerce. 1973. GPO. Supplementary and historical data for the economic statistics published in the "Survey of Current Business".

<u>County and City Data Books:</u> 1972. Bureau of the Census, U.S. Department of Commerce. GPO. Presents statistical information on business, manufacturers, Governments, agriculture, population, housing, vital statistics, bank deposits, and other subjects. Issued every several years.

<u>Data Sources for Business and Market Analysis.</u> Frank, Nathalie D. Scarecrow Press, Inc., 52 Liberty Street, Box 656, Metuchen, N.J. 08840. Provides market research information, its origins and retrieval. Gives basic sources and specific references for the study of business trends.

<u>Directory of Business and Financial Services.</u> 1974. Edited by Mary M. Grant and Norma Cote. Special Libraries Association, 235 Park Avenue, South, New York, N.Y. 10003. An annotated listing of several hundred business, economic, and financial services.

<u>Editor & Publisher Market Guide.</u> Annual. 1975. $20. Editor & Publisher Company, 850 Third Avenue, New York, N.Y. 10022. Tabulates current estimates of population, households, retail sales for nine major sales classifications, income for States, counties, metropolitan areas, and 1,500 daily newspaper markets. For each area, gives information on transportation and utilities, local newspapers, climate, and employment. Includes State maps.

<u>McGraw-Hill Dictionary of Modern Economics.</u> 1973. 2d ed. $19.95. McGraw-Hill Book Company, Inc., 1221 Avenue of the Americas, New York, N.Y. 10020. Defines more than 1300 terms currently used in economics, marketing, and finance. It also describes approximately 200 Government and private agencies, and nonprofit associations concerned with the fields of economics and marketing.

<u>Rand McNally Commercial Atlas and Marketing Guide.</u> Annual. 1975. $90 (Leased on an annual basis.) Rand McNally & Company, Box 7600, Chicago, Ill. 60680. An extensive U.S. Atlas presenting marketing data in the form of maps and area statistics.

<u>SM's Survey of Buying Power.</u> 1974. Part I - $25; Part II - $10. "Sales Management", 633 Third Avenue, NEW York, N.Y. 10017. Gives population, income, and retail sales estimates for State, county, and metropolitan areas (as defined by "Sales Management Magazine).

<u>Sources of Business Information.</u> Coman, E.T., Editor. 1964. $11. Berkeley, University of California Press, Berkeley, Calif. 94729. Guide to general sources with coverage for specific fields of business and industry.

The Statesman's Year Book. Revised annually, edited by S.H. Steinberg and John Paxton. 1973-74. $13.95. St. Martin's Press, Inc., 175 Fifth Avenue, New York, N.Y. 10010. This book is a storehouse of information on the United Nations, all countries of the world, and each of the 50 States of the United States.

Statistical Abstract of the United States: 1974. Bureau of the Census, U.S. Department of Commerce. GPO. The standard summary of national statistics, includes information on the labor force, population, business enterprises, and national income.

Statistical Services of the United States Government. Annual. Bureau of the Budget. GPO. Serves as a basic reference document on U.S. Government statistical programs.

Statistics Sources. 4th ed. $45. Edited by Paul Wasserman. Gale Research Company, Book Tower, Detroit, Mich. 48226. Arranged in dictionary style, it cites periodicals, yearbooks, directories, and other compilations issued by State, Federal and foreign agencies, associations, companies, universities, and other organizations.

PERIODICALS - U.S. GOVERNMENT

The following are some of the basic Federal Government periodicals which contain business and general economic reports and are widely used by businessmen for keeping abreast of developments in their specific areas of interest.

Construction Review. U.S. Department of Commerce. Monthly. GPO. Brings together virtually all the Government's current statistics pertaining to construction, plus some nongovernment statistical information.

Current Industrial Reports. Bureau of the Census, U.S. Department of Commerce. Lists of titles and prices available from the Bureau of the Census, Washington, D.C. 20233. These reports give information at the factory level for different industries on inventory, production, shipments, and other business activities.

Current Business Reports. Bureau of Census, U.S. Department of Commerce. Includes a series of four reports: Weekly Retail Sales Report; Advance Monthly Retail Sales Report; Monthly Retail Trade; and Retail Annual Report. GPO. Estimated sales of retail stores by kinds of business and some data for regions and metropolitan areas.

Economic Indicators. Prepared for the Joint Economic Committee by the Council of Economic Advisers. Monthly. GPO. Presents tables and charts dealing with prices, employment and wages, production and business activity, purchasing power, credit, and Federal finance.

Federal Reserve Bulletin. Board of Governors of the Federal Reserve System, Washington, D.C. 20551. Monthly. $20 a year; $2 a copy. Has monthly tables of financial and business statistics. Interest rates, money supply, consumer credit, and industrial production are some of the subjects included. Special articles cover the state of economy, financial institutions, statistical methodology.

Monthly Labor Review. U.S. Department of Labor. Monthly. GPO. The medium through which the Labor department publishes its regular monthly reports on such subjects as trends of employment and payrolls, hourly and weekly earnings, working hours, collective agreements, industrial accidents and disputes, as well as special features covering such topics as automation, and profit sharing.

<u>Monthly Wholesale Trade Reports: Sales and Inventories.</u> U.S. Department of Commerce. Monthly. GPO. This periodical includes statistics and articles on significant economic developments. It presents statistics on national income, business population, manufacturers sales, inventories, and orders. Carries special articles on personal income, foreign trade, and other aspects of the economy.

SECTION TWO

BUSINESS ACQUISITION –START UP

7

Information Sources

7.0   The second section of this book seeks to show you how to focus your attention on the particular business venture you have in mind. The intention is to research your intended business in such a way that a detailed loan proposal can be prepared that would convince a banker of your knowledge and business ability. More importantly, the research is required to convince yourself that a particular business is the right one for you. Thus, even if you have sufficient funds to completely finance an acquisition or start up yourself, you should still go through the process of business analysis to make an informed decision about that business.

In the following chapters we will examine each aspect of business activity and integrate the analysis into a formal business plan. You will be shown where you can find data on each factor and how to use it. In fact, more data that you can possibly use is published annually by private and governmental sources. It will take you several months of reasonably active research to put all the facts together on a particular business. However, in view of the rewards, psychological as well as financial, from a successful small business, there can be no doubt that an initial investigative effort is well worth it. More importantly, it may enable you to avoid making a fatal mistake.

7.1   BUSINESS SELECTION

You may have a very clear idea of what type of small business you wish to own. You may, for instance, be experienced in printing and decide that with a little capital you could start and manage your own print shop. Alternatively, you may have no particular idea of just what small business you would like to be in, but would be attracted to anything that seems profitable. Unfortunately, there are no hard and fast rules about which types of business are more profitable than others and which should be definitely avoided. For instance, McDonald's restaurants have long been considered to be a superior investment, but even McDonald's have had at least one failure. Thus, any business can do well or poorly dependent upon the business conditions and management situation of the business.

If you want somewhere to browse to get an idea of how risky a given type of business is, or to gain some idea of how much equity capital you need to create a given income for yourself, then the two references discussed below are invaluable. They do not cover every conceivable business, but they do cover every general category of business so that you can gain a very good idea of

7/Information Sources

business costs and returns. If, for instance, you want to start a "Widget" manufacturing company, then you are on your own. If, however, you want to start a more typical small business such as a bakery shop or even a detective agency then data on these has been tabulated. Before discussing the two guides themselves, you should be introduced to the SIC codes. The SIC codes - or Standard Industrial Classification codes - were created by the U.S. Office of Management and Budget to serve to classify various businesses for government statistical purposes. The latest classification, published in 1972 and updated via a small supplement in 1977, is entitled "Standard Industrial Classification Manual". The SIC codes are now widely used by both government and industry to classify customers and suppliers by business category. The SIC code itself is a four digit number, which is a subset of a three digit industry group number. For example, SIC #3652, Manufacturers of Phonograph Records is a subset of SIC #365, Radio and TV Receiving Equipment Manufacturers.

The two guides listed below tabulate the data compiled from analysing thousands of financial statements. They are both updated and published annually, so that current data is always available.

1. Annual Statement Studies
   Robert Morris Associates (RMA)
   Philadelphia, PA

2. Almanac of Business and Industrial Financial Ratios
   Leo Troy, PhD
   Prentice Hall, Inc., Englewood Cliffs, N.J.

Probably the best place to locate these publications is either at your local university library or in the business section of your main city library.

Both guides publish roughly comparable data. The RMA guide covers 305 lines of business, the Troy guide about 170. The RMA guide divides each business type into four asset categories from $0 to $50 million, whereas the Troy guide provides ten asset categories from $0 to $100 million and over. RMA provides rather more financial ratios than Troy.

- Almanac of Business and Industrial Financial Ratios (TROY)

    This guide is the simplest to understand and the most straight forward to apply for our purposes. Suppose, for example, you were interested in an apparel and accessory shop. The Almanac, in its 1977 edition, indicates that the average ratio of Net Income (after all taxes) to Net Worth (owner's investment) for apparel shops with total assets below $100,000 is 34.2%. It further indicates that the average of Total Liabilities to Net Worth is 1.1. Thus, if you invested $48,000 of your own money and borrowed $52,000, your after tax net annual income would be approximately $16,500.

    In case you are discouraged by this seemingly low rate or return, you should be aware that the data in "Almanac" is compiled from IRS returns, so that operating cost is maximized and net income minimized. However, the data is fairly valid when used on a comparative basis when looking at the differences between various businesses.

- Robert Morris Associates (RMA)

    The data provided by "RMA" is somewhat more informative because three data points are provided for each financial ratio. For instance, the median data point is given; the median being midway between the strongest and weakest percentages of all the financial statements analysed. Also, the upper quartile point is given, which is midway between the median and the strongest percentage. Likewise, the lower quartile point is given, which is midway between the median and the weakest percentage. The median is used, rather than the average, since it provides a more accurate reference point thus eliminating the influence of non-typical data.

Thus, the 1977 version of RMA provides the following data for "Women's Ready-to-Wear" shops:

SIC #5621; for shops with total assets between $0 - $250,000

#	Ratio	Upper Quartile	Median	Lower Quartile
1	% Profit/Net Worth	44.4%	22.2%	4%
2	Debt/Worth	0.4%	1.0%	2.8%
3	% Profit/Total Assets	19.4%	8.6%	1.3%

Two things can be seen from these figures; 1) there is a 10 to 1 variation in % profit to net worth between the upper quartile and lower quartile, that is 44.4% to 4% and 2) businesses tend to borrow more and more the less profitable they are, indicated by dividing ratio #1 by #3; the upper quartile borrowing being approximately 1:1 with equity, the lower quartile being 3:1 with equity.

Thus, again assuming you invested $50,000 and borrowed $50,000, your median return would be $11,100 per year and your upper quartile return would be $22,200 per year. RMA also provides other data to judge return by providing the median % Officer's Compensation/Sales as 7.2 and the Median Sales/Total Assets as 2.5. Thus, if your assets totalled $100,000, your sales would be $250,000, giving a median officers' compensation of $250,000 x 0.072 = $18,000. Using the upper quartile numbers provided for both ratios, the officers compensation would amount to $32,000. It must be understood that the last calculation assumes that the various quartiles of the ratios are strictly related, which is really not true.

However, taking data from RMA and Almanac, it would appear that a $50,000 investment in a median apparel shop would provide you an income of $15,000 to $20,000, and an upper quartile store would provide over $30,000.

The RMA quartile figures of % Profit/Net Worth for other businesses are 1) for restaurants: 85.1%, 37.1%, 10.7% and 2) for women's clothing manufacturers: 21.0%, 5.0% -10.3%. Again, note the wide variation in profitability, and that, in general, a restaurant is far more profitable than a clothing manufacturer. Indeed, the lower quartile of clothing manufacturers is shown operating at a loss. However, an upper quartile clothing manufacturer is more profitable than a lower quartile restaurant.

7/Information Sources

The attraction of high profits in the restaurant business is one reason so many open, but an equally common observation is that many die.

In summary, therefore, the RMA median figure for % Profit/New Worth gives a measure of the general profitability of a business type. The range of the upper and lower quartiles give a measure of the risk. Thus, two businesses that both have a median figure of 50% are generally equally profitable, but the one that has an upper to lower quartile range of 60% to 5% is much risker than the other with a range of 40% to 20%.

It should also be noted that it is possible in high leverage situations to show a high Profit/Net Worth ratio, which seems very attractive. High leverage occurs when the company has a high debt to equity ratio. In this situation, you should also look at the Profit/Total Assets figure to judge how profitable the company really is.

SOURCES FOR BUSINESS PURCHASE

You may by now have a general idea of which type of business you would be interested in. There are three general methods of entering the small business field.

1. The acquisition of an existing business.
2. The purchase of a franchise business.
3. The opening of an entirely new business.

- In the case of an entirely new business you will have to start from the ground up - selecting your location and business premises, obtaining furniture, equipment and inventory, and then building up a customer base for the business via advertising or salesmen, and so forth. Essentially, therefore, you buy no "good will", but have to establish your own reputation over the first few years. This start-up period can be very expensive, since the cost of establishing yourself will almost certainly outrun income.

- A franchise business is attractive to many since the franchise provides much in the way of good will and, additionally, much start up help. The best franchisors offer very structured management assistance and start up plans, which cover everything from participation in group purchases to appearance and service standards for your franchise. However, this very structure limits the entrepreneurs' freedom of operation. You are usually required to buy your equipment and supplies from the franchisor. The franchisor may own your building and land and require a percentage of your sales.

The franchise method of business entry can be very successful, but many have been spectacular failures. The franchise company and its agreement should be studied with the utmost care by you and your legal advisor before signing any agreement.

The following information sources on franchises are invaluable:

1) Directory of Franchising Operations
   Pilot Industries Inc.
   347 Fifth Avenue, N.Y., N.Y. 10016
   This is an annual publication which lists the names and addresses of franchisors.

2) International Franchise Association, Inc.
1025 Connecticut Avenue
Washington, D.C. 20036
The IFA is a non-profit industry association for franchisors. It will provide information on the financial condition and integrity of any specific franchisor.

3) Franchise Index/Profile
Superintendent of Documents
U.S. Government Printing Office, Washington, D.C. 20402
This is a 56 page SBA publication (stock #045-000-00125-3), costing $2.00, that presents an evaluation process for investigating franchise opportunities. The Index describes what to look for in a franchise; the Profile is a worksheet for listing the data.

4) Franchising
Bank of America, Dept. 3120 P.O. Box 37000
San Fransico, CA 94137
This is a publication in the series "Small Business Reporter" and is free from a BA office or $1.00 via mail.

5) Advice For Persons Who Are Considering An Investment In A Franchise Business
Consumer Bulletin #4, Federal Trade Commission
Washington, D.C. 20580

6) Facts About Franchising
National Better Business Bureau Inc. 230 Park AVe. N.Y., N.Y. 10017

A few good books on franchising are:

1) The Franchise Handbook
Jan Cameron, Crown Publishers, 1970

2) How to Get Started in Your Own Franchised Business
David D. Selts, Farnsworth Publishing Co., Inc., 1967

3) Franchising: The Complete Investor's Handbook
Robert Dias and Stanley Burnick, Hastings House, 1969

4) Franchising: Trap for the Trusting
Harold Brown, Little-Brown and Co, 1969

Another not unsubstantial advantage of entering into a franchise operation is that there are usually several stores of a particular franchise in your local area. The owners of these franchises can be approached for their opinion about the franchise operation and its net income possibilities. These people are usually more than happy to share their experience with you to help you get started.

Information concerning locations and cost of entry of a particular franchise can be solicited from writing directly to the franchisor listed in the "Directory of Franchising Operations".

- Buying an existing business will usually, but not always, require a larger initial investment than starting the same type of business from scratch. You are in a sense having to reward the business owner for his initial struggle to establish that business. On the balance sheet, of course, this extra amount is listed as "goodwill" once you purchase a business at a price above the value of its tangible assets. There is no question that the extra price paid for "goodwill" is well worth it, and every entrepreneur should consider seriously buying an existing business before trying to start a completely new one. The reasons are obvious; there is much less risk of failure when purchasing an established business; in the long run the higher start up expenses of a completely new business will just about equal the extra cost of goodwill paid for an existing business; you get to a profit situation much more quickly; the psychological strain will be less severe. It should be pointed out that even if you do buy an ongoing business, it will take some months before your cash flow becomes positive. Thus, you will need some working capital in addition to the price you pay for the business. The calculation of just how much working capital will be needed is discussed later in the book.

There are several ways of finding businesses for sale:

1) Family, friends or business associates will often hear of someone wanting to sell their business. The business owner may want to retire, to move or to go into a different business. If, for instance, friends or associates know of your interest in owning a business, they will probably inform you of the opportunity. This type of acquisition should not be disregarded since many very good deals can be had by this method. However, the entrepreneur is cautioned to investigate like businesses from other sources for comparison purposes.

2) The classified column in the advertising section of your local newspaper will often carry a section on "business opportunities". This column will sometimes carry advertising on financing and sources of finance.

3) Business brokers are in the business of bringing buyers and sellers together. A good broker is one who has thoroughly evaluated the businesses he has on his books and also knows the buyer's ability to pay for and manage such a business. However, many brokers are merely con-artists, who are, in fact, under no legal obligation to volunteer any factual information to you in this "arms-length" transaction. In selecting a business broker it is obviously best to seek one who is known for his competence and integrity. Ask your commercial loan banker, your lawyer and your local Better Business Bureau for recommendations. Deal with someone who has been in business for at least five years.

In no case should you deal with a broker without first obtaining the advice of your lawyer, who will make sure that you see all the documentation you require in order to make an informed judgement about a business. Remember that the broker is the legal agent of the seller and as such has a fiduciary duty to act in the best interests of the seller and not the buyer.

You will find a listing a business brokers in your area in your "Yellow Pages".

BUSINESS INFORMATION

As you get more serious about a particular type of business you should start to learn as much as you can about that business. This knowledge will not only serve to help you in your management operations, but will initially help to impress your professional advisers on your abilities. Your business image is especially important in setting the stage for successful business entry. Clearly, professional advisors who respect you will believe that you will be successful and thus worthy of extra attention. They will probably make no special effort for individuals who appear to be incapable.

The sources of information on a particular business are:

1. Encyclopedia of Business Information Sources

   Paul Wasserman, Editor, Gale Research Company, Book Tower, Detroit, Michigan, 48226, Third Edition - 1976. This book lists a) Handbooks and Manuals, b) Trade Associations and Professional Societies, c) Periodicals, d) Directories and e) Statistical Sources on over 1300 types of business. Thus, this encyclopedia will lead you to the main sources on each particular business.

2. Industry Surveys

   Standard and Poors Corporation, 345 Hudson St., N.Y., N.Y. 10014 This publication covers the past performance and future trends of 69 major domestic industries, from Accident Insurance to Zinc. 1500 companies are covered showing ratio comparisons and balance sheet comparisons for ten year periods.

3. 1979 U.S. Industrial Outlook Projection to 1983

   U.S. Department of Commerce, U.S. Government Printing Office. This publication projects industrial trends over the next five years for 200 industries.

4. Business Profiles

   The Bank of America has published business start up advice booklets on 29 specific small businesses. See Section 4.2 for further details.

5. The Starting and Managing Series

   SBA publications - U.S. Government Printing Office, Washington, D.C. 20402. The SBA has published 19 booklets covering the start up aspects of specific small businesses. Only four of these are currently available:

   - Starting and Managing a Pet Shop 045-000-00065-6 40 pgs $.75
   - Starting and Managing a Small Retail Music Store 045-000-00107-5 81 pgs $1.30
   - Starting and Managing an Employment Agency 045-000-00109-1 118 pags $1.30
   - Starting and Managing a Small Shoe Store 045-000-00127-0 104 pgs $1.35.

   However, the 19 publications have been grouped together and published by Drake Publishers, Inc. in three volumes at $4.95 each volume.

   Volume Two: Retail Camera Shop, Retail Flower Store, Carwash, Bookkeeping Service.

   Volume Three: A Building Business, Employment Agency, Retail Jewelry

7/*Information Sources*

Store, Retail Hardware Store.
Volume Four: Retail Music Store, Retail Drug Store, Drive-In Restaurant, Small Restaurant, Antomatic Vending Machine Business, Shoe Repair Shop.

6) Management Assistance Publications

Small Business Administration   The SBA publishes a) Counseling notes on 25 business and b) Bibliographies of reference sources on 19 different businesses. These are available free of charge by calling toll free 800-433-7212 (Texas only call 800-792-8901). The complete list of free management assistance publication is compiled on SBA publication SBA 115A. Note, the for sale list is available on publication SBA 115B.

8

Buying An Existing Business

8.0 When considering the purchase of an existing business there are some very important intangible factors to be considered, as well as the tangible factors that can be evaluated by an examination of the business operating records.

The primary intangible factors arise from taking over an ongoing concern and are as follows:

1. Bad Will – is there a legacy of bad will surrounding the business, such as a bad reputation, dissastisfied customers, and so on?
2. Personnel – will the new personnel stay with you? Do you think that they should stay; will you be able to manage them?
3. Management Skill – do you have the management skill for this particular business? Could you learn it? What would be the effects of your learning period?
4. Prior Ownership – why is the owner really selling the business? Are there undisclosed factors involved?

The answers to these intangibles do not lie in any documentation but can be uncovered by questioning the right people. Formulate your questions and go and ask your local banker, suppliers, creditors, customers, employees, former owners and, of course, your would be competitors. From all of this you should be able to build up a reasonably accurate picture of the business.

8.1 FINANCIAL SOURCES

The most important tangible data is, of course, financial. There are four main sources of this data; 1) financial statements, 2) income tax returns, 3) internal records, and 4) external sources.

The seller will usually, at the request of the buyer, prepare a set of financial statements. Even if the seller "warrants" his statements, the buyer should ask a CPA to make an audit of the financial statements, looking especially hard at certain critical items as discussed below. The CPA may, after his audit sign a standard certificate which states that in his opinion the accounts fairly reflect the financial position of the business. If he has difficulty in making such a statement he will either qualify his certificate or state that he is unable to make any opinion.

The buyer should request the financial statements for at least the past five

8/Buying An Existing Business

years, and longer if possible.

Income tax returns should also be requested for the same periods. Corporations and partnerships show balance sheet data whereas sole proprietorships do not. It must be understood that income tax statements are prepared for different purposes other than financial statements and, therefore, often present a somewhat different financial picture.

Internal data, such as purchase receipts, sales records, cash budgets, cost control sheets, etc. all help to broaden the picture. The buyer should also insist that the seller provide a cash flow projection for the next year after the sale.

External data is also available from many sources. Suppliers, bankers, public tax records are sometimes available. A very useful piece of information is a credit rating report on the business, such as a Dun and Bradstreet report. This information is only directly available to subscribers to the credit rating service, but there are ways, such as a friendly banker, to obtain such reports.

In the case where there are no financial statements, then the buyer is forced to construct his own version of the financial statements based on the other available sources.

BALANCE SHEET EVALUATION

The balance sheet contains information on the assets and the liabilities of the business. Each particular item should be investigated for its own sake, but also so that ratios can be constructed to compare with like businesses.

- Cash and Marketable Securities

    The cash is the sum of the petty cash account and the amount in the business checking account. Any securities should be stated at their market value (whatever their original cost).

- Accounts Receivable and Allowance for Bad Debts

    The primary task here is to determine how much of the accounts receivables is collectible. Bad debts must be deducted - an overall industry average figure being approximately 0.15% of sales. However, more accurate figures for a particular type of business may be obtained from a) Almanac of Business and Industrial Financial Ratios, see Section 7.1, or b) Cost of Doing Business - Dun and Bradstreet leaflet (see your local library). Next the accounts must be "aged", that is grouped by the number of days outstanding. Long overdue accounts are probably not collectible, and the bad debt allowance may need to be revised accordingly.

    Invoices should be checked against signed shipping receipts to establish that the goods have been received but not paid for. Large clients can be contacted to verify specific accounts.

- Notes Receivable

    In a small business notes receivable should be negligable or non-existent. If they do exist it usually means that a client has defaulted on a payment and has signed a note. This is obviously a bad sign and a low percentage should be placed on the value of notes collectible unless there is good indication to the contrary.

145

- Inventories

    Each item in the inventory must be valued and aged. In a retail or wholesale operation the value to be used is the lower of the cost or replacement value. In a manufacturing business, the raw materials are valued in the same manner, the work in process and the finished inventory are valued by the added direct labor and indirect costs involved in each process. In this valuation activity the services of a professional appraiser may be required. The next step it to age the inventory. In many instances the inventory is worth less with increasing age because of obsolescence. Occassionally, the inventory, although listed at full cost, is largely worthless because it is defective.

- Prepaid and Deferred Items

    These are prepaid expense items that will be valuable to the business in the future. Examples of these items are prepaid taxes, insurance, office supplies, advertising expenses and so forth. The buyer should examine each item to determine if he can make full use of the prepaid item. If he cannot, for example the prepaid advertising may show a picture of the present owner, then the value will have to be prorated.

- Property, Equipment and Furnishings

    These items are difficult to value directly, and their current market value may not truely reflect their worth to the prospective buyer. The only true method of valuation, unless the new buyer is contemplating liquidating the business, is to value the assets based on their income generating capacity.

- Depreciation

    Depreciation is recorded on the owner's books and is the amount that he has allowed for wear and tear on the fixed assets of the business. The amount of depreciation should never be used to try to arrive at the value of the fixed assets, since it is merely an allowance made for income tax purposes and does not usually reflect the true aging process undergone by an asset.

- Intangible Assets

    Usually, the amount recorded for patents, trademarks and goodwill on a small business is usually very small. Occassionally, goodwill will appear if the present owner purchased the goodwill and has not amortized it over a period of years.

    You should carefully check with local business people, local bankers, customers, employees, etc., to make sure that the business does indeed have a store of goodwill behind it. Some businesses have a store of bad will because of bad business practices, employee relations or some other failing.

We now turn our attention to the liabilities section of the balance sheet:

- Accounts Payable

    Again, accounts payable should be aged to see how far the current owner

8/Buying An Existing Business

is behind with payment to his suppliers. If the present owner is in financial difficulties he may be a long way past due with his payments to the point of creditors applying mechanics liens on the assets of his business. The responsibility for payment of goods that have, perhaps, already been sold is a matter for your lawyer to settle in the purchase contract for the business.

- Notes Payable

    These are very similar to accounts payable. Perhaps the cleanest method of disposing of these is to arrange that the current owner be responsible for the payment of all outstanding notes payable.

- Taxes Payable

    Whatever point in time a business is purchased there will always be an amount of accrued tax liability to either Federal, state, county, city or other local authority. Every tax item should be thoroughly evaluated, especially FICA and sales taxes, to establish the responsibility for payment and that there are no unpaid tax liabilities current on which interest penalties must be paid.

    Partnerships and sole proprietorships are not liable for Federal or state income tax on current income. In addition, any underpayment of past taxes are the liability of the new owner, unless otherwise stipulated.

- Long Term Liabilities

    Documentation should exist stating the terms and conditions of any long term liability - such as a mortgage or a long term note. Again the responsibility for payment of these liabilities must be established.

- Other Liabilities

    There may be other liabilities that are not documented on the balance sheet, either by accident or design. For example, inventory may have been ordered but not received so that both the inventory and the liability for its payment have not appeared on the books.

    Another very important class of hidden liability arises from the past operations of the business. Faulty merchandise may have been sold to customers that will be returned in the future. There may be potential legal problems and costs arising from the faulty completion of a past contract. The firm's insurance coverage may not be sufficient to cover past claims against it.

    These matters are very difficult to establish in detail. However, almost any business has some potential liability of one sort or another. Very often, it is difficult for the current owner to be certain of just what the potential claims against his business might be as a result of his past operations. Even if he does know, he may be unwilling to speculate. However, any such claims clearly have a potential impact on the future earnings of the business.

- Owner's Equity

    This is, of course, the difference between the business' assets and liabilities, and represents the amount of owner's interest in the business. It does not, in fact, represent the value of the business to a purchaser. Owner's equity must be adjusted to account for any re-evaluation of the total assets and the total liabilities of a business. Clearly, if contigent liabilities are added to the total liabilities, for instance, the value of the owner's equity is reduced accordingly.

8.3 INCOME STATEMENT EVALUATION

- Net Income

You must establish that the reported income was actually received over the period stated. You should check the income stated with the totals for each month as recorded in the company's books. You should, in turn, check the reasonableness of the recorded monthly income figures by comparing them with the month over month sales ratios of like businesses. In the women's specialty retailing industry, for example, the average sales in December is 11.6% of the years total, whereas it is only 6.7% in February.

Thus, in any business there are usually seasonal income peaks which "fingerprint" that particular industry. You should compare the monthly sales of the business under consideration both with general industry ratios and with that business' prior year ratios. Any significant discrepancy between any month over month comparison should be investigated.

In general, the reference sources provided in Section 7.2 should lead you to the ratios for the business of your particular interest. However, two references are useful in this regard:

1. Survey of Current Business (2 parts)
    U.S. Department of Commerce
    Government Printing Office
    Washington, D.C. 20402

    This monthly publication includes statistics and articles on significant economic developments. It presents statistics on national income, business population, manufacturing and retail sales, inventories and orders.

2. Barometer of Small Business
    Accounting Corporation of America (1974)

    This publication presents, in bar chart form, a monthly index of sales trends tabulated from the financial records of clients of the Accounting Corporation of America. These records cover a wide range of industrial and commercial businesses.

- Expenses

The amount of each component of business expense should be compared with industry norms. In this case the industry norms can be found from the "Almanac of Business Ratios" and "Robert Morris Associates" publication (see Section 7.1). The various ratios must be consistent from year to year and with industry norms. Again, any discrepancy should be investigated.

One item of contention can be the owner's salary. Often this is deflated for income tax purpose and inflated for business sale purposes. It can be inflated by minimizing the expenses charged against the business. The actual value of each expense item must be checked. The rent, for example, can be checked against the prevailing values in the business area. The lease agreement may have set the rent at a low value and may be due to expire. The insurance coverage may have been cut back. The advertising budget may have been reduced. Needed repairs and maintenance may have been deferred. The amount set aside for depreciation may be unrealistically low. The methods of predicting just what the various components of expense should be will be discussed in a later section.

NOTE - A couple of expense items to watch for are:

- Common ownership situations, where a larger parent concern has operated the business being sold. The problem to be aware of is the possibility that the parent has, in fact, performed many management functions for the business without properly charging for them. Such functions could be group employee benefits or group bookkeeping services.

- Low occupany charges can result where the business owner also owns the building. This building can also be fully depreciated and thus cause no rent or depreciation charge to appear on the books.

RATIO ANALYSIS

There are several companies publishing ratio data for wholesalers, retailers and manufacturers. However, we shall use Robert Morris Associates data (see Section 7.1) since it is probably the most current and is used by bank loan and credit officers. In fact, RMA is a product of the commercial banking community.

As a first step the current financial statements of the business under investigation should be analysed and adjusted in the manner described in the preceeding two sections. Next the various accounts are grouped and presented as amounts and percentages of the whole as shown below.

Pleasure Boats, Inc.
Balance Sheet, Dec. 31, 1977

Assets ($K)	Amount	%	Equities ($K)	Amount	%
Cash & Equivalent	25	8.4	Notes Pay (S.T)	88	29.7
Accts Rec.	20	6.4	Cur. Mat. LTD	7	2.4
Inventory	193	65.2	Acc. Payable	29	9.5
Other	2	0.7	Accrued Exp.	9	3.0
Total Current	240	81.1	Other	26	8.8
Net Fixed Assts	50	16.9	Total Current	158	53.4
Intangibles	1	0.3	Long Term Debt	33	11.1
All Other Non-current	5	1.7	All Other Non-current	4	2.4
Total	296	100.0	Net Worth	101	34.1
			Total Equities	296	100.0

Pleasure Boats, Inc.
Income Statement, Year Ended Dec. 31, 1977

	Amount ($K)	%
Net Sales	770	100.0
Cost of Sales	599	77.8
Gross Profit	171	22.2
Officers Comp.	30	3.9
Lease/Rental Exp.	12	1.5
Depreciation	5	0.7
Interest	11	1.4
All Other Operating Exp.	83	10.7
Profit Before Taxes	30	3.9

RMA publish 16 ratios grouped in five principal categories:

- Liquidity - a measure of the ability of the business to pay for its liabilities.
- Coverage - a reflection of the ability of the business to pay for its debt obligations.
- Leverage - reflects the amount of debt the business owes in relation to owner's equity.
- Operating - indicates the management performance.
- Expense Items - reflects the effect on business operations of key expense items.

Liquidity Ratios

1. Current ratio. This is found by dividing the current assets by the current liabilities, i.e.

    $$\frac{\text{Current Assets}}{\text{Current Liabilities}} = \frac{240}{158} = 1.52$$

    The higher the value of this ratio, the greater is the possibility that the business can pay for its current liabilities.

2. Quick Ratio or Acid Test. This is a sharper test of liquidity than the current ratio, since it reflects those items that are either cash or can be quickly converted to cash to pay for current liabilities.

    $$\frac{\text{Cash \& Equivalents + Accounts Receivable}}{\text{Total Current Liabilities}}$$

    $$= \frac{25 + 20}{158} = 0.28$$

    A 1:1 quick ratio is sometimes considered normal. However, in this industry inventories are high and lower quick ratios are the norm.

3. Sales/Accounts Receivables Ratio. This ratio gives a measure of how fast credit sales are collected. The higher the value of this ratio, the faster accounts are being collected, which implies a) lower working capital is needed, and b) there are probably fewer uncollectible accounts.

    $$\frac{\text{Net Sales}}{\text{Accounts + Notes Receiable}} = \frac{770}{20} = 38.5$$

8/Buying An Existing Business

Another measure of this is the average number of days that receivables are outstanding, i.e.,

$$\frac{365}{\text{Sales/Account Receivables}} = \frac{365}{38.5} = 9.5 \text{ Days}$$

This is an unusually short time and reflects one fact that boats are "high ticket" items, which are usually financed by commercial loan companies and not by the boat dealers themselves. Thus, the boat dealer quickly collects his payment from the commercial loan company.

Notice that this type of business is critically dependent on commercial financing being available at a price acceptable to the buyer of a small boat.

4. Cost of Sales/Inventory Ratio. This reflects the number of times the inventory turns over during the year and has to be replenished. Thus,

$$\frac{\text{Cost Of Sales}}{\text{Inventory}} = \frac{599}{193} = 3.1$$

The average number of days an item is in inventory can also be calculated:

$$\frac{365}{\text{Cost of Sales/Inventory}} = \frac{365}{3.1} = 118 \text{ Days}$$

Various interpretations can be placed on this ratio.

- A short inventory time can imply a high volume, high turnover business with lower working capital needs and good management.
- A high inventory time can either reflect obsolete, unattractive merchandise or an increased inventory build up.

Note, both the receivables or inventory turnover ratios are not particularly sound ratios as presented, since seasonal fluctuations are not taken into account and where, therefore, comparisons with like businesses can be misleading. One attempt to improve the ratio would involve averaging beginning and end of year inventories and receivables. A better method would be to average the monthly values of inventory and accounts receivable across the entire year. Data may be available from the financial records of the business to make this possible. At the very least, you should recognise at what point in the business cycle the books were closed in order to understand the state of the inventories and receivables.

5. Sales/Working Capital Ratio. This measures the efficiency of using working capital, so that a high ratio means that less working capital is needed to support a given volume of sales. This implies high inventory turnover and short credit collection periods. Thus,

$$\frac{\text{Sales}}{\text{Working Capital}} = \frac{\text{Sales}}{\text{Current Assets - Current Liabilities}}$$

$$= \frac{770}{240-158} = 9.4$$

Note that a very high ratio indicates growing current liabilities, which implies a potential creditor payment problem.

Coverage Ratios

6. Earnings Before Interest and Taxes/Interest. This is one indicator of the firm's ability to service its debt out of current profits. Thus,

$$\frac{\text{Earnings + interest}}{\text{Annual Interest Expense}} = \frac{30 + 11}{11} = 3.7$$

This ratio indicates the firms ability to meet its interest payments from its earnings. A high ratio indicates that the firm could pay for additional debt it required. Note, however, that the stated earnings reflect somewhat the variable amount taken out as owners compensation. If, for example, the owner were to take out a smaller salary, there would be more earnings available to improve this ratio.

7. Cash Flow/Current Maturing Long Term Debt. This ratio indicates the firm's ability to pay the principal of the current portion of the long term debt from its cash flow. Cash flow is here defined as the net income plus depreciation, depletion or amortizing expense (these are items which are charged as expenses but do not require any cash payment to be made during the year by the business). Thus,

$$\frac{\text{Cash Flow}}{\text{Current LTD}} = \frac{30 + 5}{7} = 5.0$$

Naturally, not all the cash flow is available to service long term debt, but it is a good measure of the debt coverage.

Leverage Ratios

Leverage ratios are a measure of how much a firm is dependent on debt financing compared with owner's equity. A highly leveraged firm with a large debt burden can earn higher revenues with a given amount of owner's equity if it can, at the same time, earn a large enough profit to properly service the debt. It is a precarious position because any cut back in revenues will expose such a firm to the possibility of defaulting on its debt servicing requirements.

8. Fixed Assets/Net Worth. This ratio measures the amount of owner's equity invested in fixed assets. Of course, if a high proportion of the fixed assets are leased this ratio becomes distorted. Thus,

$$\frac{\text{Fixed Assets}}{\text{Tangible Net Worth}} = \frac{50}{101} = 0.5$$

9. Total Liabilities/Tangible Net Worth. This is the direct ratio of the amount owing to external creditors compared with the amount invested in the business by the owner. The lower this ratio, the more the security of the creditors and the greater the borrowing capacity of the business. Thus,

$$\frac{\text{Total Liabilities}}{\text{Tangible Net Worth}} = \frac{195}{101} = 1.9$$

Operating Ratios

10. Percentage Profits Before Taxes/Tangible Net Worth. This ratio reflects the profits generated by a given investment. However, since owner's salaries are expensed prior to showing profits and can be adjusted, this

8/*Buying An Existing Business*

ratio is not as meaninful as it might appear. Thus,

$$\frac{\% \text{ Profit}}{\text{Tangible Net Worth}} = \frac{30 \times 100}{101} = 30\%$$

It must be noted that this amount of profit does not pass free and clear to the business owner, since corporate income tax must be paid (if the business is incorporated) and long term debt repaid.

11. Percentage Profits Before Taxes/Total Assets. This ratio reflects the profit generating capability of the business' assets. Note, however, that fully depreciated fixed assets can cause distortions. Thus,

$$\frac{\% \text{ Profit}}{\text{Total Assets}} = \frac{30 \times 100}{296} = 10.1\%$$

12. Sales/Net Fixed Assets. This ratio reflects the revenue generating capability of the net fixed assets (after depreciation). Again heavily depreciated assets can distort this ratio. Thus,

$$\frac{\text{Sales}}{\text{Net Fixed Assets}} = \frac{770}{50} = 15.4$$

13. Net Sales/Total Assets. This is an overall indicator of the revenue generating capability of a business. Thus,

$$\frac{\text{Net Sales}}{\text{Total Assets}} = \frac{770}{296} = 2.6$$

Expense To Sales Ratios

The following three ratios characterise the amount of supporting expenses required to generate sales. It is a measure of operating efficiency for the sales effort.

14. Percentage of Depreciation + Amortization/Sales. For this business, the value of this ratio is:

$$\frac{5 \times 100}{770} = 0.65\%$$

15. Percentage of Lease or Rental Expenses/Sales. For this business, the value of this ratio is:

$$\frac{12 \times 100}{770} = 1.56\%$$

16. Percentage Officer's Compensation/Sales. For this business, the value of this ratio is:

$$\frac{30 \times 100}{770} = 3.9\%$$

USE OF RATIO ANALYSIS

It is very worth while to calculate the 16 RMA ratios just described. In doing so you begin to get a good "feel" for the operational characteristics of the business. With luck, you will be able to compare the RMA ratios for the business that interests you with the averages for the industry as a whole. More importantly RMA publishes the upper and lower quartile values for each ratio.

Any particular ratio that seems to be outside the normally expected limits should be thoroughly investigated.

8.6 TREND ANALYSIS

A more powerful method of exploring the operating characteristics of the business is the use of trend analysis. In this technique, the various ratios are calculated for the past five years. If a particular ratio shows marked decrease or increase over a period of years, or shows a sudden change after a period of stability, the reason for the change should be explored.

Another trend analysis technique is to examine the variation, in amount and percentage, of selected categories of the income statement. In this respect, Troy's "Almanac of Business and Industrial Financial Ratios" published 12 operating factors as a percentage of net sales. A simple example of this method is shown below:

	1972 $K(%)	1973 $K(%)	1974 $K(%)	Troy Value %
Net Sales	623 (100)	693 (100)	770 (100)	100
Gross Margin	237 (38)	243 (35)	246 (32)	34
Wages	46.7 (7.5)	55.4 (8)	69.3 (9)	8.2
Advertising	13.3 (2.1)	31.2 (4.5)	11.5 (1.5)	2.5
Rent	25 (4.0)	25 (3.6)	25 (3.2)	4.0
Profits	56 (9.0)	58.9 (8.5)	61.6 (8.0)	8.5

You will note that the percentages for each are not far from those given in Troy. However, the trends are revealing:

- The percentage gross margin is declining .
- The cost of wages is rising faster then sales.
- Advertising has fluctuated, but not had much influence on the upward sales trend.
- Rent has declined as a percentage of sales, falling to below the norm. Its steady value may mean a long term lease - when does it expire?
- Profits have fallen from above average to below average, although they have increased in value over the three year period. This is not an encouraging trend.

Again, this type of analysis gives you a "feel" for the expenses of the business, and should enable you to judge when any expense item is out of line.

8.7 MARKET ANALYSIS

In the previous section, the sales growth trend was discussed. This gives an indication of the probable future growth, but not enough to be conclusive. The methodology presented in section 6.1.1 should enable you to define future market potential for your type of business. Some further factors to consider are:

- Population Changes - these may be vital to your product. It may be the type of product that responds to total population changes, or, perhaps, only to young married women. The predictions of changes in census tract information will be helpful here.

- Income Changes - the income to consider here is the net spendable income rather than gross earnings. The amount spent for different types of goods

8/Buying An Existing Business

and services depends on the level of per captia income. Your business may be influenced by changes in district, city, region or national income levels.

- Competiton - this factor may be one reason why a business is being sold. Often, successful businesses are copied by many competitors, thus decreasing the average income for all. You must define your marketing area, define your competitors and assess their significance. A key clue is to discover how many competitors have entered and left your market area during the last year. You should try to assess the advertising effort, promotional effort, physical appearance, pricing strategy and reputation of your competitors. Often, you can assess a competitor's sales volume, by counting the number of his sales people, floorspace, or valuing his displayed inventory. Industry standards that give the ratios of the sales volume to these operating factors are published for most industries; see

  - Robert Morris Associates, Annual Statement Studies; see industry cost references in RMA's appendix.
  - Encyclopedia of Business Information Sources (see Section 7.3).

Data on the number and type of businesses (by SIC code) in specific census tract areas is published by the U.S. Department of Commerce, Bureau of the Census in its publication County and City Data Book, 1977, G.P.O.

If you can, by various means, obtain Dun and Bradstreet reports on your competitors you will find a wealth of data on their ownership affiliations, income and balance sheet history, credit payment record and past operating history. The Dun and Bradstreet credit rating reports are provided to subscribers, usually financial institutions, for the purposes of judging the creditworthiness of a particular business.

An assessment should be made of the sales volume of the business compared with the total sales volume for the market area. Given comparisions of number of sales people, floor space, inventory, etc., is the business getting its fair share of the total sales volume? If it has a markedly higher or lower sales volume than its calculated market share, you should try to discover what factors are causing the disparity. Perhaps, when you rate factors such as brand selection, advertising, sales person skill, location, external appearance, internal atmosphere, pricing and so on, the reasons for the disparity will become apparent. Perhaps the customer services offered cause the difference. You must, however, form a judgement as to whether the factors can be maintained, if favorable, or changed if they are detrimental.

- Location - it is said that there are three vital factors in the success of a retail store - location, location and location. It is true, as we all know, that traffic patterns develop in a particular shopping area such that certain locations always seem to be busy whilst others always seem to be quiet. You might perform a simple count of the number of potential shoppers passing the business location in selected periods of the week compared with the numbers passing competitive locations.

The status of the location should be investigated to determine if any plans exist for rezoning, highway changes, or general rebuilding programs. You should look at the possibility of floorspace expansion should the business volume require it.

8.8 LEGAL ASPECTS OF BUSINESS ACQUISITION

The major aspect to be settled in buying an ongoing business is how to properly transfer title of both the assets and the liabilities. Each particular asset must be examined and called out in the purchase agreement. If any particular asset is left in question, you can anticipate future trouble about its legal ownership.

Liabilities are a much more serious aspect of business transfer, since many contingent liabilities can arise in the future because of past business operations. Some information exists only in the sellers head, but a great deal is documented. Obviously, a buyer should make special effort to research all sources for information concerning the legal aspects of any business he is contemplating purchasing.

- Outstanding Contracts - at the instant of transfer most businesses will have contracts outstanding for the purchase or sale of merchandise or services. Typically, only contract rights and not contract obligations may be transferred to a third party without the consent of the individual or company with whom the contract was made. For example, even if the buyer takes over the lease as part of the purchase contract, the seller remains liable for payment of the unexpired portion of the lease should the buyer default.

  It is important for the buyer to review all contract documents, such as leases or loans, to determine if they are transferable to him. Very often, contracts will expressly prohibit their assignment to third parties. It may be that the only way the buyer can assure himself the rights to a contract is to renegotiate it in his favor. Typical examples of contracts that may cause trouble are credit arrangements, prior manufacturing agreements and liens. The buyer should examine carefully all such contracts <u>before</u> any purchase agreement is signed. In particular; insurance coverage should be examined for completeness of coverage and transferability; accounts receivable should be examined for collectibility - it may be that these should remain with the seller; all financing agreements should be examined for repayment terms and conditions; any employment contracts; stock options; etc. Purchase contracts should be noted, expecially for repayment terms.

- Evidence Of Ownership - it is important to establish that the seller owns clear title to all fixed assets - land, buildings, machinery, furniture and equipment. The abstractor's certification for each piece of land should be examined for any mechanics liens, tax liens, unpaid assessments or remaining mortgages. Receipts for equipment and ownership titles of automobiles and trucks should also be asked for where such title evidence is lacking. The possibility is that the item in question is rented, leased, on approval, borrowed or event stolen.

- Public Records - separate records exist for chattel morgages, trust receipts, assignment of accounts receivables, conditional sales contracts. Any liens against these items can usually be discovered from the Office of Records. In addition, liens on real estate will usually show up on the title abstract.

- Court Records - court records may reveal judgements or lawsuits against the business, which involve liens against fixed assets. Thus, a buyer of corporate stock or a buyer who assumes liabilities in his purchase must particularly concern himself with such possibilities. Not withstanding any search of court records, liabilities may still exist. Again, the buyer must question employees, vendors, salesmen, bankers, insurance agents, and anyone else familiar with the business to discover potential liability situations.

- Tax Liabilities - the various tax liabilities of a business were discussed in Chapter Three. Clearly, in acquiring an ongoing business you will be acquiring some accrued tax liability. Has adequate funds been set aside for payment of these obligations? Have past taxes been paid or are there any tax assessments still outstanding? A check with the relevent tax collection agencies will reveal the current situation.

- Legal Aspects Of Property - if you buy a building and land you should check the boundaries and zoning regulations. In addition, you should verify that the building codes are not being violated. There may be limitations to any changes dictated by zoning or building codes that could limit the use of your building or make futher expansion impossible.

    The city, county or state planning department should be consulted for future proposed changes concerning zoning, highways, access, flood plane, sewage areas, etc. These potential or planned changes may be enough to make business continuance at this location impossible.

9 VALUATION OF AN ACQUIRED BUSINESS

At some point in your discussions with the owner of the business, the question of the price to be paid for the business must be faced. This is the most difficult aspect of the negotiations since both parties normally want to obtain the best deal for themselves. Be aware that you as a buyer have some advantage since you are free not to buy this particular business, not to buy at this time or to select from several other business opportunities. The seller, on the other hand, has only the one business to sell and probably has a good reason to be out of it reasonably quickly.

In placing a value on a business there are two basic methods to be used depending on the situation:

1. Asset Valuation - this method is <u>only</u> used in the situation where the business as such is not operating very profitably and you want to pick up the assets of the business either for incorporation into an existing business or to use for a different type of business. <u>Never</u> make the mistake of thinking that you can buy an ailing business and turn it around; you had best change its entire image and start again.

    The seller might suggest that you pay the book value or the replacement value for the assets. The book value, of course, is the value of the assets shown in the accounting records of the company and may be no where near their market value. The replacement value is the cost of going to various suppliers and buying exactly the same items, less of course an allowance for wear and tear.

Both these methods tend to favor the seller, for in actual fact he can only hope for the liquidation value of his assets. The liquidation value is the price he would obtain if he held an action to sell his assets to knowledgeable buyers.

It may be that the buyer is only interested in part of the inventory or part of the fixed assets. Since the buyer is saving the seller the time and trouble of an auction and the uncertainties of collecting the proceeds, he should offer somewhat under the liquidation value of the assets. The greater the proportion of the assets he buys the futher below liquidation value his offer should be. This may seem heartless, but you can rest assured that if you were the seller that is what you would receive. The liquidation valuation is the price you pay for failure and that price can be high. As a would be entrepreneur you should recognize the price of failure as well as the rewards of success. In terms of placing a liquidation value on the assets of the business, you should turn to experts for advice; pay a used equipment dealer to visit the business with you and price the equipment; ask a wholesaler to place a value on the existing inventory.

2. Return On Investment - this method is used when you are purchasing an ongoing, profitable business that you intend to operate. You should, of course, go through and value the assets as descirbed in Section 8.2. However, the overriding concern is whether or not the business is a good investment for your time and effort. You could stay working for someone else and invest your money in a T Bill, which provides a safe return these days of about 10%.

The first step is to create a pro-forma income statement for the next year of operations. This must be based on a realistic assessment of both the sales trend and the trend of operating costs. Using the purchase of a retail store as an example, we have:

Quality Gifts, Inc.
Pro-forma Income Statement For The
Year Ending December 31, 1980

Net Sales	$200,000
Cost Of Goods Sold	120,000
Gross Margin	80,000
Operating Expenses*	70,500
Profit	$ 9,500

* Includes owner's salary of $16,500.

The next step is to reasses the balance sheet items, such as the inventory, to produce a corrected version of the balance sheet as was described in Section 8.2.

Quality Gifts, Inc.
Balance Sheet, December 31, 1979

Assets($)		Liabilities($)	
Cash	10,000	Notes Payable (ST)	7,000
Acc. Rec.	14,000	Current LTD	3,000
Inventory	40,000	Acc. Payable	14,000
Total Current	64,000	Accrued Exp.	4,000
Fixed Assets	12,000	Total Current	28,000
Other	4,000	Long Term Debt	12,000
Total Assets	80,000	Owner's Equity	40,000
		Total Liab. + N.W.	80,000

It is interesting to see how much cash is required to run this business using the corrected figures. You will note that if we include other assets in with fixed assets we have a simple equation:

Current Assets + Fixed Assets = Current Liabilities + Long Term Debt + Owner's Equity.

Rearranging this we have:

(Current Assets - Current Liabilities) + Fixed Assets = Long Term Debt + Owner's Equity

Or,

Working Capital + Fixed Assets = Long Term Debt + Owner's equity

Current Assets-Current Liabilities is called the Working Capital, which is the amount of money required to finance the buying and selling of inventory.

In this case the amount of money required to run the business is $36,000 for working capital plus $16,000 for fixed assets (etc.). This amount is funded by $40,000 of owner's equity plus $12,000 of long term debt for a total of $52,000. Thus, on a balance sheet assets basis the business is valued at $52,000 without any considerations for goodwill. However, its final asset valuation depends on the disposition of the various portions of the current assets and current liabilities. Suppose, for example, that the current owner retains the cash and the accounts receivable, but agrees to pay all the current liabilities. The business is then worth, on an assets basis, $52,000 - (10,000 + 14,000) + 28,000 = 56,000, which also equals the value of the total assets less cash and accounts receivable.

Suppose the buyer pays $56,000 in cash for the business, his operating profit would be higher than $9,500 since he would not be paying deductible interest on the long term debt. In this case the total long-term debt outstanding is $15,000 ($12,000 shown as long term debt plus $3,000 shown as current portion of long term debt). Let us assume that the interest cost is $1,500 (10% of outstanding debt). Thus the buyer's profit will be $11,000 for an investment of $56,000, or a return of 19.6%.

If the buyer is satisfied both with the salary ($16,500) and with the return on his investment (19.6%) then the business would be purchased right at asset value. Alternatively, if the total profit, after adjusting for not paying interest, were $13,000 and the buyer required a 20% return on his investment, he would be prepared to pay $13,000 divided by 0.2 or $65,000. In this case he is paying $65,000 - $56,000 or $9,000 for goodwill.

Again, if the business profit, after adjustment for not paying interest were only $10,000, the buyer would offer $50,000 to maintain a 20% return.

You will notice that the amount of owner's salary has a major effect on these calculation because of its influence on profits. You will want to be certain that the quoted owner's salary is reasonable for this type of business. Here Robert Morris Associates "Annual Statement Studies" comes to our aid to quote the median and quartile percentages of the owner's salary with respect to net sales.

You will also note that if the buyer is required to pay for any current liabilities the purchase price should be reduced by the corresponding amount. Thus, if, in the first case where the business is sold at asset value, the buyer was required to pay for accounts payable of $14,000, the business would be valued at $56,000 - $14,000 or $42,000.

It is worth making a final point that the buyer could further increase his return on investment by resorting to leverage. Suppose, for example, that in the first case where the business is worth $56,000 the buyer provides $28,000 of his own money and borrows $28,000 at a 10% interest rate. Thus, his annual profit would be reduced to $11,000 - (28,000 x 10%) or $8,200. Let us further assume that the borrower chooses not to pay off the long term debt, but only pay interest on it. Thus, his actual return is now $8,200 divided by $28,000 or 28.3%. You can see, therefore that any return on investment calculations can be distorted by the amount of leverage - the only accurate calculations being the return on total money required (the buyer's own funds plus any borrowed funds).

8.10 THE PURCHASE CONTRACT

Once the purchase price has been agreed, the various conditions surrounding the sale must be put down in a written agreement. Two other major considerations will also have been taken into account:

- The effects of taxation on both the buyer and seller.
- The assumption of any business liabilities by the buyer.

If the buyer purchases stock rather than assets he automaticaly assumes past liabilities because of the legal continuity of the business. The buyer may want to limit contingent liabilities by including a clause in the purchase contract that specifically indemnifies the buyer against these liabilities. The buyer can gain further assurance by requiring that part of the purchase price be held in escrow against the possible contingent liabilities.

The buyer should also want clauses in the agreement to protect him against undisclosed liens, against the seller competing against him locally or any changes that take place in the business between the time of first agreement and the closing of the deal.

The purchase agreement, therefore, should contain clauses covering the following items:

8/Buying An Existing Business

- The date and parties to the contract.
- The full description and address of the business premises.
- The purchase price and a full accounting of what is being purchased.
- The terms of payment must be specified, that is, the amount of downpayment and the amount of amortized payment over a specified number of years at a specified interest rate. The seller may request some form of security for payment of the balance of the purchase price. This security can take the form of a chattel mortgage on equipment, inventory, etc., which were part of the assets of the business.
- The method of determining just what adjustments to the final purchase price are to be made at the actual time of takeover. These adjustments arise because of the fact that in an ongoing business the stated assets change from day to day; for example the inventory may rise or fall.
- If the buyer is prepared to assume any liabilities and contracts, such as leases or mortgages payable, these must be listed.
- The seller should make expressed warranties of certain items. These items should include; warrantees of good and unencumbered title to all assets specified in the sale, financial statements, unspecified (contingent or otherwise) liabilities, contingent lawsuits, adverse business influences, and the veracity of all statements and material supplied to the buyer.
- The buyer's rights are protected during the period between the signing of the contract and the actual physical takeover. This is most important, since a dramatic change in fortunes such as a fire could wipe out an unprotected buyer. In this regard, two specific clauses are necessary:

  a) Statement that the seller assumes all risk of a loss through fire, theft, etc. during the interim period. If the loss is sufficient to close down the business to a specified extent, the buyer must have the right to withdraw from the agreement.

  b) The seller must operate the business in a satisfactory manner to serve the best interests of the seller. He must maintain accurate records such that the process of adjustments can take place fairly. He must give the buyer full access to the business premises and financial records during this time.

- In situations where it is appropriate, the seller can be asked to sign a covenant not to compete with the buyer or his successors. This situation most commonly occurs where a purchaser has paid a considerable amount for goodwill.
- The time, date and place of closing should be specified together with any conditions on both parties at the time of closing, such as exchanging documents or records, etc.
- A final clause idemnifies the buyer as a result of the seller's breach of warrantee or contractual obligations. Often a part of the purchase price is placed in escrow against the possibility of such a breach, and a method of resolving a buyer-seller dispute without resorting to litigation is specified.
- The agreement must be signed by both parties and witnessed.

11 FINALIZING THE TRANSACTION

Apart from signing the purchase agreement there are certain other important aspects to be attended to before the transaction is complete.

- **Bulk Sale Act**

    This act requires that a seller of a business provide a warranted list of creditors to the buyer and that the buyer informs the creditors of the sale. The Act protects creditors from situations where the seller might abscond with the proceeds of the sale without settling with his creditors. Thus, creditors are given an opportunity to attach the proceeds of the sale if necessary. Failure to properly comply with the Bulk Sale Act may result in an impounding of business assets. Thus, the buyer should make certain that all the requirements of this Act have been met before closing the sale.

- **Financing The Sale**

    The buyer needs three categories of funding, 1) purchase price funds, 2) working capital funds, 3) mess-up factor funds. We will see later how to calculate the total for these funds. Before signing the purchase agreement the buyer must make sure that he has adequate funding available. The various sources of capital, including the seller, were discussed in Chapter Five. The buyer must have a signed loan agreement, or other funding arrangement with these various capital sources.

- **Documenting The Business Form**

    The buyer(s) may decide to enter business as a partnership or a corporation. The various agreements or business form, which specify ownership share, etc, must be filed before signing the purchase agreement. Any change of business name must be filed and the business entity placed on record for taxation purposes (see Chapters Two and Three).

9

Starting A New Business

9.0   There are many situations in which it is attractive to start a completely new business. Perhaps a new shopping mall is opening up in your area and you decide that a standard type of retail store, such as a fast-food restaurant, would be profitable. Or perhaps you have a new retail business in mind, such as a shop specializing in things that will become collectors items in ten to twenty years time. You may have a new product idea, in which case you have to decide on its commercial viability, whether you want to manufacture and sell it yourself, or whether you want someone else to manufacture it or sell it for you.

No matter what type of new business you decide to enter there are many more unknowns than if you bought an existing business. Perhaps some people are attracted to the idea of a new business because of the lower entry cost. A completely new business may indeed provide a lower entry cost, but the longer term starting costs over the first two years may be the same as buying an existing business. This is because a completely new business takes time to establish a reasonable sales volume, during which time the business is usually operating at a loss. Thus, the new businessman must have enough money to establish the business, pay for shopfitting, equipment, etc., and have enough further capital to carry him through the unprofitable start up period. A great many new businesses go under precisely because the owner does not have the funds to last out during the initial lean period, which can be up to two or three years. However, the longer a new business can stay in operation, the greater chance of survival it has, since it is usually continually building up new clients and connections. This is why so many new businesses are started on a part-time basis or started and operated by one spouse, so that continuing income is provided from the regular employment of the other spouse. Once a business is built up to a reasonable level, the working spouse can either hire a manager or take over himself/herself on a full time basis.

9.1   BUSINESS ANALYSIS

Before thinking of entering a particular type of business you clearly need to understand as much about that business as possible. Where the business is similar to many others located in the same general area you can find out the profitability, market segment, sales volume, and so on, of your competitors, as described in Section 8.6. You should also consult Robert Morris Associates "Annual Statement Studies" to satisfy yourself concerning the general profitability of your type of business (Section 7 1).

In addition you should consult the references given in the Encyclopedia of

Business Information Sources (Section 7.3) in order to be thoroughly familiar with the operating aspects of your type of business.

9.2 MARKET ANALYSIS NONUNIQUE BUSINESS

Retailing

When considering starting a new business, which will be in competition with existing similar businesses, the main question to be asked is whether or not there is sufficient over-all market volume to support another business in the market place. This question was discussed in Section 6.1.2, and essentially involves finding the average number of people and sales volume required to support a particular type of store. In this respect Sales Management magazine's "Buying Power Index", which is published every July, is an excellent reference to the sales potential of your particular area. The buying power index for particular items varies greatly from area to area depending on many demographic factors, such as income, age, family size, ethnic background, and so forth.

It may turn out that there is sufficient present sales volume to justify the existence of another store, especially if the existing stores are not highly regarded by their present customers. Perhaps they are doing little in the way of providing service, promoting themselves or keeping their stores well stocked, neat, clean and attractive. Under these circumstances, another similar business that is really more customer orientated will do well. Clearly, the factors of local competition just described can only be uncovered by personal investigation. You may come across consumer surveys performed by the local Chamber of Commerce or University. Some college business schools welcome the opportunity to engage in a real market research project under the supervision of a professor. Costs for such a survey are modest, but would answer most questions concerning market potential, products sold, various deficiencies of existing stores, poorly served areas, prices and customer attitude. The usual cost of such studies are no more than the cost of conducting the study, perhaps $500 to $1000. Such studies are conducted by mail, by telephone or by personal interview in a shopping area.

If either no consumer attitude survey has been conducted in your area concerning your type of store or if no college is willing to conduct one, you may gain a great deal of insight by conducting your own. Typically, your own survey might best be conducted by telephone over, say, a three week period and perhaps gain replies from several hundred people. You can select telephone numbers at random from your telephone book inside your intended market area. Clearly, women are more likely to be home during the day time hours and men can usually be contacted during the evening or at the weekend. You must write down a series of questions to be asked and practice them on family and friends to make sure that the questions make sense. The questionnaire would follow these general lines, although you can ask specific questions if you wish (for example; which brand of lawn mower would you buy next when your present one wears out?).

1. At which store do you shop for XXX?
2. Where is it located?
3. Why do you shop there?
   — Best selection of merchandise

- Lowest prices
- Most convenient
- Best Service

4. How often do you visit the store?
5. How far do you travel from your home to the store; 0-1 mile, 1-2 miles, 2-3 miles, or over 3 miles?
6. Do you shop at the same store now as you did a year ago? If not, which store did you shop? Why did you change?
7. Which brands of merchandize do you prefer to buy?
8. Do you prefer to use a charge card? Which charge card?

You notice that just these eight questions alone will provide you with insight into why people shop, where they do and what attracts them. It will also indicate what brands of merchandise are most popular and whether or not to install a charge card service - you should be able to predict the volume of cash sales versus charge card sales.

After you have checked the local business factors, you should check the average number of customers serviced by existing stores in your market area. The typical number of people required to support various kinds of retail stores, taken from the 1967 U.S. Census of Business: Retail Trade, is tabulated below.

Store	Number	Store	Number
Lunchroom	840	Jewelry Store	8400
Grocery Store	910	Radio & TV Store	8720
Gasoline Station	920	Florist	8860
Cocktail Lounge/Bar	1790	House Appliance Store	9560
Drugstore	3700	Retail Bakery	10150
Furniture Store	5980	Sporting Goods Store	12400
Women's Ready Wear	6240	Department Store	34580
Hardware Store	7320	Cigar Store	35770

You should assemble the various factors together–population, spendable income local business conditions–to determine if another store of a particular category makes sense in your business area.

Wholesaling

It is sometimes possible to break into existing wholesale distribution networks, although rather greater capital is required than is typical in most small businesses. Again the key factor, after conducting a market analysis similar to the one just described for retail operations, is how efficient your competing operation will be. New plants can be located on the edge of town, which have lower rent, ample space and the latest in efficient storage and transportation equipment. Often, good access to interstate highways and major regional airports are key factors in success. Naturally, you must have a detailed understanding of your target market and type of goods handled. A good general marketing information source for wholesalers is the "Monthly Wholesale Trade Reports: Sales and Inventories" published by the Bureau of Census, U.S. Department of Commerce GPO. This report provides details of trends in sales and inventories and provides geographic data

Mananufacturing

Again, the same question applies. Is there room for you to enter the market?

Your market, in this case, can be local, regional, or national. In fact, the decision will probably boil down to a cost/performance trade-off; that is, whether or not you can produce a given level of quality in a product at a competitive price. If you can, indeed, deliver either a superior quality or a cheaper product then you can effectively compete and take market share away from existing businesses.

Information on directories providing the names of business firms who buy goods for resale is given in the Small Business Bibliography No. 13 entitled "National Directories for Use In Marketing", which is available free by phoning toll free 800-433-7212 (Texas only 800-792-8901 . Information concerning manufacturers themselves can be found from a) the U.S. Industry Directory, b) MacRae's Blue Book and c) Thomas' Register of American Manufacturers (for further details see Section 4.5). The current level of manufacturing output can be found from consulting the "Survey of Current Business", U.S. Department of Commerce. G.P.O.

Another way of determining the market potential in your local business area is to phone the particular commodity buyers who work for larger businesses in your area and determine their buying needs, pricing requirements, contract terms, and so forth. By this means, which amounts to a "bottoms up" approach rather than a tops down approach, you can fairly accurately guage just how large the local market is and how much of it you might be able to capture.

Local Expansion

Some areas of the country, especially the "sunbelt region" and cities like Houston and Dallas in particular, are in the middle of a hectic growth period, which requires a host of small business to feed, house, supply and generally cater to the growing population. In this situation, small business opportunities abound and any competition that exists within the completely new market areas is not so much with existing businesses as with other newcomers. In this new melting pot situation those businesses that have thoroughly prepared themselves in knowing and responding to their market's needs will survive.

9.3 MARKET ANALYSIS - UNIQUE BUSINESS

The success of any unique business idea depends on its acceptance in the marketplace. The idea must be capable of practical fomulation as a consumer or business product. Do not make the mistake of thinking that just because you believe your idea is a good one, it will gain widespread acceptance. The basic marketing questions to be answered are:

1. Exact definition of your product
2. Definition of the customers for your product
3. Definition of the location of your customers
4. Definition of how many potential customers exist and, therefore, the potential sales volume

- Product definition - no product can be all things to all people. However, it must satisfy one or more of the basic motives that individuals have for buying something:

    1. Prestige - the product will enhance the stature of the individual owning it (examples - Rolls Royce, Cadillac)

9/Starting A New Business

2. Comfort - the product will provide for physical or mental wellbeing (examples - wool blanket, well fitting shoes)
3. Health - the product will enhance the health of the owner (examples - jogging shoes, vitamins)
4. Conveinence - the product will save time and effort (examples - microwave oven, automatic car wash)
5. Economy - the product is cheaper than existing ones
6. Security - the product will provide for the safety or the financial future of its owner (examples - T Bills, real estate)

The product may appeal to several needs simultaneously. Clearly you need to identify the particular needs your product will appeal to. This is essential in order to identify the demographics of your potential customers.

- Customer Definition - once you have defined your product you must define who is likely to buy it a) by demographic classification if the product is consumer orientated, or b) by SIC numbers, asset size, number of employees, etc., if you have a commercial or industrial product. You may not, of course, be able to pin-point customer characteristics exactly but you should put reasonable ranges on each particular characteristic.

If, for example, you decide to make T shirts for a newly franchised basketball team in your area, you could assume that your market would mostly comprise males between say the ages five through 15, from families with incomes in the $8,000 through $40,000 per year categories.

- Customer Location - basically where are they located? Take the case of a special computing service that is suitable for small firms in the professional and technical fields. The most promising clients seem to be accountants, architects, medical offices, engineers and legal offices. The question to be answered is where is the highest concentration of these types of businesses. You can use "County Business Patterns", which is published annually by the Census Bureau, G.P.O. In this instance we look at a report for New York State of businesses having 1, 2 or 3 employees in each category of interest.

County	Total Of 4 Groups	Medical (SIC 80)	Legal (SIC 81)	Engineering Articitects (SIC 891)	Accounting (SIC 893)
Bronx	841	694	112	10	25
Kings	2374	1762	467	35	110
Nassau	2321	1450	554	79	198
Queens	1891	1399	344	41	107
Richmond	265	177	67	8	13
Rockland	316	213	72	15	16
Westchester	1505	1061	305	53	86

Clearly, Kings and Nassau county have the highest number of applicable offices.

- Customer Volume - data is also available on the potential sales volume by looking at income levels for individual consumers - Census Tract Statistics (from Census of Population and Housing Census Tracts) or retail sales by

167

looking at Census of Business: Retail Area Statistics or County Business Patterns G.P.O , which provides information on employment and payroll statistics.

It should be pointed out that exact information is never possible, but that by looking for data from several sources to cross check it and by applying your own judgement to the data you should be able to arrive at some reasonable figures.

9.4 NEW BUSINESS LOCATION

When you start a business from scratch you are free at least to locate the business where you choose. Location is vitally important in most businesses so that you must learn how to locate your new business in the most advantageous area. The factors that determine the best site for location depend on the type of new business that you have in mind.

Retail

There is no question that location plays a key role in the success of a retail store. In locating to a new city, the factors to consider are, 1) the size of the city's trading area, 2) its population and the population trends within that city, 3) the total purchasing power and its distribution within the city, 4) the total retail trade potential for your specific retail store, 5) the number, size and quality of the competition.

Having chosen a particular city, the next step is to decide on a particular area in which to locate. In this case the factors to consider are 1) the demographic changes within the area, 2) the general appearance of the area, 3) the particular zoning regulations in the area, 4) the quality and number of competing stores, 5) the quality of the access routes to the area, and 6) the customer appeal of a particular shopping district.

Much of the data listed above can be found from figures provided by the Bureau of Census. In actual fact, the Census Bureau now collects and publishes data formerly published by other agencies. If you have difficulty locating a particular data source look for the Bureau of the Census's "Guide to Programs and Publications", which is a 227 page book with an 11 page index (1974 edition). The usual areas for which data is available are:

- Groups of States: nine divisions, grouped in four regions
- Standard Metropolitan Statistical Areas (SMSA's) are usually counties clustered around a central city with at least 50,000 population.
- State Economic Areas (SEA's) are groups of counties
- Counties
- Cities
- Census Tracts, which are small areas averaging about 4,000 inhabitants, tabulated for 233 SMSA's.
- Central Business Districts (CBD) are one or more census tracts covering the downtown business area
- Major Retail Centers (MRC) are concentrations of retail stores outside the CBD in SMSA's, which include both suburban shopping centers and traditional neighborhood shopping areas.
- Census Blocks are, in most cases, city blocks.

9/Starting A New Business

The information provided by the Bureau of Census data can answer the following questions:

1. How many people live in your trading area?
2. What is the exact population breakdown; by age, by sex, by race, by country of origin, by educational level, by income, by occupation, by home ownership percentage and by home appliances available to them.
3. Family size breakdown
4. Age of the community itself
5. The value of the homes owned and the amound paid for rent
6. The average age and quality of the homes
7. The degree of automobile ownership

Once you have specified the demographics of your customer, you can compare each census tract in the city for the best fit to your demographic requirements. You might usefully compare the tract's demographics to the averages for the city, the region, the state and America as a whole. If the demographic characteristics of your tract are significantly different you should investigate and understand the reasons for any difference since this may make for a unique selling opportunity.

You might see a segment of data such as this

	Tract 1	Tract 2
Number of rented units	1,860	320

Note, tract 1 has almost six times the number of rented units as tract 2. This would suggest a market for the type of merchandise used by apartment dwellers, such as small portable appliances.

Census block data give even more detailed information, sometimes down to blocks with less than 10 individuals.

You can also obtain retail trade information compiled by county, by SMSA, by cities and by central business district. Retail data is not tabulated by tract. The retail data includes the number of retail stores, retail sales, number of paid employees, and payroll by kinds of business. The Census of Business is taken every five years and published in the years ending in 2 and 7 - for example 1977 and 1982.

You now come to the point of picking out a specific site in which to locate your retail business. You may want to locate near a larger store, for example a well frequented supermarket, in order to benefit from the existing traffic flow. You may indeed want to locate near a particular group of residents. The factors to find out are 1) the amount of traffic passing the site, 2) the amount of traffic actually intercepted by the site, 3) the complementary nature, hopefully, of adjacent stores, 4) the amount of direct competition, 5) the availability of parking and good site access 6) the costs associated with the site.

- Traffic Count

    A traffic count is more important for some stores than others. Experience with your type of business should enable you to count the number of individuals who form your potential clientele. You might, for example, want to count young mothers with children. Thus, you must first establish the demographic characteristics of your clientele and then proceed to make your count. You should select a few half-hour periods during the day and repeat this over several days including the weekend period. You should be aware of peak shopping periods, such as just before Christmas and the Easter period, so that you do not arrive at inflated counts. You may derive the total potential sales by determining the proportion of passersby who enter the store and become purchasers. Your earlier studies should have provided the information on the average value of each customer purchase and thus you can estimate the annual potential sales volume

The types of goods you sell can also influence your store location.

Conveinence Goods - cigarettes, milk, (frequently bought items) - depend purely on the quantity of pedestrian traffic.

Shopping Goods - higher priced items, requiring more shopper effort to select good buys, are more influenced by the quality of the pedestrian traffic. Thus, you should choose a location for the particular demographic characteristics you require.

Specialty Goods - unique high priced items - depend on selling high prices items to individuals who are already sold on such items. Location, in this case is not so important.

- Automobile Count

    Many retail operations rely principally on drive-in traffic for their customers. The quantity and quality of the automobile traffic along a particular highway can be determined in the same way as pedestrian traffic. In addition, traffic flow may already have been measured by your local county or city highway department. Again, the types of goods you sell influence the type of vehicle traffic you wish to pass by your location. Convenience goods are most easily sold to people going to or from work. Note however, that certain establishments should be located on the inbound flow side of the street to catch the morning traffic - dry cleaners, for example. Alternatively, other shops should be located on the other side of the street to catch the homebound traffic flow - convenience food stores, for example

    You may want to catch customers on a planned shopping trip to a major shopping center. In this case, you should be located on the left hand side of the street approaching the shopping center.

    Service businesses, such as gasoline stations, restaurants and motels should be located to catch the maximum flow created by a recreational or pleasure facility

- Locating in a Shopping Center

    One question you will have to face is whether or not to locate in a shopping center. A shopping center is specially created to attract customers by offering a broad mix of stores, easy access, good parking facilities, weather protection and safety. The stores will group together for joint advertising often directed at specific demographic segments.

9/Starting A New Business

The large shopping center developer will look for one or more major retail stores, such as J.C. Penny or Sears, to act as a magnet for the rest of the stores. The developer will then seek to fill the rest of his space with good complementary stores that will be successful. Obviously, you must qualify in the developer's mind as a smaller store that will enhance the entire shopping center. For your part you must conduct your own study to determine if the present or future customer demographics are suitable for your type of business. You must perform an analysis of your particular location within the center; main arteries are more frequented than side entrance ways. You will be expected to pay a percentage of your gross sales in rent, typically five to seven percent. You will also have to pay maintenance and joint promotion fees. You will also have to pay for the shopfitting in your store

There are three classifications of shopping center:

1. Neighborhood - where a large supermarket is usually the leading store and where the other stores serve the needs of the local neighborhood.
2. Community - where a variety or junior department store is usually the leading store and where there are more specialty shops; shops having wider price ranges and assortment of merchandise.
3. Regional - where there is one or more nationally known stores and customers are drawn from a wide area. The large enclose mall is typical of a regional shopping center.

In making your selection of where to locate you retail business, you will soon realize that vastely different rents per square foot are charged, typically $5 per square foot per year in older, less attractive locations up to $15 per square foot for attractive, modern shopping center locations. You will also find that you must select your store area in given incremental sections - the smallest rentable space being approximately 800 square feet (a small ice-cream store) but more typically around 1,000 square feet. You can then rent in increments of this smallest size, that is 1,000, 2,000, or 3,000 square feet, and so forth.

In the final analysis, you must decide whether the sales volume generated by a particular site is sufficient to justify the rent being asked. It may be that older locations with typically lower rents actually provide a better return for your rental dollar than newer, more expensive locations. However, only detailed investigation on you part will provide the answer.

- **Small Wholesaler's Location**

The chance for introducing new wholesaling opportunities lies mostly with new types of business that spring up from time to time. In the past twenty years, for example, there has been a large growth in small electrical consumer appliances. Another newer wholesale area is the popularity of Scandinavian designed furniture, glassware and other housewares. These situations give the small businessman the opportunity to enter the wholesaling field.

The selection of a particular town depends upon the size of the market and the stength of the competition. These factors have been previously discussed in the section on market analysis. The particular section of town chosen depends primarily on the advantages of locating in the wholesale district or some other location in town. It would appear that the small wholesaler is better off locating out of the older, wholesale district of town where rents are high, traffic congestion is present and where it is difficult to find the location for an efficient, modern operation.

The small wholesaler must choose his location depending on his type of business. If he delivers to a number of local retailers by truck he needs to locate his warehouse centrally with respect to his clients, but having good access to his supply routes, which can be primarily by air, by sea, by rail or by truck. Alternatively, if he is the "cash and carry" variety where retailers drive to him, he must locate centrally and select a site providing good access and good truck loading facilities.

- **Small Manufacturer's Location**

A factory, with its heavy equipment and its large installation cost, is difficult and expensive to move once you have chosen a location. For these reasons, a factory site must be chosen with particular care. In making the decision on a location you should consider the following factors:

- Location To Market - you should be close to your future customers. This will enable you to provide quicker service and lower freight costs.
- Access To Raw Materials/Suppliers - you should have close access, with reasonable freight rates, to your raw material needs, or to your other suppliers.
- Availability Of Labor - your location should be accessible to local labor. The local labor should possess the skill you need in your particular manufacturing operation. The cost of labor is another important factor, along with the productivity of the local labor force.
- Adequacy and Cost Of Utilities - your business may need a great deal of heat, light, power or water. You should check to see if they are available at rates you can afford.
- Local Business Climate - some cities positively attract business by offering tax incentives and other benefits.
- Possibility for Future Expansion - you may need to expand your operation in the future. Thus, you should ensure that your site can be expanded either by acquiring adjoining buildings or land.
- Site Selection - in choosing the actual site for your plant you should study the local topography (for slope and foundation questions)
- Local Community - is the local community conducive to providing a stable work force. Adequacy of local schools, police, fire department, hospitals, etc. should be checked out.

The factors listed above should be tabulated for each site investigated and the site that provides the best combination for low distribution and manufacturing costs should be chosen.

There are many local agencies that would be helpful in establishing your location. At the state level, a Planning Commissioner or Industrial

Development Commission usually can provide information on plant location and business matters (such as tax rates and utility cost). At the local level the Chamber of Commerce also privides similar services, but has a greater knowledge of prevailing local conditions.

5 BUSINESS FORMATION PLAN

The business formation plan, shown in the chart below, is the timetable describing each of the steps required before you actually open your business. Such a plan is required for you to establish your new business in a timely, orderly manner without things "falling through the cracks" and causing last minute scrambles. Starting a new venture from scratch requires many more start up tasks than if you were buying an existing business. Many tasks must be done in parallel in order to avoid long delays.

The planning chart, known as a Gantt chart, is prepared by writing down every activity you can think of that is required before you can open your business. These tasks can then be grouped into major categories, such as legal requirements, and so forth. The next step is to estimate how long each activity will take and note the time relationships between the various tasks. For example, you cannot start preparing your loan proposal until you have completed your business study. Thus, each activity is moved back and forth across the chart until the proper time slot for it has been found. You can tell from the completed chart when a particular task has to be started in order to be completed in time for the next step. Obviously, a delay in completing a given task may delay the entire business opening plan. This chart will enable you to make predictions concerning the magnitude of the delay. The start and completion of each task are denoted by an S and a C respectively. Key events in the plan are denoted by ● .

The chart describes a typical start up situation. The various steps are:

1&2   Business Study

You must conscientiously set a start date and begin the various aspects of the business study. Doing this study you thoroughly familiarize yourself with business operations, its costs and its market potential.

3   Financing Your Business

Your loan proposal package can now be prepared from the results of your business and cost study. The proposal (covered in Chapter 11) asks for specific funding in support of your future business needs. The approval of your loan application is a key event, which implies that you can go forward with your business plans.

4   Legal Requirements

Towards the end of your business study and before you have completed your loan proposal, you should obtain a competent legal adviser. Once you have obtained your loan you will need to establish the legal existence of your business and have someone available to look over the various contractual commitments you will soon be making.

5.   Site Selection

One of the first contractual commitments will involve arranging to buy or

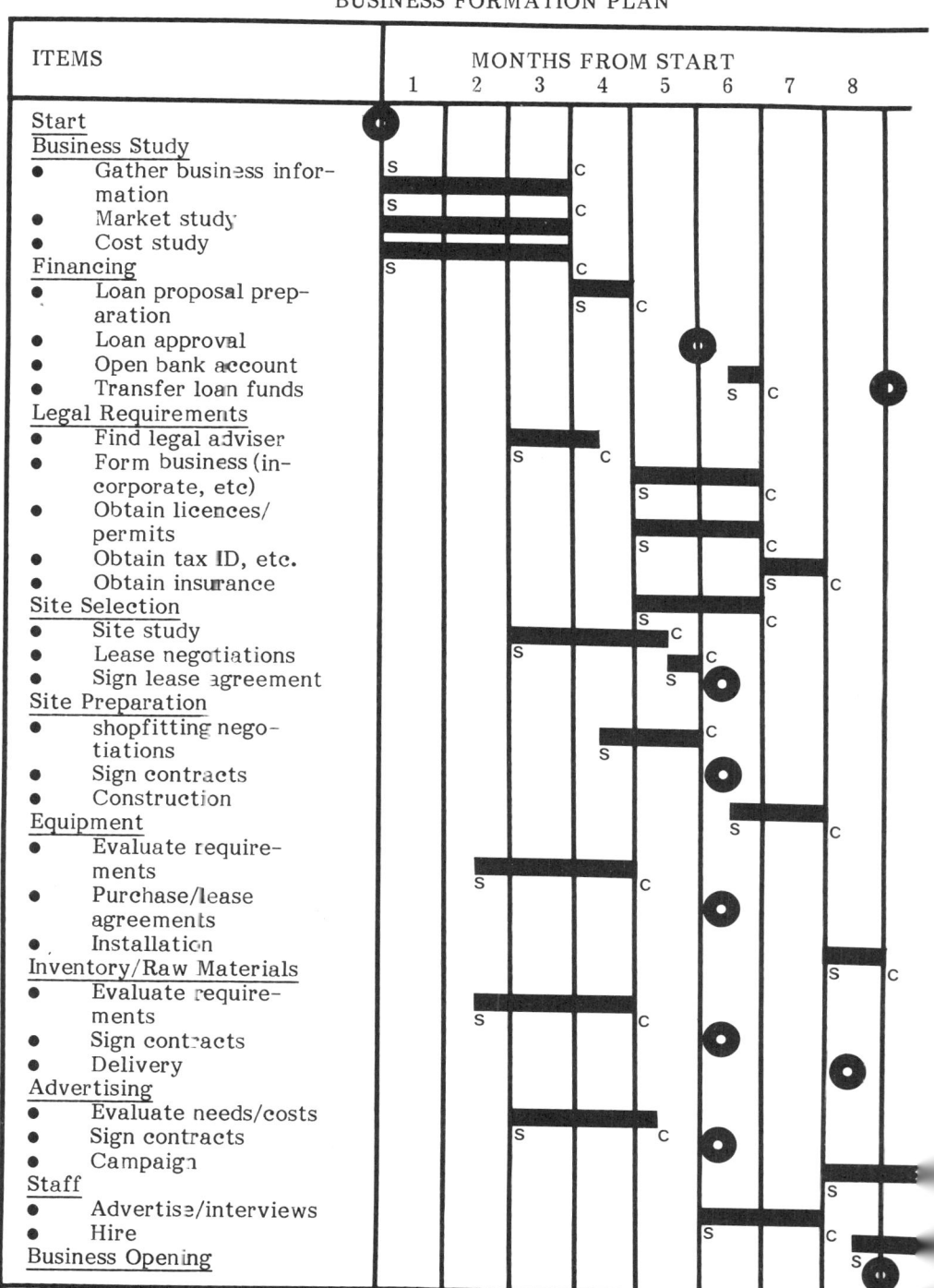

to lease your business premises. The most sensible arrangement appears to be to lease the premises on a reasonably short-term basis. Remember that a sole proprietorship or members of a partnership would be legally bound to pay the unexpired portion of the lease in the event of a business failure. The purchase of a building and its land only makes sense if a) the purchase is a good investment in its own right and b) the entrepreneur has sufficient funds to cover his other start up expenses.

6. Site Preparation

   The business premises must be outfitted and decorated. A business sign must be manufactured and any theme or logo considerations worked into the overall design.

7. Equipment

   You will need various types of equipment, plant and furniture. Again, you must make the decision either to buy or to rent. It seems sensible to initially rent with an option to purchase an item later on once the business becomes established. Note that should your business fail you will only be able to sell your equipment or funiture at distressed prices.

8. Inventory/Raw Materials

   You will establish in you business study the amount and type of inventory or raw material you need to begin business. You will also establish the lead times required to order particular items and to order sufficient quantities to carry you through your first selling period. In certain industries you may need to reorder many months ahead to be sure of catching a given manufacturing cycle. You can often specify that your order is delivered in separate shipments that are phased over a particular time period

9. Advertising

   If the sales of your business are strongly dependent upon seasonal events, such as Christmas, it would be best to open your business just before the start of the major selling season. Your advertising campaign, given the lead times of the various advertising media, should be designed to enhance the appeal of your freshly stocked inventory or new product idea. The suggested advertisement timing and advertising practices can be found in "Annual Time Table of Retail Opportunities", which is published annually by the Bureau of Advertising, American Newspaper Publishers Association, New York

   If your business relies heavily on leads from the Yellow Pages, you should note that the deadline for obtaining Yellow Page listing is usually in the mid-summer period prior to an October publication.

10. Staff Selection

    You may require several months to hire the right staff – salespeople, machine operators, cleaning staff and so forth. Make sure you understand the laws relating to hiring and discrimination (Chapter Two) and make a practice of checking references. Should you order a credit bureau report you must notify the applicant in writing with three days.

11. Opening Day

You have the funding, the inventory, the staff, have taken advantage of every PR opportunity and are set for the grand opening. Make the most of this event, the general buying public is curious to sample a new business if brought to its attention forcefully enough. You will need the best possible sales push to help out your initial cash flow problems.

10

Financing A Business

The amount of capital required to finance the start up costs of purchasing an existing business or establishing an entirely new one is the subject of this chapter. The amount of income available from a business is, of course, related to the amount of capital invested in the business.

PURCHASE OF AN EXISTING BUSINESS

As always, it is easier to estimate the financing required to take over an existing business than the financing required to start a new business. In this former situation there are several methods of approach depending on your particular needs.

Ratio Method

This method is useful in arriving at a quick estimate of the capital funding requirements for a particular business. You might visit the business and be able, with a practiced eye, to ascertain the following:

- Amount of total square footage occupied by the business
- Value of the inventory

Knowing the total square footage you can arrive at an estimate of the rent paid for that particular premises by inquiring with the real estate agent about the rent per square foot charged for his space plus any percentage of total sales charge. You can now turn to either Robert Morris "Annual Statement Studies" or Troy "Almanac of Business and Industrial Financial Ratios" that will provide the average values of the ratios net sales to rent and net sales to inventory. Using these ratios you should be able to calculate the expected net sales for the business.

Another easy check to determine how profitable the business is is to count the number of sales employees. The average retail sales per employee is published by the National Cash Register Company (NCR) in their booklet "Expences in Retail Business" (other ratio data and cost of doing business data can be found in the Appendix of the Robert Morris publication). It may turn out that the store is selling more than the average for its size and rent and thus you can use Robert Morris' upper quartile figures for making ratio estimates. Alternatively, if you observe few sales people and few customer sales at normal peak selling periods you can conclude that the store is below average and you can use Robert Morris' lower quartile figures.

Using an apparel store as an example, suppose that your visit indicates that the store is approximately 2,000 square feet in total area (including a small office and store room), that the total inventory is $75,000 (sale's value) that the store normally is staffed by 3 people with 4 on Saturdays and that the store generally seems busy. Using the Robert Morris ratios and NCR data, you quickly arrive at the following:

- Typical sales per square foot of total space is $105, thus giving an estimated total annual sales of $210,000.
- Typical net sales to the sale's value of inventory is 3.1, thus giving an estimated total annual sales of $232,000
- The business is paying $6 per square foot for space or a total of $12,000 per year. Since the average rent is 6% of sales, you would expect a sales volume of $12,000 divided by 0.06 or $200,000 per year.
- The average employee sells 10 times her own wage costs during the year.

Assuming that the average employee costs $7,500 per year to employ, she should sell about $75,000 worth of merchandise. Since there are 3.2 people selling (0.2 covers the extra person on Saturday), the total sales volume expected is $75,000 x 3.2 or $240.000 per year.

Estimate Of Purchase Price

The figures derived above point to a shop selling somewhat above average with an estimated cost of inventory of $75,000 times 0.6 or $45,000 and an annual sales of $240,000.

The total of owner's salary and net profit before taxes is about 15% of net sales. Thus, this business should generate a total of $36,000 for its owner. An upper quartile business should provide 9.4% of net sales for the owner's salary, so that 5.6% is profit or $13,400. Applying our 20% return in investment rate, the business should sell for about $67,000. Since fixed assets are about 40% of inventory, they are valued at $18,000. This would imply that the business goodwill is valued at $67,000 - 45,000 - 18,000 or $4,000.

Estimate Of Cash Flow Needs

The next step is to see what the on-going cash flow (working capital) requirements are to support the business. The sales are about $20,000 per month, so that the cost of merchandise sold is $12,000 (60% of sales value), and the operating expenses (25% of sales) are $5,000 per month.

Assuming you were purchasing this business with $37,000 of your own funds and $30,000 of borrowed funds, you would pay back your loan (principal and interest) at about $1,000 per month. Thus the cash flow would be as follows:

	Month 1	Month 2	Month 3	Month 4
Sales ($000's)	20	20	20	20
Collections	7	14	20	20
Expenses				
• Merchandise Purchased	—	12	12	12
• Operating Expenses	5	5	5	5
• Loan Repayment	1	1	1	1
Total Expenses	6	18	18	18
Net Cash Flow	1	(4)	2	2
Cumulative Cash Flow	1	(3)	(1)	1

It is further assumed that about one third of the sales of the first month are collected in cash in the first month, one third in the second month and the last third in the third month, and so forth. You have to order merchandise to replace that sold and it must be paid for starting in the second month. The net effect of the cash flow situation is that you are $3,000 down at the end of the second month and only come into the black by the fourth month. Thus at least $3,000 is needed to finance the cash flow requirements. In addition, if your personal cash needs are $1,500 per month you will need at least $4,500 over the first three months.

Estimate Of Start-up Fees

Start-up fees would cover legal payments, licences, insurance and so forth. Let us assume that $2,500 is required.

Total Capital Requirements

- Purchase Price $67000
- Cash Flow Needs   7500
- Start-up Fees   2500
- Mess-up factor   10000
- TOTAL $87000

From the above you will note that you need about $87,000 to take over this business. A $10,000 wedge is included (the mess-up factor) to tied you through any unforseen problems

Bottom-Up Method

This method of estimating new business finance needs is used when you have come to the point of deciding to buy a particular business. In this case you actually know the various financial numbers that we were estimating in the ratio method. You would obviously know the purchase price. The month over month receipts and expenditures recorded in the business ledgers for the prior year provide the basis for a better estimate of the cash flow requirements. In terms of your legal fees, etc., you would obviously seek actual quotations for the various licences and services you need. The mess-up allowance can still be left at $10,000. Thus, you can finally arrive at a very accurate estimate of your start up capital requirements. You can then take those numbers to a banker to obtain the correctly sized loan for your needs. In this way you borrow no more than you actually need and place less of a repayment burden on your new business.

Required Income Method

It may be that what you really want to know is how much capital investment you will need to achieve a specific income from a business. You can easily do this by inverting the "ratio method" discussed previously. Suppose, for example, you decide that you must obtain a total of $40,000 from a business. You must also decide which particular type of business you are interested in and find its financial ratios from one the various sources previously mentioned

- Percentage of total of salary + pre-tax profit to sales is 15%. Thus total required sales is $\dfrac{40{,}000}{0.15}$ = \$267,000

- Cost of goods sold (assume goods cost 60% of their sale price is
 0.6 x 267,000 = \$160,000

- The inventory required (assuming the ratio of cost of goods sold to inventory is 3.1) is $\dfrac{160{,}000}{3.1}$ = \$52,000

- The amount of fixed assets needed (assume ratio of fixed assets to inventory is 0.41) is
 52,000 x 0.41 = \$21,000

- Assume that the amount of goodwill = \$10,000

- Assume that \$10,000 will cover start-up costs and cash flow needs
 = \$10,000

 Total capital required = \$90,000

Since bankers and other financial institutions are reluctant to lend more than 50% of your capital requirements, it appears that you need at least \$45,000 of your own funds in order to start in this business.

10.2 STARTING A NEW BUSINESS

The most important aspect of starting a completely new business is to estimate your future sales over the first 18 months. This is also a very difficult estimating task but is the critical factor in determining how much start-up capital you need. Another aspect to bear in mind is that some businesses operate on essentially a cash basis while others have a heavy credit component. For example, a dry cleaning store cleans an article in, say, six hours and is usually paid in cash later the same day. On the other hand, a manufacturer may produce an article over, say a two week period and not receive payment for that article until it is delivered four months later. During this period, of course, the manufacturer must pay for his raw material, his labor and his operating costs. Thus, the manufacturer requires a large amount of working capital, whereas the working capital needs of the dry cleaner are relatively modest.

These aspects will be discussed in more detail in two examples. The first example concerns a retail store and the second example a manufacturing operation.

10.2.1 Starting A New Retail Store

The first step is to estimate your projected sales over the first 18 months or so of the existence of your new business. The methodology in doing this was described in Sections 9.2 and 6.1.2. A word of caution is needed, however, since although you may decide that your sales over the first two or three months will not be very high you will need to have a full inventory in order to give your store a well stocked appearance. If you skimp on initial inventory you may discourage future sales growth by giving the initial customers the impression

10/Financing A Business

that you carry an inventory of very limited selection. If your business has several seasonal selling periods, such as occur in women's apparel stores, you will probably have to sell off your outstanding merchandise at cost (via a sale) before the new season starts in order to make room for the next season's merchandise. In addition, you will need to order your apparel merchandise from the various fashion shows approximately four months ahead of when you plan to sell it. In stocking your store for the fall period you might decide that your inventory should be as follows:

Item	Size	Unit Cost	Total
300 dresses	9-14 emphasis	@30	$9,000
200 knits	10-14 emphasis	@35	$7,000
60 sport suits	9-13 emphasis	@70	$4,200
400 skirts	9-16 emphasis	@30	$12,000
600 blouses	28-36 emphasis	@20	$12,000
Miscellaneous hats, handbags, jewelry			$4,000
TOTAL			$48,200

Thus, the total cost of goods for inventory is $48,200. Since the ratio of the sale's price of merchandise to cost in women's apparel is 0.6, the sales price of the inventory is $80,300. Since the average inventory turnover is 3.1 times per year you would normally expect to sell $80,300 times 3.1, or $248,930 per year. This would amount to an average monthly sales of $20,700. However, since the fall period is a peak selling season you normally project a higher sales volume for this period. The normal sales volume would be as follows:

	Oct	Nov	Dec	Jan	Feb	Totals
1. Normal Sales ($000's)	$21	$23	$29.3	$18.8	$16.8	$108.9
2. Projected Sales ($000's)	$11	$15	$20	$12	$10	$ 68.0
3. Cost of Projected Sales ($000's)	$ 6.6	$ 9	$12	$ 7.2	$ 6	$ 40.8

Since your store is new, you would expect to sell below normal for this period (row 2). The cost of your goods sold is shown in line 3. You will notice that by the end of February you project to have sold merchandise worth $40,800, whereas you originally stocked $48,200 worth of merchandise. It is assumed that during January-February you clear out $7,400 worth of stock at specially reduced prices. In January you sell items at 20% above cost and in February you sell items at cost - the "Final Clearance Sale". Thus, your January and February clearance sales may look as follows:

	January	February
Clearance sales	6,500	2,400
Cost of goods	5,000	2,400

Since your inventory mostly arrives in late September, with some in October you must pay for it (on a 30 day credit basis) in October and November. Thus, the composite gross cash flow for your first selling season would be as follows:

181

	Oct.	Nov.	Dec.	Jan	Feb.
Sales ($000's)	11	15	20	18.5	12.4
Cost of goods sold	6.6	9	12	12.2	8.4
Revenues	4	8	15	18	16
Payment for mechandise	30	18.2	0	0	25
Gross cash flow	(26)	(10.2)	15	18	(9)
Cumulative gross cash flow	(26)	(36.2)	(21.2)	(3.2)	(12.2)

From the above table you can see that even if there were no other costs involved you would need at least $36,200 to support your inventory costs. You should estimate all your other start up costs as follows.

- Legal Costs

    When you have decided on your business form, you must pay legal fees to officially establish your business and pay for any licences or permit fees. You should obtain quotes from your lawyer concerning, say, incorporation fees and the cost to approve any contracts you will enter (see Section 9.5). Thus you budget your legal payment schedule as follows:

	Jul	Aug	Sep	Oct	Nov	Dec
Legal Consultation	50	100	100	100	50	50
Incorporation	0	700	0	0	0	0
Licences/Permits	0	200	0	0	0	0
TOTALS	50	1000	100	100	50	50

- Site Preparation Costs

    You will, of course, need to remodel the store to your needs and to buy a sign to put over the door. Again, quotes for both of these can be obtained in advance to enable you to budget for these items. Usually store remodelling cost run anywhere from $8 to $20 per square foot, thus the remodelling cost of a 2,000 square foot store might cost $24,000. Another $6,000 would be needed for furniture and equipment. Thus, your site preparation payment schedule would be:

	Aug	Sep	Oct	Nov
Store Sign	0	2000	0	0
Remodelling Cost	4000	16000	4000	0
Furniture/Equipment	0	4000	2000	0
TOTALS	4000	22000	6000	0

- Insurance

    You will discuss with your insurance agent the amount and type of coverage you need for your store. You are then usually required to pay in advance on a semi-annual basis. Thus, you might arrange to pay $425 in October and another $425 in April.

- Employee's Salaries

    You must decide how many paid employees, beyond your family members,

10/Financing A Business

you need to operate your store. In the start up period it is best to use the minimum number possible and use part time help for peak selling periods during the week or during the season. Knowing your projected sales and the amount sold per salesperson will give you the number of salespeople you require.

- Telephone

  You will, of course, need a business telephone. You will be charged an installation fee and also for calls at the business rate. Your local telephone company will provide you with the costs.

- Supplies

  Supplies are items such as typewriter ribbons, paper clips, cleaning fluids, etc., that you need to operate your business, but which you do not sell. You must project, knowing the nature of your particular business, a reasonable amount for this item.

- Repairs and Maintenance

  This item covers the cost of keeping your store in shape, but should not be very high for a new business unless you have purchased a great deal of used equipment. Again, you should make sensible estimates of your expenditures.

- Advertising

  With a new store, you must expect to advertise heavily in order to get your business known and to attract customers. Spend as much as you can that makes sense given the advertising options described in Chapter Six. A few enquiries with the local media should enable you to create an advertising budget that will reach your target market.

- Car and Delivery

  You will find that you are, at the very least, often meeting suppliers and driving to pick up merchandise. The costs of such transportation should be calculated based on projected mileage and vehicles required (you may need a delivery truck).

- Administration

  Here again, you will incur costs in running the paperwork side of your business. You may need to pay a bookkeeper or a CPA to keep your books and taxes in order.

- Rent and Utilities

  You will establish rental costs for your location in your site survey. You will probably be required to pay one month's rent as deposit and a month's rent at the beginning of each month. Utility costs can be estimated by talking to other business renters in the same commercial area.

-Prinicipal and Interest Repayments

  You may have to borrow funds to start your business. Local banks typically lend up to say $35,000 at about three percentage points above the prime rate. Let us assume that you decide to borrow $35,000 at 15%, which implies a monthly repayment of about $830 each month for a five year period.

- Taxes

    If you consult the tax calendar given in Section 3.2 you will note that the various tax payments are required at roughly quarterly intervals for a small business. There are two major tax categories:
    1. Taxes based on sales volume - sales tax paid to your state tax authority.
    2. Taxes based on employee/owner income - income, FICA, and unemployment taxes paid to both State and Federal governments.

I) Sales Tax - taking New York State as an example, the collection periods and filing dates are as follows:

Collection Period	Dec 1-Feb 31	Mar 1-May 30	Jun 1-Aug 31	Sep 1-Nov 30
Filing Date	March 20	June 20	Sept. 30	Dec. 20

You would use form ST-100 to make your return; the particular percentage varies depending on the particular county in which your business is located. Niagara county in upstate New York requires a sales tax rate of 7%.

The amount of sales tax charged and collected is shown in the table below.

	Oct.	Nov.	Dec.	Jan.	Feb.
Sales	11.0	15.0	20.0	18.5	12.4
Sales Tax Charged	0.77	1.05	1.4	1.26	0.87
Revenues	4.0	8.0	15.0	18.0	16.0
Sales Tax Collected	0.28	0.56	1.05	1.26	1.12

You will remember that the IRS requires retail stores to use the accrual accounting system for recording their sales. In this case you see that you record your sales and sales tax although the revenue from the sales has not yet been received. Thus, for the months of October and November you owe a total of $1,820 in sales tax but you have only collected $840. This under collection is caused, of course, by your credit sales. In the next quarter your total sales taxes are $3,530 whereas you collect $3,430 and required, therefore, a further $100. As the months go on the collections generally balance taxes due and this problem goes away, but you will need about $1,100 in cash flow to cover these early tax payments.

II) Employment Taxes - let us assume that apart say from unpaid help provided by your wife and daughter, you have only one full time employee who is paid $600 per month. The various employment taxes are as follows:

a) State unemployment insurance @ 2.6% of first $4,200 earned.
b) Federal unemployment insurance @ 3.2% of first $4,200 (but State unemployment insurance can be deducted). In this case the State unemployment insurance is higher than the Federal unemployment insurance tax and can, therefore, be ignored.
c) State income tax - for a single employee with one exemption earning $600 per month the withholding amount would be $19 per month.
d) Federal income tax - for a single employee with one exemption earning $600 per month, the withholding amount would be $90 per month.
e) Social Security taxes (FICA) would amount to $37 per month paid by both employer and employee (using a 6.13% rate).

10/Financing A Business

The various tax payments are tabulated as shown below:

	Oct	Nov	Dec	Jan	Feb
Wages Paid	600	600	600	600	600
State Unemployment Insurance	—	—	—	Jan 31 $65	—
State Income Tax	—	—	—	$57	—
Federal Income Tax	—	—	—	$270	—
FICA	—	—	—	$220	—
TOTAL	—	—	—	$612	—

It is assumed that you, the owner, have a full time job elsewhere and are no tax burden on this business. Otherwise you would have to deduct employment or self employment taxes for yourself

NOTE: You see how the addition of just one part time or full time employee multiplies your paperwork problems.

- Owners Salary

    If you were working in your store on a full time basis you would need an amount each month to cover your living expenses. Even though the business may not be earning enough to pay you anything you should include what you need since it does represent a drain on your cash reserves.

- Miscellaneous

    Various expense items have been discussed above, but these do not represent an exhaustive list. If you are aware of any significant expense items you should include them in your projected cash flow needs.

PROJECTED CASH FLOW

You have estimated both your revenue from sales and your various expenses. You are now in a position to create a projected cash flow statement that will show you how much cash you need and when you need it. Note, sales tax is not added to the sales or cash flow except as noted above to pay for the accrual imbalance (total of $1100).

You will notice that the maximum amount of negative cash flow is $81,220 occurring in November. Allowing a further $9,000 or so as a safety margin it appears that you need about $90,000 to start your business. Since you decided on a $35,000 bank loan, you need $55,000 of your own funds in order to start. You will also notice that you do not need your bank loan until October when your expenses begin to mount.

Even if you were able to sell you merchandise on a cash basis, you would still need about $67,000 in starting capital. You may want to offer discounts for cash payment in order to improve your early cash flow. You can also see that if you were able to take an extra month and prepare the site largely on your own, by painting and decorating the store yourself, you could well save $10,000 to $15,000 in start up cost for the further expense of an extra month's rent (this may be negotiable with the realtor).

PROJECTED CASH FLOW DURING START UP PERIOD

ITEM	Jul	Aug	Sep	Oct	Nov	Dec	Jan	Feb	Mar	Apr	May	Jun
Sales	—	—	—	11.00	15.00	20.00	18.00	12.40	14.00	13.00	15.00	17.00
Collections	—	—	—	4.00	8.00	15.00	18.00	16.00	14.80	13.10	14.00	15.00
DISBURSEMENTS												
Purchases	—	—	—	30.00	18.20	—	—	20.00	8.00	4.00	—	16.00
Salaries	—	—	—	0.56	0.56	0.56	0.56	0.56	0.56	0.56	0.56	0.56
Telephone	—	—	0.05	0.15	0.15	0.15	0.15	0.15	0.15	0.15	0.15	0.15
Insurance	—	—	—	0.43	—	—	—	—	—	0.43	—	—
Supplies	—	—	—	0.20	0.10	0.10	0.10	0.10	0.10	0.10	0.10	0.10
Outside Labor	—	—	—	0.08	0.08	0.08	0.08	0.08	0.08	0.08	0.08	0.08
Repairs and Maintenance	—	—	—	—	—	—	—	—	—	—	—	—
Advertising	—	—	1.00	1.00	1.00	1.00	0.30	0.30	0.50	0.50	0.30	0.30
Car and Delivery	—	0.10	0.10	0.10	0.10	0.10	0.10	0.10	0.10	0.10	0.10	0.10
Administration	—	—	0.10	0.10	0.10	0.10	0.10	0.10	0.10	0.10	0.10	0.10
Rent and Utilities	—	—	2.00	1.00	1.00	1.00	1.00	1.00	1.00	1.00	1.00	1.00
Principal & Interest	—	—	—	0.83	0.83	0.83	0.83	0.83	0.83	0.83	0.83	0.83
Taxes	0.05	1.00	—	—	—	1.00	0.01	—	0.10	0.61	—	—
Legal	—	4.00	0.10	0.10	0.05	0.05	0.05	0.05	0.05	0.05	0.05	0.05
Site Preparation	—	—	22.00	6.00	—	—	—	—	—	—	—	—
TOTAL DISBURSEMENTS	0.05	5.10	25.35	40.55	22.17	4.97	3.88	23.27	11.57	8.51	3.27	19.27
Net Cash Flow	(0.05)	(5.10)	(25.35)	(36.55)	(14.17)	11.03	14.12	(7.27)	3.23	4.59	11.73	(4.27)
Cumulative Cash Flow	(0.05)	(5.15)	(30.5)	(67.05)	(81.22)	(70.19)	(56.07)	(63.34)	(60.11)	(55.52)	(43.79)	(48.06)

2.2 Starting A Manufacturing Business

You can estimate the start up capital requirements of a small manufacturing business by using a bottom-up estimation approach similar to the retail store calculation. However, the manufacturing start-up costs are somewhat different in nature from the retail store since the manufacturer has to spend heavily on equipment and raw materials in order to make his inventory. In addition, labor is required to fabricate the product. The manufacturer may not be able to deliver and be paid for his product for several months

Your market survey should indicate how many items you are able to sell over a particular period. This information will indicate how much manufacturing capacity you require, how much labor you require, and also your raw material requirement. The size of a manufacturing plant will in turn indicate rental, utility, cleaning and other operating costs. You can also estimate when you will receive payment from your production process (you may, if you are lucky, be able to obtain some prepayment charges). Setting all of the various expenses out in detail in a cash flow chart will enable you to accurately predict your initial capital requirements.

11

Your Loan Proposal

11.0   You may have sufficient funds of your own to start a new business venture. If you do not, however, a key step will be to obtain a loan from a bank or other financial institution. You will note from the business formation plan described in Section 10.5 that only when you have obtained your loan can you commit yourself to the other major steps in starting your business.

The loan proposal package that you prepare to submit to your bank's commercial loan officer is the culmination of all of your researches into a business of your own. By now you know what business you want to get into, why you like that business, just how much money you need, and how you will spend it.

The loan proposal format described in detail in this chapter can also be used to seek a loan once your business is well established and needs further capital for expansion.

The particular loan proposal package presented below is for the purchase of an existing apparel store, "Annabell's", to be operated by the purchaser and his wife. The package is detailed enough to satisfy SBA requirements and those of almost any bank.

The loan proposal format would differ only slightly if you were starting a new business. You would certainly want to emphasis your market projections section and provide data on your site selection process. Remember to add life and casualty insurance coverage and your proposed lease agreement.

A loan for business expansion would be very similar to this proposal, except you would emphasis the effects of the new assets on increased cash flow and net profits.

<u>LOAN PROPOSAL</u>
<u>FOR</u>
<u>MR AND MRS. J. SMITH</u>

<u>PURCHASE OF ANNABELL'S</u>
<u>APPAREL STORE</u>

<u>DECEMBER 10, 1979</u>

TABLE OF CONTENTS

- 1.0 Summary
- 2.0 Personal Resumes
- 3.0 Personal Financial Statement
- 4.0 Personal Credit References
- 5.0 Basic Proposal
    - 5.1 Personal Situation at Present
    - 5.2 Market Prospects
    - 5.3 Competition
    - 5.4 Personnel
- 6.0 History of Business
- 7.0 Financial History of Business
    - 7.1 Five-year Profit and Loss Comparison
    - 7.2 Five-year Balance Sheet Comparison
    - 7.3 Operations Analysis
- 8.0 Profit and Loss Projections
    - 8.1 Twelve-Month Projection
    - 8.2 Footnotes
    - 8.3 Five-Year Projection
    - 8.4 Footnotes
- 9.0 Cash Flow Projections
    - 9.1 Twelve-Month Projection
    - 9.2 Footnotes
- 10.0 Balance Sheet Projections
    - 10.1 Balance Sheets for 1981, 1982
    - 10.2 Footnotes
- 11.0 Loan Request
    - 11.1 Amount/Use
    - 11.2 Proposed Collateral
    - 11.3 Estimated Average Balances
    - 11.4 Proposed Repayment Terms
- 12.0 References

11/Your Loan Proposal

1.0 <u>Loan Application Summary</u>

Applicants names	John Smith
	Mary Jane Smith
Address	65 Highridge Circle
	Dallas, TX 75247
Amount Requested	$30,000
Terms Requested	Five years, no prepayment penalty
Interest Rate	Current small business rate
Security	Business assets
	Personal guarantee
Debt/Equity Ratio (after loan)	$30,000/$32,000
Purpose Of Loan	This loan will enable the applicants, Mr. and Mrs. Smith to purchase "Annabell's" apparel store. A sales price of $42,000 includes inventory, furniture, fixtures and goodwill. A cash payment of $42,000 is required. No agreement or cash deposit has been made. It is intended to take over the business on February 1, 1980.

2.0 Personal Resumes

Husband

Name	John Smith
Address	65 Highridge Circle Dallas, TX 75247
Phone	881-9114
Personal	Born: March 16, 1943 Married, two children Social Security Number 814-91-9143
Education	B.S.E.E. SMU, Dallas, 1964 MBA SMU, Dallas, 1973
Business Experience	Southern Datamatics Corp Dallas, TX 1964 - 1971 Electrical design engineer on military electronics computers, radar Scientific Dynamics Corp Dallas, TX 1971-Present Product planning manager of military and commercial electronics, experienced in preparation of product proposals, budgeting, and business analysis.

Wife

Name	Mary Jane Smith
Address and Phone	Same as John Smith
Personal	Born: June 2, 1949 Social Security Number 752-99-1155
Education	Business diploma, Dallas Business Institute 1971
	Fashion Merchandizing (15 credit hours) Richland College, 1973 - 1975
	The Fashion School, Dallas, (40 credit hours) Dressmaking/Tailoring, 1977
Business Experience	Nash - Frazier Department Store 501 Westbrook Street Dallas, TX 75201 Duties: Salesperson in the softgoods department. Softgoods buyer. 1971 - 1975
	"Young Elegance" 16915 Briarwood Avenue Dallas, TX 75201 Duties: Managed store; supervised three salespeople, bought merchandise, kept books.

3.0 Personal Financial Statement (Mr. J. Smith)

FINANCIAL CONDITION AS OF NOVEMBER 15, 1979

ASSETS

Cash	Checking	$	450
	Savings		12,000
Securities (Schedule 1)	Marketable		24,000
Real Estate (Schedule 2)	Homestead		110,000
Cash Value Life Insurance - Net (Schedule 3)			---
Automobiles			6,000
Other Personal Property			18,000
TOTAL ASSETS			**$170,450**

LIABILITIES

Notes Payable	$	-----
Mortgage Payable (Schedule 2)	Homestead	35,000
Taxes Owing		-----
Other Liabilities		-----
Total Liabilities		35,000
Net Worth		135,450
TOTAL LIABILITIES & NET WORTH		**$170,450**

ANNUAL INCOME

Salary	$ 32,000
Bonus	---
Dividends/Interest	500
Other	---
TOTAL INCOME	$ 32,500
Taxes Paid (1978)	$ 6,280

CONTINGENT LIABILITIES

Any Contingent Liabilities	-----
Total	-----

SCHEDULES

SCHEDULE 1 - STOCKS OWNED BY J. SMITH

Number Of Shares	Company	Traded	Market/ Share	Wholly Owned	Pledged	Value
100	AT&T	NYSE	50	Yes	No	$5,000
100	Xerox Corp.	NYSE	55	Yes	No	$5,500
100	Exxon	NYSE	85	Yes	No	$8,500
60	Eastman Kodak	NYSE	100	Yes	No	$6,000
					TOTAL	$24,000

SCHEDULE 2 - REAL ESTATE - HOMESTEAD

Market Value	Type Appraisal	Cost	Year Acquired	Monthly Payment	Related Indebtedness		
					Lien Holder	Original Amount	Present Balance
$110	M.A. 1	$55K	1974	$460	Dallas Savings	$42K	$35K

SCHEDULE 3 - LIFE INSURANCE

Company	Face Amount	Loan Value	Policy Loan	Beneficiary
Scientific Dynamics Group Policies	$150,000	None	None	Wife

4.0 *Credit References*

    4.1   *Dallas State Bank*   *Checking account: 6312-9914*

          8111 Houston Road   *Savings account: 2165-3128*
          Dallas, TX

    4.2   *First Dallas Savings*   *Savings account: 35-16512-02*

          325 S. 14th Street
          Dallas, TX

    4.3   *Texas Savings & Loan*   *Mortgage Loan: 6154-91-36512*

          7915 Charles Avenue
          Dallas, TX

5.0 BASIC PROPOSAL

The loan amount is required to provide funds for inventory and working capital in the purchase of a ladies' ready-to-wear apparel shop (retail) by the partnership of JOHN SMITH and his wife, MARY JANE SMITH.

5.1 PERSONAL SITUATION AT PRESENT

Both JOHN and MARY JANE SMITH are working at present. It is intended that JOHN SMITH remain in his present employment as Product Planning Manager, Scientific Dynamics Corporation, whilst his wife, MARY JANE SMITH, would leave her current employment and take over full-time operations management of "Annabell's", the retail store intended for purchase. JOHN SMITH will provide ongoing financial support via his employment, management expertise and guidance, especially of inventory control (unit and dollar types) and financial analysis.

5.2 MARKET PROSPECTS

The store rents 1,700 square feet in a one-story brick building in good condition. It is located in a suburban business section on a well-traveled street in North Dallas. The premises are neat and the fixtures and furnishings are in satisfactory condition (store partially remodeled approximately 19 months ago).

The merchandise is ladies' ready to wear in the medium to higher priced lines, specializing in suits, dresses, sportswear and a limited assortment of accessories, including jewelry. Sales are to women in the medium to upper income level in the suburban shopping area of North Dallas.

The advertising thrust in the period after purchase and merchandise appeal will be primarily towards working women in the 25-35 age segment. This matches the largest segment of female population growth of 16 7% over 1975-1980[1].

However, an even higher proportion of women in the 25-35 age range are entering the workforce, providing an annual increase of 9.9%[1]. These women have a greater requirement for a variety of clothes than do those who remain at home and are a factor in the upturn in the dress industry.

The fashion trend itself is towards a softer, dressier look in ladies' apparel, which will result in a higher outlay per ticket item.

In terms of demographics [6], *the population growth of North Dallas has slowed down but can be expected to grow overall by approximately 3% per annum; highest growth is in the far North Dallas area (north of LBJ Freeway) at approximately 6.2% per annum. Its population of approximately 200,000 has an average family annual income of $30,400. The average per store consumer spending on ladies' apparel over the 62 stores in this area is $205,000. The average population increase in the North Dallas area since 1970 has been 4.3% per year.*

Given the increasing overall population and the increasing female working population, a conservative estimate of the growth in ladies' apparel sales of 5% seems warranted.

5.3 COMPETITION

There are eight other apparel stores within a one mile radius. Each is reasonably well established offering a similar type of merchandise to "Annabell's". However, "Annabell's" is in a superior location, in terms of traffic count, to all but one of its competitors. It is prejected that by superior location, more advertising and selective merchandising "Annabell's" should be able to achieve the average store sales for this area.

5.4 PERSONNEL

Is is intended to retain the services of the present three employees; one of whom is full time and two are part time. Mrs. Smith intends to work at the business on a full time basis.

[1] *After 1980, the primary age segment for growth will be the 35-44 age range.*

6.0 HISTORY OF BUSINESS

Present business name, location:

> *Annabell's*
> *13625 Northwest Road*
> *Dallas, TX*

11/Your Loan Proposal

Telephone: (214) 661-2951

SIC No.:   5621, Ladies' Read to Wear

The business was started as "Fashion-House" in January, 1972, at this location by Tirelle's of Arlington, Texas. On October 1, 1973, Ann and Fred Johnson purchased this location for $9,600 cash derived from savings. At that point, the business name was changed to "Annabell's". Its trading history is clear, its current condition is good and the sales/net income trend is up. Ann Johnson is running this business on a full time basis. Fred Johnson has been offered an attractive promotion to the West coast in his current employement as regional sales manager for a national food company. The Johnson's want to sell their Dallas business and relocate to the West coast.

7.0 Financial History Of Business

7.1 FIVE-YEAR PROFIT/LOSS COMPARISON
(in 000's Dollars)

ANNABELL'S

Fiscal Year Ended October 1	1975	1976	1077	1978	1979
Total Net Sales	80.2	118.4	142.9	156.4	166.9
Cost of Sales	44.9	67.5	84.3	96.9	100.2
Gross Profit on Sales	35.3	50.9	58.6	59.5	66.7
OPERATING EXPENSES*					
Employee Salaries	6.2	11.4	12.3	13.6	14.3
Telephone	0.6	0.6	0.8	1.2	1.5
Insurance	0.4	0.5	0.6	0.7	0.8
Supplies	0.7	1.3	2.2	2.4	2.7
Outside Labor	0.5	0.6	0.6	0.7	0.8
Repair and Maintenance	0.5	0.6	0.6	0.7	0.7
Advertising and Promotion	2.1	2.3	2.5	3.2	3.5
Car and Delivery	0.4	0.4	0.6	0.8	0.8
Bad Debts	---	---	0.3	0.3	0.3
Administration/Legal	0.9	0.9	1.0	1.0	1.0
Rent/Utilities	9.2	10.6	11.8	11.8	12.6
Taxes	0.9	1.1	1.3	1.4	1.5
Interest	1.1	.4	1.0	1.2	1.8
Depreciation	2.4	2.4	2.65	2.65	3.95
Total Operating Expenses	25.9	34.1	38.25	41.65	46.25
Net Income Before Taxes	9.4	16.8	20.35	17.85	20.45

*Excluding proprietor's salary

FIVE-YEAR BALANCE SHEET COMPARISON

ANNABELL'S

Fiscal Year Ended October 1	1975	1976	1977	1978	1979
ASSETS					
Cash	$ 2,700	$ 4,100	$ 5,500	$ 5,100	$ 6,200
Accounts Receivables	6,700	9,500	12,100	15,200	14,300
Inventories	18,500	21,400	26,400	29,200	33,600
Total Current Assets	$27,900	$35,000	$44,000	$49,500	$54,100
Equipment	$ 1,750	$ 1,750	$ 2,150	$ 2,150	$ 2,150
Furniture and Fixtures	15,250	15,250	16,500	25,500	25,500
Less Depreciation	2,400	4,800	7,450	10,100	14,050
Net Fixed Assets	$14,600	$12,200	$11,200	$17,550	$13,600
Total Assets	$42,500	$47,200	$55,200	$67,050	$67,700
LIABILITIES					
Accounts Payable	$ 5,400	$ 5,200	$ 5,700	$ 7,200	$ 8,100
Current Long-Term Debt	6,500	5,000	4,000	7,000	5,500
Accrued Expenses	4,100	3,700	4,700	7,500	6,300
Other	1,600	2,300	1,200	3,700	4,300
Total Current Liabilities	$17,600	$16,200	$15,600	$25,400	$24,200
Long-Term Debt	$15,500	$10,000	$ 5,000	$13,000	$ 6,000
Total Liabilities	$34,100	$26,200	$20,600	$38,400	$30,200
Net Worth	$ 8,400	$21,000	$34,600	$28,650	$37,500
Total Liabilities & Net Worth	$42,500	$47,200	$55,200	$67,050	$67,700

7.3 OPERATIONS ANALYSIS

The sales volume of the business has steadily grown over the past five years, although Net Income Before Taxes has stabilized over the past three years. The Return on Sales of 11-12% is around the trade average for this size and type of business. The business has maintained adequate liquidity; its Quick Ratio[1] being better than 0.8:1 over the period. Accounts Receivables cycle have been kept under control at about 30 days[2], the Net Trade Cycle[3] being approximately 65 days. The Owner's Net Worth as a percentage of total assets has steadily increased, with a modest long-term debt of $6,000 outstanding.

Footnotes

1. Quick ratio is Cash + Accounts Receivables divided by Current Liabilities.
2. Account Receivables cycle is the Account Receivables divided by the Total Annual Sales multiplied by 365, and gives the average number of days the Account Receivables is outstanding.
3. Net Trade Cycle is the Accounts Receivable Cycle + Inventory Cycle.

11/Your Loan Proposal

ANNABELL'S

ADJUSTED BALANCE SHEET FOR DECEMBER 1, 1979

ASSETS

Cash	$ 7,400
Accounts Receivables	18,600
Inventories	25,000
Total Current Assets	$51,000
Equipment	$ 3,150
Furniture and Fixtures	25,500
Less Depreciation	14,150
Net Fixed Assets	$14,500
Total Assets	$65,500

LIABILITIES

Accounts Payable	$ 8,400
Current Long-Term Debt	5,100
Accrued Expenses	5,800
Other	4,500
Total Current Liabilities	$23,800
Long-Term Debt	$ 7,000
Total Liabilities	$30,800
Net Worth	$34,700
Total Liabilities & Net Worth	$65,500

8.0 PROFIT AND LOSS PROJECTIONS

8.1 PRO FORMA INCOME STATEMENT

ANNABELL'S

Year Ended February 1, 1981

Total Net Sales (1)	$176,400
Cost of Sales (2)	105,800
Gross Profit on Sales	$ 70,600

OPERATING EXPENSES (3)

Employee Salaries and Overhead	$ 14,520
Telephone	1,800
Insurance	850
Supplies	2,880
Outside Labor	960
Repairs and Maintenance	720
Advertising and Promotion	4,100
Car and Delivery	840
Bad Debts	660
Administrative/Legal	1,110
Rent and Utilities	12,000
Taxes and Licenses	1,600
Interest	3,800
Depreciation	1,580
Total Operating Expenses	$47,420
Net Income Before Taxes	$23,180

8.2 FOOTNOTES ON INCOME STATEMENT PROJECTION

Note 1 - Net Sales

Month over month sales projections were calculated from the past sales performance of "Annabell's". Correlation was also obtained with data taken from "Barometer of Small Business" published in 1974 by Accounting Corporation of America. It is assumed, as discussed in Section 5.2 that the market will grow by 5% per year.

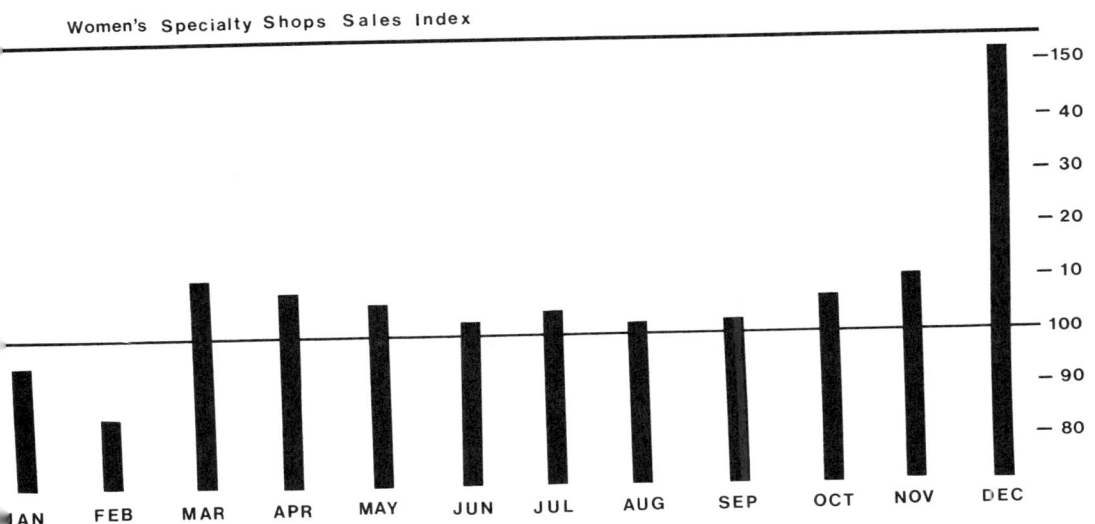

Note 2 - Cost Of Sales (Accrual Basis)

The cost of sales is projected to be 60% of sales. This is based on past "Annabell's" data of local buying conditions at the Dallas Apparel Mart. Industry comparisions are given in note 4: ACA - Barometer of Small business, Troy - Almanac of Business ratios, Dun and Bradstreet - Cost of Doing Business Survey.

Note 3 - Operating Expenses *(Cash Basis)*

- *Salaries* - The current employees will be retained with Mary Jane Smith substituting her services for the present owner, manager Mrs. Johnson.
- *Telephone* - Projection based on historical experience of 1.0% of sales.
- *Insurance* - $850 insurance quotation obtained from Allied Insurance Company to cover up to $40,000 of inventory, $15,000 of equipment for fire and theft. Also, $300,000 public liability and workman's compensation. Business interuption insurance of $20,000.
- *Supplies* - Based on historical ratio of 1.6% of sales.
- *Outside Labor* - Based on an estimate of $120 per year increase in cleaning costs.
- *Repairs and Maintenance* - Estimated on historical experience of 0.4% of sales.
- *Advertising* - A larger advertising budget is allowed to negate the effects of change of ownership and to ensure a 5% minimum increase in sales.
- *Car and Delivery* - An extra $40 is projected to cover extra fuel costs over 1979.
- *Bad Debts* - Based on historical experience of 0.3%.
- *Administration/Legal* - A slight increase is allowed to cover extra settling down costs after business take over.
- *Rent and Utilities* - Based on negotiated continuation of current lease terms.
- *Taxes and Licences* - FICA taxes at 6.1% for employees, 3.6% of first $4,200 of employee pay for unemployment tax and local taxes.
- *Interest* - $3,800, the first year interest payment on the $30,000 loan at 13%.

11/Your Loan Proposal

- *Depreciation* - Calculated using a straight line depreciation method on the following assets:

Item	Cost	Life	Depreciation Amount
Cash Register	$1,500	10 yrs	$150
Calculator	100	10 yrs	10
Office Furniture	800	10 yrs	80
Display Stands	6,800	9 yrs	755
Showroom Furniture	3,700	8 yrs	462
Lighting Fitments	1,250	10 yrs	125
TOTALS	$14,150		$1,580

Note 4 Industry Average Operating Expenses

The pro forma operating expenses were estimated using data from "Annabelle's" past accounts and estimates of current business conditions. For comparision, the averages for apparel stores is presented below using several sources of industry data.

	Barometer of Small Business	Almanac of Business Ratios	Dun & Broadstreet (partnerships)	Annabell's projected
Operating Expenses	(1973)	(1977)	(1975)	
Sales	100%	100%	100%	100%
Cost of sales	62.2	61.0	63.9	60
Gross Profit	37.8	39.0	36.1	40.0
Controllable Expenses				
Outside labor	0.7	--	1.73	0.6
Operating supplies	1.8	--		1.6
Wages	9.0	--	9.0	8.2
Repairs	0.6	--	0.4	0.4
Advertising	1.8	1.9	--	2.3
Delivery	0.6	--	--	0.5
Bad debts	0.02	--	0.2	0.3
Admin./Legal	0.6	--	--	1.6
Miscellaneous	0.4	--	--	--
Total Controllable Exp	15.5	--	--	15.5
Fixed Expenses				
Rent	2.5	5.4	3.6	7.1
Utilities	1.2	--	--	--
Insurance	0.6	--	--	0.5
Taxes	0.7	2.2	1.9	1.0
Interest	0.1	0.6	0.5	1.8
Depreciation	0.7	1.1	0.9	0.9
Total fixed expenses	5.8	--	--	11.3
Total Expenses	21.3	26.3	24.1	26.8
Net Profit*	16.5%	12.7%	12.0%	13.2%

* Including proprietor's salary

11/Your Loan Proposal

FIVE-YEAR PROFIT AND LOSS PROJECTION

CONDENSED PRO FORMA INCOME STATEMENT
(in 000's Dollars)

ANNABELL'S

Five Years, Each Ending February 1

	1981	1982	1983	1984	1985
Total Net Sales (1)	176.4	185.2	194.5	204.2	214.4
Cost of Sales (2)	105.8	111.1	116.7	122.5	128.6
Gross Profits	70.6	74.1	77.8	81.7	85.8
OPERATING EXPENSES (Less Interest) (3)	43.7	46.5	48.8	51.3	53.8
Interest	3.8	2.3	1.6	0.8	0.8
	47.4	48.8	50.4	52.1	54.6
Net Income Before Taxes	23.2	25.3	27.4	29.6	31.2

Footnotes To Five-Year P&L Projection

Note 1. The total net sales are projected to grow at a compounded rate of 5% per year.

Note 2. The cost of sales is projected at 60% of the sales price.

Note 3. Operating expenses (less interest) are projected to remain at about 25% of net sales.

Net income will grow by approximately 50% in five years on a sales increase of 22% principally because the loan has been paid off and interest costs deminish.

209

9.0 CASH FLOW PROJECTION

9.1 ANNABELL'S 12 MONTHS' CASH FLOW PROJECTIONS - 1980
(in 000's Dollars)

ITEM	FEB.	MAR.	APR.	MAY	JUN.	JUL.	AUG.	SEP.	OCT.	NOV.	DEC.	JAN.
Net Sales (1)	12.20	15.20	14.70	14.80	14.60	13.90	14.40	14.50	14.90	15.30	19.30	12.60
Collections (2)	4.07	9.14	14.03	14.90	14.70	14.43	14.30	14.26	14.60	14.90	16.50	15.73
DISBURSEMENTS (3)												
Employees' Salaries	1.21	1.21	1.21	1.21	1.21	1.21	1.21	1.21	1.21	1.21	1.21	1.21
Purchases	—	8.70	8.40	8.40	8.40	7.92	8.04	8.10	8.40	8.70	11.10	7.44
Telephone	0.15	0.15	0.15	0.15	0.15	0.15	0.15	0.15	0.15	0.15	0.15	0.15
Insurance	0.85	—	—	—	—	—	—	—	—	—	—	—
Supplies	0.24	0.24	0.24	0.24	0.24	0.24	0.24	0.24	0.24	0.24	0.24	0.24
Outside Labor	0.08	0.08	0.08	0.08	0.08	0.08	0.08	0.08	0.08	0.08	0.08	0.08
Repairs and Maintenance	0.06	0.06	0.06	0.06	0.06	0.06	0.06	0.06	0.06	0.06	0.06	0.06
Advertising	0.40	0.40	0.35	0.35	0.35	0.30	0.30	0.30	0.35	0.40	0.50	0.10
Car and Delivery	0.07	0.07	0.07	0.07	0.07	0.07	0.07	0.07	0.07	0.07	0.07	0.07
Bad Debts	—	0.06	0.06	0.06	0.06	0.06	0.06	0.06	0.06	0.06	0.06	0.06
Administration & Legal	1.00	0.01	0.01	0.01	0.01	0.01	0.01	0.01	0.01	0.01	0.01	0.01
Rent Utilities	1.00	1.00	1.00	1.00	1.00	1.00	1.00	1.00	1.00	1.00	1.00	1.00
Principle and Interest	1.19	1.19	1.19	1.19	1.19	1.19	1.19	1.19	1.19	1.19	1.19	1.19
Taxes	—	—	0.40	—	—	0.40	—	—	0.40	—	—	0.40
Total Disbursements	6.25	13.17	13.22	12.82	12.82	12.69	12.41	12.47	13.22	13.17	15.67	12.01
Net Cash Flow	(2.18)	(4.03)	(0.81)	(2.08)	(1.88)	(1.74)	(1.89)	(1.79)	(1.38)	(1.73)	(0.83)	(3.72)
Cumulative Cash Flow	(2.18)	(6.21)	(5.40)	(3.32)	(1.44)	(0.30)	(2.19)	(3.98)	(5.35)	(7.09)	(7.92)	(11.64)

9.2 FOOTNOTES FOR CASH FLOW PROJECTION

Note 1 - Net Sales

See Note (1), Section 8.2

Note 2 - Collections

Past Annabell's experience indicates that approximately one-third of all sales are in cash and are therefore collected in the month sold. The average days receivables outstanding is 41 (versus 45 for industry average indicated by Robert Morris Associates). It is therefore conservatively estimated that the second third is collected in the second month following the sale and the last third in the third month.

Note 3 - Disbursements

The disbursements were made as indicated in detail in note 3, Section 8.3. Note, there is no allowance made for any salary or compensation drawn by the owner/manager Mrs. Smith. It is assumed that during the first year she will be entirely supported by Mr. Smith.

You will note that during the first two months of operation disbursements exceed collections due to the lag in collections. This results in a maximum negative cash flow of $6,210, that is extra funds required by the business. However, as the year continues the cash flow improves; the net year-end cumulative cash flow being $11,650.

10.0 Balance Sheet Projection

10.1 ANNABELL'S

PRO FORMA BALANCE SHEETS

(Status after purchase and at the end of first year)

	A Feb 1, 1980	B Feb 1, 1981
ASSETS		
Cash	$20,000	$31,640
Accounts Receivables	0	14,840
Inventory	25,000	20,720
Total Current Assets	$45,000	$67,200
Equipment	$ 1,600	$ 1,600
Furniture & Fixtures	12,550	12,550
Less Depreciation	0	1,580
Net Fixed Assets	14,150	12,570
Goodwill	2,850	2,850
Total Assets	$62,000	$82,620
LIABILITIES		
Accounts Payable	$ 0	$ 7,920
Current L-T Debt	10,480	6,000
Accrued Expenses	0	0
Other	0	0
Total Current Liabilities	$10,480	$13,920
Long Term Debt	19,520	13,520
Total Liabilities	30,000	27,440
Net Worth	32,000	55,180
Total Liabilities & Net Worth	$62,000	$82,620

11/Your Loan Proposal

10.2 Footnotes On The Projected Balance Sheets

Cash - The total of initial working capital plus cash reserve, $20,000, is projected to be $31,640 at February 1, 1981. The increase of $11,640 is shown resulting from the cumulative cash flow projection (Section 9.1).

Accounts Receivables - The $14,840 balance results from the difference between the total annual sales, $176,400, and the amount collected, $161,560 (see cash flow Section 9.1).

Inventory - The inventory is projected to decline to $20,720 in 2/1/79, which is a more natural lower level after the peak Christmas sales.

Net Fixed Assets - Predicted to decline to $12,570, based on a depreciation charge of $1,580 (see Section 8.2, Note 3).

Goodwill - Remains unchanged at $2,850.

Accounts Payable - Represents the amount of goods on hand that have not been paid for. These goods are found by recognising that the cost of goods sold during the year, $105,800 (projected income statement, Section 8.1) equals the drop in inventory (25,000 - 20,720) plus the amount purchased, $93,600 (sum of goods purchased, cash flow- Section 9.1) plus those purchased but not yet paid. Thus,

$105,800 = 4,280 + 93,600 + $ Accounts Payable

Accounts Payable = $7,920

Long Term Debt - Started at $30,000, of which $10,480 was paid off during 1980 leaving a total of $19,520 ($6,000 to be paid in 1981 and $13,520 in later years).

Net Worth - The owner's equity has risen from $32,000 to $55,180 or $23,180, which is the net profit shown in the income statement (Section 8.1).

11.0 Loan Request

11.1 Amount/Use

The amount requested by this loan proposal is $30,000, which, when added to $32,000 to be supplied by John Smith, will be used to purchase and operate "Annabell's".

Source of Funds

- Bank Loan $30,000
- Owner's Capital   32,000

    TOTAL $62,000

Use of Funds

- Purchase of Inventory (as of 12/1/79) $25,000
- Purchase of Furniture/Fixtures and Goodwill   17,000
- Working Capital to Underwrite Cash Flow   10,000
- Cash Reserve   10,000

    $62,000

11.2 Proposal Collateral And Conditions

It is proposed to use short and long terms assets as collateral for this loan, based on term provided by the Uniform Commercial Code.

- Inventory at $25,000 value
- Furniture and fixtures at $14,150 value

The borrower will maintain insurance on inventory and long-term assets and will provide the lender with quarterly financial statements.

11/Your Loan Proposal

1.3 Estimated Average Balance

The estimated working capital fluctuations due to cash flow (shown in 8.1) should provide an estimated average balance of $7,630. It is intended to hold approximately $5,000 in the bank as Certificates of Deposit.

1.4 Proposed Repayment Terms

- Amount of Loan $30,000
- Interest   13%
- Repayment Period   5 years
- First Year Monthly Payment $1,190

2.0 REFERENCES

Fashion Industry
Periodicals

- Women's Wear Daily, Fairchild Publications, Inc.
- Fashion Digest, Traghagen School of Fashion
- Harper's Bazaar, Hearst corporation
- Vogue, Conde Naste Publications

Books

- Can a Smaller Store Succeed, Jane Cahill, Fairchild
- Inside the Fashion business, Jamon & Judelle, Wiley

Industry Data

1. Survey of Buying Power, Sales & Marketing Management, July, 1978, Bill Publications
2. Annual Statement Studies, Robert Morris Associates
3. Barometer of Small Business
4. Women's Dresses, Fairchild Fact File, 1976
5. 1972 Census of Retail Trade, U.S. Department of Commerce
6. Geographic Profile, Dallas Times Herald (1978)
7. Standard & Poors Industry Survey - Apparel 2/78
8. Cost of Doing Business, Dun & Bradstreet
9. Almanac of Business and Industry Ratios, Troy

12

Conclusion

12.0 It is hoped that you have learned a great deal in reading the previous eleven chapters. You should have prepared yourself to understand the financial, legal, tax and personal implications of starting your own business. You should have selected your advisers, selected a location and written up a detailed loan proposal. Your next step is to plan your schedule implementing your acquisition process, the major milestone of which will be to secure funding. In visiting your bank make sure; a) you understand your proposal thoroughly - have your legal adviser check it over and ask you questions concerning any inconsistencies, and b) look your best - wear a dark business suit to project a respectable, business like image.

It is hoped that this small book will have prepared you for what lies ahead. Make sure, however, that you gain some experience in a particular line of business before fully committing yourself. Remember, it is sometimes best to start in a small way, perhaps in your spare time if possible, to gain experience. A recent Dun and Bradstreet study on retail failures gave lack of experience as the cause of failure in 49% of all unsuccessful ventures. Incompetence accounted for about 46% and dramatic occurences of neglect, disaster and fraud only accounted for 5% of failures.

A finer breakdown of the causes of failure is provided in the table on the next page.

An examination of the apparent causes of failure reveals that inadequate sales is the most common single defect. Thus, you should make sure you understand what your market is and what it wants. Then you can cater to that market.

Inventory difficulties is caused by not managing your inventory properly, that is buying the wrong items or not being able to obtain what you wish to sell. One point to remember is not to retain slow moving items beyond their selling season. Get rid of slow moving items by a series of sales (of increasing reductions) to improve cash flow to fund new items that will sell. The lesson here is not to be afraid to buy - but be prepared to sell at a loss if necessary.

Competitive weakness is obviously caused by inability to understand and respond to competitive pressures It is most important, as has been emphasised, to have sufficient reserve funds to withstand a price war, increase advertising, take advantage of wholesale discounts or the liquidations of suppliers.

Do not discount, however, the other causes of business failure. Make sure your health, marriage and self discipline are in good shape. In addition make sure

12/Conclusion

that your insurance is adequate.

The final piece of advice must be - work hard and good luck.

CLASSIFICATION OF RETAIL FAILURES

Underlying Cause Of Failure		Apparent Causes	%
Neglect	Due To	Bad Habits Poor Health Marital Difficulties Other	2
Fraud	By Principals Seen In	Misleading Names False Financial Statement Premediated Overbuy Irregular Disposal of Assets Other	1
Lack of experience in line; lack of management experience; unbalance experience, incompetence	Seen by	Inadequate Sales Heavy Operating Expenses Receivables Difficulties Inventory Difficulties Excessive Fixed Assets Poor Location Competitive Weakness Other	48 10 1 16 1 3 16 1
Disaster	Insurance Could Have Helped In	Fire Flood Burgulary Employee Fraud Strike Other	1

100%

INDEX

A

Accidental Death, Life Insurance, 78
Accounting, 6-42
    Accrual Basis, 6
    Cash Basis, 6
    Double Entry, 7
    Hybrid Basis, 6
    Single Entry, 7
Accounts Receivable, 27, 103, 108
Accounts Payable, 28, 146
Adjusted Balance Sheet, 149, 203
Advertising, 124-127
Age Discrimination Act, 60
Almanac Of Business Ratios, 137
Annual Statement Studies, 137
Assets, 26, 145
Assignment Of Leases, 107
Associations, 95
Automobile Traffic Count, 170

B

Bad Debts, 81, 145
Balance Sheet, 24
Balance Sheet Evaluation, 145
Bank Of America, 92
Bankers Rules, 110
Banks, 102
Borrowing Money, 73
Brand Policy, 124
Broker, 127
Bulk Sale Act, 162
Business Advice, 86
Business Analysis
    Ratio Method, 177
    Bottom-up Method, 179
    Required Income Method, 179
Business Acquisition, 144-162
Business Checkbook, 9
Business Development Organization, 115
Business Formation Plan, 173
Business Guides, 94
Business Profiles, 93
Business Selection, 137
Buying A Corporation,
    Tax Aspects, 71

C

Cash, 26, 145
Cash Flow, 31
Celler-Kefauver Act, 57
Civil Rights Act, 60
Chattel Mortgage, 108
Clayton Act, 56
Collapsible Corporations, 75
Collateral, 107
Commercial Finance Companies, 112
Consumer Finance Companies, 113
County & City Data Book, 119
Copyrights, 54
Corporate Leasing, 76
Corporation Formation, 70
Corporations, 43
Coverage Ratios, 152
Credit Cards, 19
Credit References, 197
Current Assets, 27
Customer Definition, 167
Customer Location, 167

D

Deductible Expenses
    Entertainment, 81
    Insurance, 87
    Interest, 81
    Rents, 81
    Salaries, 81
    Taxes, 82
    Travel, 81
    Wages, 81
Deferred Asset Items, 146
Depreciation, 79-81
Direct Mail Advertising, 125
Directories, 95
Distribution Methods, 127
Dividends, 78
Double-entry Bookkeeping, 8
Doubtful Accounts, 27, 145
Drop Shipper, 128

E

Economic Information, 133
Employer ID Number, 64
Endorser, 107
Equal Credit Opportunity Act, 60
Equal Employment Opportunity Act, 60
Equal Pay Act, 60
ESOTS, 76
Excise Tax, 67
Expenditure Recording, 16
Extraction Of Corporate Income, 77
E & P Market Guide, 119

F

Factoring, 106
Fair Credit Reporting Act, 58
Family Trusts, 77
Farmers Home Administration, 114
Federal Reserve System
    Regulation Z, 59
Federal Trade Commission, 57
Federal Unemployment Tax, 65
Federal Withholding And Social Security Taxes, 65
Financial Consultants, 115
Financial Statements, 23
Financing, 88, 99-116, 177
Finders, 115
Fiscal Year, 8, 72
Fixed Assets, 72
Floor Planning Financing, 106
Franchise Businesses, 139

G

General Partnership, 44
Goodwill, 72
Group Health Insurance, 78
Gross Profit (income), 30
Guarantors, 107
Guide To Customer Markets, 119

I

Income Recording, 14
Income Statement Evaluation, 148
Income Tax Appeal, 83
Incorporation, 48
    In Delaware, 49
Insurance, 5
Installment Financing, 106
Institute Of Federal Taxation, 85
Intangible Assets, 28, 146
Interest Rate, 109

Internal Revenue Code, 85
Investment Bankers, 115
Inventories, 27, 103, 146
Invoices, 10
IRS Publications, 83

L

Labor-Management Relations Act, 62
Leasing, 72
Leverage Ratios, 152
Liabilities, 28, 45
Life Insurance Companies, 113
Limited Partnership, 44
Liquidation, 78
Liquidity, 150
Loan Proposal Request, 188-215
Local Development Companies, 114
Location Of A New Business, 168
Long-term Bank Loans, 105
Long-term Liabilities, 29, 147
Loss Carryover, 73
Loss Corporation, 76
Low Occupancy Charges, 149

M

Magazine Advertising, 125
Manufacturer's Agent, 127
Manufacturing, 165
Market Analysis, 154
    New Business, 164-166
    Unique Business, 166
Market Definition, 117
Market Forecasting, 123
Market Services, 118
Marketing Plan, 117
Marketable Securities, 26, 145
Merchant, 128

N

Name (ficticious) Registration, 47
National Labor Relations Act, 61
Net Income, 30, 148
Newspaper Advertising, 125
Notes Payable, 29, 147

O

Operating Expenses, 30
Operating Ratios, 152
Occupancy Factor, 120
Occupational Safety And Health Act (OSHA), 60
Outdoor Advertising, 126

Owner's Equity, 20, 147

P

Partnership, 43, 74
Partnership Basis, 74
Patents, 55
Payroll Accounting, 19
Penetration Factor, 120
Pension Benefits, 79
Permits, 50-51
Personal Financial Statement, 194
Personal Holding Company, 76
Personal Liability, 45
Petty Cash, 21
Prepaid Expenses, 28
Pricing Policy, 124, 129-131
Procurement Assistance, 88
Product Line, 123
Profit/Loss Comparison, 200
Pro-forma Statements, 23
Property Exchange, 70
Prentice-Hall Federal Taxes, 85
Pull Product, 124
Push Product, 124
Purchase Contract, 160
Purchasing A Business, 177

R

Rack Jobber, 128
Radio Advertising, 125
Ratio Analysis, 149
Recordkeeping-Taxes, 69
Retail Store Start-up, 180
Retailer's Association, 118
Retailing, 164
Retirement Plans, 78
Residential Buyer, 127
Risk In Loans, 110
Robert Morris Associates, 137
Robinson-Patman Act, 57

S

Sale-Lease Back, 115
Savings Account, 109
Savings And Loan Companies, 113
Self Employment Tax, 65
Selling Agents, 127
Single Entry Bookkeeping, 8
Sherman Act, 56
Shopping Centers, 170, 171
Short-term Bank Loan, 103
Small Business Administration, 86
Special Agent, 82

Sole Proprietorship, 43, 74
Split-run Advertising, 125
Statistical Abstract For
   The United States, 119
Statistics For States And
   Metropolitan Areas, 119
Standard Federal Tax Reporter, 85
Stock
   Common Stock, 49
   Preferred Stock, 49, 71
   1244 Stock, 50, 71, 73
Stock Redemption, 78
Subchapter S Corporation, 45, 71-74
Survey Of Buying Power, 119
Survey Of Current Business, 119

T

Tax Calendar, 67
Tax Credit, 79
Tax Deductions, 20, 79
Tax Deductible Benefits, 78
Tax Forms, 68
Tax-free Benefits, 45
Taxes, 64
Taxes Payable, 29, 147
Thin Corporations, 49, 75
Trade Credit, 114
Trademark, 55
Trade Secret, 54
Traffic Count, 127
Trend Analysis, 154
Trust Receipts, 108
TV Advertising, 125

U

Uniform Commercial Code, 58
Uncollectable Accounts, 19

V

Valuation Of A Business, 157

W

Waggon Distributor, 128
Wagoner Act, 62
Warehouse Receipts, 107
Wholesaling, 128, 165
Working Capital, 99

Y

Year-end Accounting, 21
Yellow Pages Advertising, 125

Another Weybridge publication of interest:

Business Profitability Data – 1980

If you want to buy or start a small business, this unique publication answers some of the most important questions you should be asking. It will answer how profitable a particular business is and how it compares with other types of business. It will also provide information on business risk, future potential, trend and much more.

The following information is provided for 261 different businesses of all types - retail, wholesale, manufacturing and service businesses:

- Average profitability for 261 businesses - defined as the amount of money generated by the business divided by the amount of money invested

- Profitability versus asset size for three asset categories
  - $0-250K assets
  - $250-1,000K assets
  - $1-10M assets

- Profitability trend - the amount of change in profitability over the last three years

- Downside risk - a measure of the profitability of the more unprofitable members of each type of business

- Upside potential - a measure of the profitability of the most profitable members of each type of business

- Total capital invested in each business

- Amount of owner's equity and long-term debt

- Total value of sales

- Officer's salary

- Net profit and total income

TO: Weybridge Publishing Company
     P. O. Box 400264
     Dallas, TX 75240

Please send _____ copy(ies) of the softbound edition of BUSINESS PROFITABILITY DATA - 1980. I enclose a $12.0 check or money order for each copy plus $1 for postage and handling. (Texas residents add 5% sales tax.)

Name _____

Address _____

City _____ State _____ Zip Code _____